1983

University of St. Francis
GEN 956 T187
Taylor, Alan R.

S0-AYG-958

The Arab Balance of Power

Contemporary Issues in the Middle East

The Arab Balance of Power

ALAN R. TAYLOR

LIBRARY
College of St. Francis
JOLIET, ILL.

Syracuse University Press   1982

Copyright © 1982 by SYRACUSE UNIVERSITY PRESS
Syracuse, New York 13210

All Rights Reserved

First Edition

Library of Congress Cataloging in Publication Data

Taylor, Alan R.
    The Arab balance of power.

    (Contemporary issues in the Middle East)
    Bibliography: p.
    Includes index.
    1. Arab countries—Politics and government—
1945–   I. Title.   II. Series.
DS63.1.T39   909′.0974927   82-3394
ISBN 0-8156-2267-8   AACR2
ISBN 0-8156-2261-9 (pbk.)

Manufactured in the United States of America

956
T187

105,641

For Bernadette

ALAN R. TAYLOR is Professor of International Relations at the American University's School of International Service in Washington, D.C. He is author of *Prelude to Israel: An Analysis of Zionist Diplomacy, 1897–1947*; *The Zionist Mind: The Origins and Development of Zionist Thought*; and co-editor of *Palestine: A Search for Truth*.

Contents

Preface   xi

1 Unity and Diversity in the Arab World   1

2 Origins of the Arab System   7
   The Salafiyya Movement   7
   Egyptian Nationalism   8
   The Arab Awakening in Greater Syria   10
   Syrian Nationalism   12
   The Regional Structure of Arab Political Development   13
   The Beginnings of Arab Solidarity   19
   The Arab League   21

3 Initial Alignments   24
   The Hashimite and Saudi-Egyptian Blocs   24
   Revolution in Syria   26
   Revolution in Egypt   29
   The United Arab Republic   32

4 Breakdown of the Arab System   36
   Collapse of the UAR   36
   The Yemen War   38
   The Cairo Negotiations and Arab Summitry   40
   The 1967 War as a Watershed   43

5 The New Pragmatism   49
   The Trilateral Alliance   49
   The Role of the PLO   56
   Crisis in Lebanon   61
   The Search for Solidarity   67

6 Polarization   73
    The Arab-Egyptian Confrontation   73
    The Iraqi-Saudi-Jordanian Axis   81
    The Syrian-Libyan Counter-Axis   89
    The Iraq-Iran War   92
    The PLO at Bay   95

7 Regional Disputes   97
    Western Sahara   97
    North and South Yemen   101
    The Red Sea and the Horn of Africa   105

8 The Arab Dilemma   108
    Legitimacy and Continuity   108
    Destabilization and Security   113
    Sources of Disunity   115
    The Road to Cooperation   118

Appendices   121

    1 Membership of the Arab League   121
    2 Arab Summit Conferences   122
    3 Arab Alignments, 1945–1955   122
    4 Arab Alignments, 1965   123
    5 Arab Alignments, 1971–1975   123
    6 Arab Alignments, December 1977–March 1979   124
    7 Arab Alignments since March 1979   124
    8 Treaty of Joint Defense and Economic Cooperation among
      the States of the Arab League. April 13, 1950   125
    9 Proclamation of the United Arab Republic. February 1, 1958   127
    10 Resolutions and Recommendations Adopted by the 4th
      Arab Summit Conference. Khartum, September 1, 1967   129
    11 The Palestine National Charter Adopted by the 4th
      Palestine National Assembly. Cairo, July 17, 1968   131
    12 The Cairo Agreement between the Lebanese Authorities
      and the Palestinian Commando Organizations. Cairo,
      November 3, 1969   135
    13 Speech by the United Arab Republic President Nasser at the
      Closed Session of the 5th Arab Summit Conference (Excerpt).
      Rabat, December 21, 1969   136
      Speech by the United Arab Republic President Nasser at the
      5th Arab Summit Conference (Excerpt). Rabat, December 22,
      1969   137

14 Resolution on Palestine Adopted by the 7th Arab Summit
    Conference. Rabat, October 28, 1974   138
15 Resolution of the Six-Nation Arab Summit Conference
    Held to Consider the War in Lebanon. Riyadh, October 18, 1976   139
16 Communiqué Issued by the 8th Arab Summit Conference
    Convened to Discuss the Ending of the War in Lebanon.
    Cairo, October 26, 1976   141
    Resolutions of the 8th Arab Summit Conference Convened to
    Discuss the Ending of the War in Lebanon. Cairo, October 26,
    1976   142
17 Palestine National Council Declaration. Cairo, March 20, 1977   144
18 Final Statement Issued by the 9th Arab Summit Conference.
    Baghdad, November 5, 1978   147
19 Resolutions of the Arab League Council Following Meetings
    of the Arab Foreign and Economy Ministers. Baghdad, March 31,
    1979   149
20 National Covenant Proposed by Iraq. Baghdad, February 8,
    1980   153
21 Joint Syrian-Libyan Declaration Forming a Unitary State.
    Damascus, and Tripoli, Libya, September 10, 1980   155

Index   159

Preface

THE PURPOSE of this book is to present a concise account of the origins of the Arab system and the course of inter-Arab politics from the foundation of the Arab League in 1945 to the present. It is also designed to offer an interpretation of these events to help explain the kaleidoscopic character of the changing relationships among the Arab states.

The complexity of the Arab system stems mainly from the ambivalent attitudes that prevail in regard to the question of unity and from the ambiguity that characterizes most official policies. The idea of a federated Arab nation extending from Iraq to Morocco is appealing to Arabs because it conjures up memories of a glorious past and dreams of a future based on internal strength and freedom from foreign influence. Yet the regional structure of the Arab world predisposes its component societies to think and act in terms of the geographic and sub-cultural compartments that separate them. This is the basic dilemma that confronts the Arabs as they try to decide how to relate to each other.

In the formulation of state policy, Arab regimes usually deal with this dilemma by articulating a commitment to the ideal of unity, while actually pursuing regional policies. Unfortunately, this involves a degree of equivocation which generally leaves the important issue of solidarity unaddressed and often obstructs attempts to achieve cooperation. The fundamental problem is the difficulty established governments have in subordinating their own prerogatives to broader Arab interests. But in the final analysis, survival and viability rest on the evolution of coordinated policies among the Arabs. The realization of such a relationship depends, however, on the ability to overcome the resistance to the diffusion of power on all levels, both domestic and international. This is the theme the present study is designed to explore.

The expression "Arab balance of power" as used in this book refers to the patterns of equilibrium, dislocation, and readjustment which unfolded in the context of interdependence among the Arab states following the foundation of the Arab League. The term "Arab system" is to be understood as an interactive relationship in which the component countries became intensely involved with each other in terms of alignment, rivalry, or the perception of common goals. Because the system was so highly diversified, the evolution of inter-Arab politics was inevitably accompanied by a preoccupation with the balance of respective interests.

I am particularly indebted to the works of Albert Hourani, Ahmed Gomaa, Patrick Seale, Malcolm Kerr, Walid Kazziha, and Fouad Ajami. I also wish to express my gratitude to the Information Ministry of Saudi Arabia for its assistance during a sabbatical leave in 1977–78, which made possible a fact-gathering visit to Saudi Arabia, Kuwait, Jordan, Syria, Egypt, and Tunisia. Further information was collected on subsequent trips to Libya in January 1980, to Jordan, Syria, and Lebanon in May 1980, to Egypt and Jordan in May 1981, and to Iraq in January 1982.

I acknowledge with deep appreciation the contributions of my student assistants—Yehuda Lukacs, Mohammed Hosseinbor, Debra Premysler, and Debora Evans—in conducting research and preparing the manuscript for publication. I am also grateful to Richard N. Tetlie and Mohammed Mughisuddin, who read the manuscript with care and made many helpful suggestions. I am further indebted to Hisham Sharabi for his recommendation that the appendices be added and for his other valuable counsel.

The expression "Fertile Crescent" refers to the region now comprising Iraq, Syria, Lebanon, Jordan, and Israel. The term "Maghreb" denotes the countries of northwest Africa—Morocco, Mauritania, Western Sahara, Algeria, Tunisia, and Libya.

This book should be particularly useful to undergraduate and graduate students of the contemporary Middle East. But it is also intended for the general reader interested in the affairs of the area and in international relations.

Washington, D.C.   ART
February 1982

The Arab Balance of Power

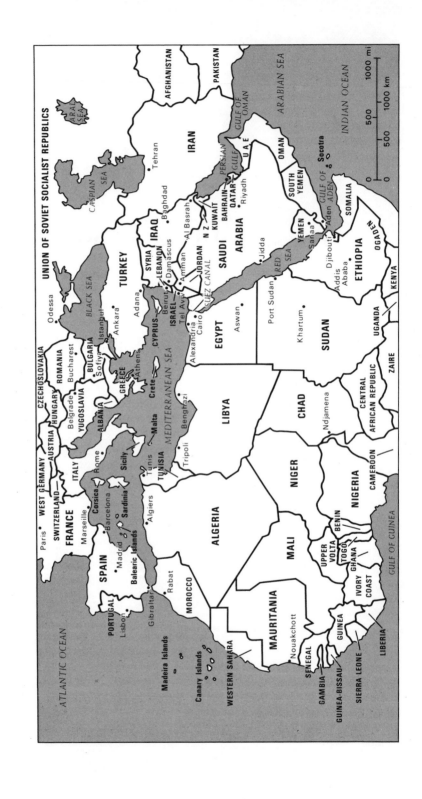

1

Unity and Diversity in the Arab World

I N THE PURELY ETHNIC SENSE, the Arabs are the settled and nomadic peoples of the Arabian Peninsula. But with the rise and expansion of Islam in the seventh and early eighth centuries A.D., the concept of what it is to be an Arab underwent a radical change. The Islamic conquests transformed the ethnic and linguistic character of the Fertile Crescent and the entire span of North Africa. In time, the majority of the peoples in these areas adopted Arabic as their native tongue and came to think of themselves as Arabs, though they were essentially a hybrid of the old Semitic and other stocks with Arab blood introduced from the Peninsula.

The Islamic tradition, of course, extended beyond the Fertile Crescent and North Africa, primarily to the north and east. But in these regions, people retained the previous indigenous languages and never assumed an Arab identity, though Arabic was institutionalized as the official medium of Islamic discourse.

In the early stages of Islamic empire-building, the conquerors constituted an Arab elite class governing a Muslim imperium. The Umayyad Caliphate (A.D. 661–750) has been called an "Arab Kingdom" for this reason.[1] Yet even during the Umayyad period, the non-Arab demographic elements had begun to challenge the Arab character of the empire, especially those who had converted to Islam and were known collectively as the *mawali*. The outcome of this confrontation was the *shuubiyya* movement, which sought to de-Arabize Islam. The Abbasid revolution in A.D. 750 endorsed this trend and made it a basis of the succeeding cali-

1. Bernard Lewis, *The Arabs in History* (New York: Harper & Brothers, 1960), pp. 64–79.

1

phate, established in the new capital of Baghdad.[2] But despite the attempts
of the Abbasid caliphs to hold the far-flung empire together by making
it more cosmopolitan and eclectic, they soon confronted powerful divisive forces.

The sectarian split in Islam between the Sunni and Shiite factions
dates back to the mid-seventh century and involved a bitter dispute over
the question of legitimate succession to the caliphate.[3] The Abbasids were
initially able to contain the problem of Shiite dissent through their
ecumenical policies. But in the ninth and tenth centuries, Shiism became a
menacingly disruptive force because it took root in distinct regional components of the empire. The combination of sectarianism and regionalism
ultimately shattered the unity of the Abbasid system, which finally came to
an end in A.D. 1258 following centuries of fragmentation in which rival
dynasties vied with each other for power and influence.[4]

There are two aspects of the Arab Empire that have particular rele-
vance to the present study. The first is that its history reflects a broad
cyclical pattern common to the area where it was situated. The Middle
East and North Africa are composed of distinct regions which during the
course of millenia have been profoundly influenced by the interaction of
two equally powerful but directly opposite forces. One of these is the
impulse of the components to unite with each other and form empires
which represent the political, economic, and cultural affinities of the
intercontinental complex. The other is the inclination of the components to assert their respective regional identities and to separate from
one another. Hence periods of unification have traditionally given way
to fragmentation, only to be followed later by new ventures in empire-building. It is a story of unity and diversity, of universalism and
particularism.

The second important aspect of the Islamic Empire has to do with its
Islamic character. Fundamental to the Islamic world view is the notion
that the Quran represents the final revelation of God to man. It is the
complete word of God and has coexisted with God from the beginning of
time. For this reason, the Islamic community as the initial recipient of the
Quran always regarded itself as having been charged with the great historical mission of transmitting the word of God to the entire world.[5] But it
was believed that this could not be accomplished unless the community

2. Ibid., pp. 80–98.
3. Ibid., p. 71.
4. Ibid., pp. 144–54.
5. Albert Hourani, *Arabic Thought in The Liberal Age, 1798–1939* (London: Oxford University Press, 1962), pp. 1–3.

retained a high degree of solidarity, or *asabiyya*. The cohesion of the Arabs in the early stages of empire-building led to a chain of victories which reinforced the conviction that the success of the Islamic mission depended on the preservation of solidarity. But when the empire began to break up and the expansion was stopped on various frontiers, a complicated psychological malaise was the result. The Muslims were confronted with the agonizing problem of dealing with the discrepancy between the ideal and the actual.

Aside from the purely Islamic perceptions of the importance of solidarity, history had taught the peoples of the Middle East and North Africa that unity was a protective shield against the ever-present threat of conquest from external areas. In particular, the Mediterranean seaway made the Middle East and North Africa vulnerable to attack by European powers, and many centuries of Graeco-Roman rule bore witness to this awesome reality. It was clear that when disunity prevailed in the eastern and southern Mediterranean, Europe was always ready to exploit the situation to its own advantage. Cohesion, on the other hand, had the opposite effect and put Europe on the defensive.

Though Islam extended far beyond what we know today as the Arab world, there remained certain components which were permanently Arabized in the sense that the inhabitants became Arabic-speaking and to at least some extent thought of themselves as Arabs. These regions include the Arabian Peninsula, the Fertile Crescent, the Nile Valley, and the Maghreb. But even here, the process of fragmentation during the Abbasid period was as pronounced as it was in the larger Islamic context. The separation of Muslim Spain under the remnants of the old Umayyad Caliphate in A.D. 756 and the rivalry between the Fatimid dynasty in Egypt (A.D. 969–1171) and the Abbasid regime in Baghdad were perhaps the most dramatic instances of division within the Arabic-speaking complex.[6] But there were a host of other conflicts in which competing dynasties identified themselves with the particularist interests of distinct regions.

One of the problems which the extended Arab world inherited from Islam was the idealism of the Islamic world view. Though the Arabic language created a common denominator in the component regions of the Arab world, it did not alter the reality that these regions are different in other respects. Each has a special history, in most cases dating back to the great civilizations of the pre-Islamic era. There are also differences in geography, local customs, and socioeconomic orientation. It is true that a

6. Lewis, *Arabs in History*, pp. 111–14, 121–30.

cooperative relationship among the Arabic-speaking components is to the mutual advantage of all of them. But in trying to preserve an integrated order as an ideal without recognizing the fact of regional diversity, the original experiment in Arab empire-building was doomed to disaster.

The basic dilemma which has always confronted the Arab world is how to construct a system of solidarity which combines a realistic approach to cooperative action with a respect for the separate identity and regional interests of the components. The early Arab empire-builders were so intoxicated with the Islamic ideal of solidarity that they could not deal with the regional factor, and this was a major cause of their failure. It is only fair to add, however, that any attempt at political unification of the Middle East and North Africa has very limited chances of durable success. But it is possible to establish modes of close cooperation if regional diversity is accepted as the basic premise.

On the ashes of the defunct Arab Empire, the Ottoman Turks built an empire of their own in the fourteenth, fifteenth, and sixteenth centuries. Aside from using the eclectic approach of the Abbasids, however, they also developed the practice of awarding maximum autonomy to the regional provinces under their appointed governors and to the non-Muslim religious sects, or *millets*.[7] This gave them an advantage in coping with the heterogeneous nature of their imperium. But pervading the whole system was the concept of an Ottoman identity, and this had the effect of submerging the national components under their rule. In a sense, the Arabs lost track of who they were under the Ottomans, and the situation even brought about an eclipse of Turkish national tradition.

While the Ottoman Empire lasted, the Arabs as a distinct people were consigned to oblivion. But when the system became dysfunctional and was beset with the aggressive intrusions of the West and Russia, the nationalities began to reassert themselves. Initially this was confined to the Balkans, where popular nationalist movements were the dominant political theme throughout the nineteenth century. In the Asiatic and North African provinces, nationalism was preceded by the separatism of local governors, but this did not stem from nationalist movements. Muhammad Ali, the Ottoman governor of Egypt who nearly overthrew the central government of the empire, was an Albanian and was interested in his own personal fortune, not the rediscovery of an Arab identity.[8] But during the second half of the nineteenth century, a deep concern with the fate of the faltering empire developed in Arab and Turkish intellectual circles. This

7. Roderic H. Davison, *Turkey* (Englewood Cliffs, N.J.: Prentice-Hall, 1968), pp. 44–45.
8. Hourani, *Arabic Thought*, pp. 261–62.

gave rise to a number of reform movements, which in the early twentieth century gradually became Arab and Turkish nationalism. But in the Arabic-speaking regions, nationalism was pluralistic in character and was organized in terms of regional and ecumenical ideologies, a phenomenon that will be examined in the following chapter.

The Arab world's historical legacy is a blend of unifying and divisive forces combined with a profound psychological concern over the impact of these forces on the destiny of the Arabs as a group. Regionalism is a deeply rooted predisposition related to history and geography. The great early civilizations in the Fertile Crescent, Egypt, and the Maghreb left a cultural heritage which can never be completely erased, and the Arabian Peninsula also has traditions which go back thousands of years. Likewise, each of these areas has a distinctive physical environment that has determined the economic and social orientation of the respective inhabitants.

The Fertile Crescent has always been a melting pot of diverse ethnic elements poured into it from the Syrian Desert and the mountain ranges to the east and north. It is a region of intense demographic movement in which the dichotomy of the desert and the sown (i.e., nomadic and settled ways of life) is the dominant reality. It is still possible to see the slow migration of nomadic peoples from the Syrian Desert into the peripheral towns of Syria, Jordan, and Iraq. Aside from mobility, the Fertile Crescent is demographically heterogeneous, and the interaction of varied peoples has given it a multidimensional social character. The site of a succession of ancient empires, its greatest cultural achievements include the concept of monotheism and the Hammurabic Code.

Egypt is quite different. The dominant geographic feature is the Nile, which is the source of fertility in an arid country. The Egyptians themselves are above all else a Nilotic people, and they relate to each other through their common experience—the river. In this sense, they are a closed society, homogeneous and fundamentally settled rather than migratory. A unique culture developed in this circumstance, and it is interesting that other Arabs attribute a particularly facile sense of humor to the Egyptians. Perhaps this gift is the natural result of having to laugh at the difficulties which a densely settled people have to confront as they try to survive in a rich but narrow belt of fertile land. Beyond this, the relics of the past are constant reminders to the Egyptians of the continuity of civilization in the Nile Valley, of their special identity and their links with the pharaonic era.

The Maghreb has its own special characteristics. Surrounded by the Atlas Mountains, the Mediterranean, and the Atlantic, the Maghrebis enjoy a more temperate climate than most Arabs to the east and an easier access to the outside world. They are also closer to Europe, with which they have interacted both economically and culturally. In history, the Maghreb was the seat of Hannibal's Carthaginian Empire, which challenged the Romans for control of the Mediterranean during the Punic Wars. It was also here that some of the earliest independent Muslim dynasties were established.

The Arabian Peninsula is also a unique geographic component of the Arab complex. Aside from being the most remote, its socioeconomic structure is quite different. The dominant reality of the Peninsula is that it is a desert subcontinent. Though bounded by settled areas in the east, west, and south, the Arabians have traditionally been a nomadic and tribal people. This has given them a strong sense of kinship, as well as the proud spirit that stems from the eternal struggle to survive in a sparse environment. Along with these predispositions, they have pronounced sentiments about honor and hospitality, the hallmarks of their culture. The Peninsula is also the home of the Arabic language and the birthplace of Islam.

It goes without saying that such differences in history, geography, and socioeconomic structure have created powerful regional inclinations in the Arab world. But the other side of the coin is the realization among all these peoples that they need to cooperate with each other. The lesson of history is that when they are divided they become the objects of foreign aggression. Following the collapse of the Achaemenid Persian Empire, the Middle East fell under Graeco-Roman control for a millennium. Then, when the Abbasid Empire became fragmented, the Crusaders established Latin kingdoms in Asia Minor and the eastern Mediterranean coastlands. Finally, the breakup of the Ottoman Empire was attended by the intrusion of the Western powers and Russia into the area, ending with its virtual partition in the early twentieth century.

The obsession among Arabs with the question of unity is not difficult to understand in the light of these traumatic experiences in their history. Indeed, the ideology of pan-Arabism gathered much of its momentum from the concern of Arabs with the problem of foreign intervention. But there still remains the issue of implementation. For despite the common interest in unity, the fact of regional diversity remains. This is the crux of the inter-Arab dilemma in our time.

2

Origins of the Arab System

THE SALAFIYYA MOVEMENT

ONE OF THE FOUNTAINHEADS of systematic political thought in the modern Arab world was the *salafiyya* movement, which first took root in Egypt. Its founder was the Persian pan-Islamic activist, Jamal al-Din al-Afghani (1839–1897),[1] who gathered a following of students at Cairo's al-Azhar University in the 1870s. Al-Afghani was deeply disturbed by the encroachments of the European powers on the Islamic countries of the Middle East and North Africa, and the message he preached to the al-Azhar students was that Muslim societies faced the threat of complete foreign domination if they did not reform themselves and stem the tide of political and social disintegration.

Al-Afghani's doctrine of Islamic reform was based on the idea of using the first Muslim generation, *al-salaf al-salih* (the venerable ancestors), as a model through which contemporary Muslims could reexamine the legitimacy of existing institutions and practices. Hence his followers became known collectively as the *salafiyya* movement. Fundamental to his thought was a belief that modern Islam was capable of reconstructing the solidarity that characterized the age of the *salaf*, and in this respect the movement was pan-Islamic rather than particularist or nationalist.

The most important of al-Afghani's disciples was Muhammad Abduh (1849–1905),[2] an Egyptian theologian who eventually became a

1. See Albert Hourani, *Arabic Thought in the Liberal Age, 1798*–1939 (London: Oxford University Press, 1962), pp. 103–129.
2. See ibid., pp. 130–60

close associate of the Persian activist. A more profound thinker, Muham-mad Abduh developed the *salafiyya* idea into a systematic philosophy of Islamic reconstruction. Ultimately he became the central figure in the re-formist circles of Cairo, and his ideas played an important role in shaping the thought of the younger generation in Egypt and in the neighboring Arab countries. Though Abduh emphasized education and reform over agitation and revolutionary change, the circumstances of his time made it inevitable that many of those he influenced would adopt a more activist stance toward Egypt's problems.

Some of Abduh's disciples followed closely in the tradition he in-augurated. The most prominent of these was Muhammad Rashid Rida (1865-1935),[3] who developed the themes of the *salafiyya* idea for nearly four decades in his journal, *al-Manar (The Lighthouse)*. Though Rida was always faithful to Abduh's teachings, he was a Syrian and reacted negatively to the Turkification policies of the Young Turk regime after the revolution of 1908. Like his Syrian compatriot, Abd al-Rahman al-Kawakibi (1849-1903), Rida ultimately began to forward the idea of an Arab Caliphate as the only institutional agency of a genuine Islamic revival. In this respect, he became related to the broader Syrian movement known as the Arab Awakening.

Many of Abduh's other disciples gradually drifted away from his Islamic approach to social and political change. Qasim Amin, Ahmad Lutfi al-Sayyid, and others looked more to contemporary Western civili-zation than to early Islam for the model on which to base reform.[4] To most Egyptians of that time, the British occupation which had been in effect since 1882 was a constant reminder of the awesome power of the West, and this promoted a general interest in Westernization as the key to Egypt's future. Eventually this secular offshoot of Abduh's movement became one of the sources of Egyptian nationalism.

EGYPTIAN NATIONALISM

A nascent Egyptian nationalism was in the making throughout much of the nineteenth century, but it was not until the end of the 1870s that a group of officers formed a semisecret organization loosely known as the National Party. Ahmad Urabi Pasha, who became a popular leader in

---

3. See ibid., pp. 222-44.
4. Ibid., pp. 161-73.

Egypt on the eve of the British occupation in 1882, was the leader of this circle, and the occupation itself was the catalyst which transformed it into a national movement. By 1907, Mustafa Kamil (1874–1908) became the dominant personality in the now formally established National Party, which gathered a significant following among students and the urban masses. At this juncture, the pan-Islamic followers of Abduh broke with Kamil and his colleagues, creating a distinction between the nationalists and the adherents of the *salafiyya* doctrine. Yet Qasim Amin and others from the secular wing of Abduh's following were attracted to Kamil's ideas and gradually became part of the nationalist movement.

In Mustafa Kamil's thought the focus of attention is neither Islam nor the *umma* (Islamic community), but an almost mystical attachment to the land of Egypt. The fervor of his sentiments is evident in one of his speeches about Egypt: "Fatherland, O fatherland: To you my love and my heart. To you my life and my existence. To you my blood and my soul. To you my mind and my speech. . . . You, you O Egypt are life itself, and there is no life but in you."[5] Islam is important because it is the religion of the Egyptian people, but it is clearly subordinated to the status of a facet of national culture. But Kamil also believed that Egyptian nationality pre-dated Islam and that there was a bond of peoplehood between the Muslims and the Coptic Christians. The essence of his doctrine is Egyptianism, an abiding dedication to the ageless continuity of the Nilotic people, which included the Sudanese as well as the Egyptians. It was what Arnold Toynbee would have called the worship of a parochial community.

Mustafa Kamil's Egyptianism was largely the product of his Western education, culminating in legal studies in France. Ahmad Lutfi al-Sayyid had a similar academic background and was deeply influenced by the European intellectual traditions of the time, especially Darwin's theory of evolution. Both of these men had relatively little exposure to Islamic learning and were easily drawn into the orbit of Western thought. As nationalism was one of the dominant political themes in late nine-teenth-century Europe, it was natural that they would develop an Egyptian version of the same concept, especially now that the country had fallen under British occupation.

What is most significant about the Western origins of Egyptian nationalism is that a new understanding of loyalties and priorities was thrust into the mainstream of Egyptian life. The Islamic ideal of an ecumenical caliph presiding over the *umma* under the *sharia* (Islamic law) was replaced with a regional patriotism in which the liberation of the

5. Nadav Safran, *Egypt in Search of a Political Community* (Cambridge, Mass.: Harvard University Press, 1961), p. 87.

fatherland and the institution of Western liberal constitutionalism were the primary goals. After Kamil's death in 1908, Saad Zaghlul became the leader of the nationalist movement and enlisted the support of large masses of the population. After World War I he headed the new Wafd Party, which led the struggle against British rule up to the Anglo-Egyptian treaty of 1936. In this context the ideology of pharaonism also developed. Tawfiq al-Hakim, one of the principal pharaonist apologists, promoted the idea of an ageless Egyptian identity with its own unique Nilotic experience and culture. In his view, Egyptian character predated Islam and the Arabization of the Egyptians, and other pharaonist thinkers looked at the country's secession from Abbasid rule under Ibn Tulun in the ninth century and the Fatamids in the tenth century as an assertion of a regional predisposition.

The overall effect of these developments in Egyptian social thought was the emergence of a distinctly Egyptian nationalism as the dominant theme in the country's political orientation. It indelibly altered the outlook of the people and remained ascendant until after the revolution of 1952, when Gamal Abd al-Nasir popularized the doctrine of pan-Arabism. But under the presidency of Anwar al-Sadat, Egyptianism was revived again and was one of the causes of the break with the rest of the Arab world in 1979.

THE ARAB AWAKENING IN GREATER SYRIA

While the *salafiyya* movement and Egyptian nationalism were in their formative phases in the Land of the Nile, similar developments were taking place in Greater Syria, known in colloquial language as *Bilad al-Sham* and comprising the western sector of the Fertile Crescent. Perhaps the dominant influence in this case was the educational activity of a group of American Protestant missionaries,[6] who had initially come to the region in expectation of a mass conversion of Palestinian Jews to Christianity. When it became evident that this anticipation was unfounded, the missionaries moved to Beirut to focus their attention on the conversion to Protestantism of Catholic and Orthodox Christians. It was assumed that this was the logical first step in drawing large masses of Muslims into the faith.

6. See George Antonius, *The Arab Awakening: The Story of the Arab National Movement* (London: Hamish Hamilton, 1938), pp. 41–43.

The basic premise of the American missionaries was that any attempt at religious conversion had to be preceded by the institution of an extensive Western educational system under their auspices. They began by founding elementary schools all over Lebanon, and later opened secondary schools and seminaries. Their crowning and ultimately most significant achievement, however, was the Syrian Protestant College, established in Beirut in 1866. This undertaking was the result of their own fund-raising operation in the United States during the early 1860s, and thus did not come under the sponsorship of the American Board of Commissioners for Foreign Missions, which directed their purely missionary activities. Essentially, this symbolized a dichotomy in the religious and educational dimensions of their work.

The Syrian Protestant College, renamed the American University of Beirut in 1920, became the center of a broad cultural movement with political implications. It not only introduced such facets of Western education as the study of science and medicine, but stimulated the rediscovery of Arab history and the revitalization of Arabic as a literary language and a vehicle for the expression of new political ideas. The translation of the Bible by the missionaries and their Arab assistants from the original tongues into Arabic was an important contribution to this linguistic renaissance. It was in this way that after nearly four centuries during which any distinct sense of Arab national identity had been submerged in the pluralistic Ottoman system, an Arab ethos was generated by American educators. The fact that the idea of Islamic reform was also beginning to take root in Syria and that two important personalities in the *salafiyya* movement—Rashid Rida and Abd al-Rahman al-Kawakibi—were themselves Syrians added significance to what the Americans had done.

It is important to understand that the Arab world, like the rest of the Ottoman Empire, was profoundly disturbed by the incursions of the European powers throughout the nineteenth century. This concern ultimately gave rise to nationalism in Egypt and to separatism in the Balkan provinces. In Syria, similar tendencies began to appear with the formation of a secret society by graduates of the Syrian Protestant College in 1875.[7] In 1880 members of this small circle put up posters all over Beirut calling for the unity and autonomy of Greater Syria. This initial manifestation of political nationalism among Syrian Christians was expressed in a different context in the writings of al-Kawakibi, a strong opponent of Ottoman despotism and one of the first to develop the idea of Islamic reform under the aegis of an Arab Caliphate.

7. Ibid., pp. 79–84.

What had started as a pair of cultural movements concerned with the rediscovery of Arab identity and Islamic reform, respectively, was translated into a political theme by the end of the century. Gradually this theme acquired an increasingly secular character, largely because of the influence of Christian publicists who advocated the introduction of Western institutions, science, and sociopolitical values. Eventually, two distinct ideological predispositions developed out of this process. The first was a fascination with the idea of an "Arab Awakening," the reassertion of Arab culture and the liberation of the Arabic-speaking peoples from the bonds of external control—whether Turkish or European—which stood in the way of their renaissance. Implicit in this notion was the idea of the reconstruction of an ecumenical "Arab Nation," an expression of the universalist predilection in Arab society. The second ideology centered on the immediate problem of continuing Turkish rule in Greater Syria and the rest of the Fertile Crescent. This became the basis of a particularist movement which is usually referred to as Syrian nationalism, though it extended into Mesopotamia and the Arabian Peninsula as well.

SYRIAN NATIONALISM

The decisive event in the formation of a distinct Syrian liberation movement was the Young Turk revolution in 1908.[8] The Young Turks were divided into two groups, one espousing Ottoman nationalism and strong central control, the other favoring decentralization and liberal policies. The former faction, known as the Committee of Union and Progress (CUP), had recruited adherents from the army who played a major role in the 1908 revolution. But after the new government was established, a power struggle ensued between the unionists and the liberals. Finally, in 1913, a group of nationalist officers seized control and promulgated a policy officially known as Ottomanism.

At first, the Arabs of the eight Ottoman provinces in the Fertile Crescent welcomed the Young Turk revolution. But when it became clear that the unionist faction was dominant and that Ottomanism involved a conscious policy of Turkification, they reacted very negatively. Syrians had close contacts with Ottoman liberals and in 1912 some of them living in Cairo founded the Ottoman Party of Administrative Decentralization.

8. See Zeine N. Zeine, *Arab-Turkish Relations and the Emergence of Arab Nationalism* (Beirut: Khayats, 1958), pp. 73–89.

But more important were a number of secret societies which advocated complete independence from Turkish rule. These included al-Qahtaniyya (1909), al-Fatat (1911), and al-Ahd (1914). Al-Fatat was perhaps the most important; the doctrine of liberation was clearly expressed in its platform, the Damascus Protocol.

The Damascus Protocol called for the independence of the Arab east, extending from the Taurus Mountains to the Arabian Sea and including the Fertile Crescent and the Arabian Peninsula. In 1915–16 it became the basis of the negotiations between Sherif Husayn of Mecca and the British, which led to Husayn's proclamation of the Arab Revolt against the Turks. Though the British interpreted the understanding very differently and in the Sykes-Picot Agreement of 1916 had made arrangements with France to partition the Fertile Crescent, Sherif Husayn and the Arabs looked to the creation of three interrelated but independent Arab states in Syria, Iraq, and Arabia.

When the war ended, the Arab provinces were detached from Turkey, but despite the attempts of Husayn's son, Faisal, and other Arab representatives at the Paris Peace Conference in 1919 to prevent the partition of the Fertile Crescent, Britain and France remained determined to implement their original plans. A General Syrian Congress, convened in Damascus in 1919, declared the independence and unity of Greater Syria as a constitutional monarchy with Faisal as king. The Congress also called for close economic ties with an independent Iraq, and rejected the idea of a Jewish national home in Palestine. But in 1920 the Supreme Council of the new League of Nations awarded mandates for a truncated Syria and a greater Lebanon to France, and for Iraq and Palestine including Transjordan to Great Britain. The mandatory administrations were imposed by force, inaugurating a long struggle of the Fertile Crescent Arabs for liberation from European control.

THE REGIONAL STRUCTURE
OF ARAB POLITICAL DEVELOPMENT

After World War I all of the post-Ottoman societies of the Middle East and North Africa were confronted with the enormous task of reconstructing themselves as successor nation-states. The nation-building process required the termination of foreign controls, the conceptualization of national identities, and the establishment of modern national institutions capable of maintaining the internal and external viability of the new sovereign entities. Paradoxically, it was the defeated Turks who were able within five years to evict all foreigners from their soil and to set up an independent Turkish state with a clear and workable national ideology. For the eastern Arabs, who had allied themselves with the victorious powers in the war, the nation-building process was far more difficult, as it was for the Arabic-speaking societies of the Nile Valley and the Maghreb.

The primary initial problem for the Arabs in general was the continuation of foreign control and influence. With the exception of Yemen and the emerging Saudi kingdom, all of the Arabs were involved in the struggle for independence for lengthy periods following the end of World War I. Great Britain retained a dominant position in Aden, the Arab sheikhdoms of the Persian Gulf, Iraq, Transjordan, Palestine, Egypt, and the Sudan. France held its colonies in Morocco, Algeria, and Tunisia, and acquired the mandates of Syria and Lebanon. Italy remained in control of Libya. What is most significant about the ensuing liberation movements is that they were highly compartmentalized, a fact which shaped the regional structure of Arab political development.

The primary centers of resistance to foreign rule were in the Nile Valley, the Fertile Crescent, and the Maghreb. In 1918 an Egyptian delegation, or *wafd*, led by Saad Zaghlul approached the British high commissioner, Sir Reginald Wingate, with a request to proceed to London to negotiate Egypt's independence with the British government. The denial of this request in London led to an eighteen-year conflict between Great Britain and the dominant Wafd Party of Egypt. The central issues were Egyptian sovereignty, British military rights in the Suez Canal and the rest of the country, and Egypt's relationship to the Sudan. Ultimately a compromise agreement was reached and its terms were embodied in the Anglo-Egyptian Treaty of 1936. Egypt became an independent country and the occupation was replaced with a twenty-year alliance under which Britain was allowed to maintain a force of ten thousand troops in the canal zone and to use Egyptian ports and airspace. Egyptian immigration into the Sudan was to be permitted with the understanding that the welfare of the Sudanese people was the guiding principle. Finally, the mixed tribunals and consular courts, under which Western residents enjoyed special privileges, were to be gradually phased out.

Aside from Egypt's distinctive history and geography, a purely Egyptian nationalism had been gradually developing during the nineteenth century and especially after the British occupation. But the intense encounter with Britain over the future of the country in the period from 1918 to 1936 was a decisive factor in the development of the strong regional sentiment which has remained the dominant theme in Egyptian politics ever since. It is true that the Egyptians recognize that they are part of the Arab world through linguistic and other cultural ties. They also think of themselves as the most important part of that world inasmuch as they have the largest Arabic-speaking population and the greatest metropolis. But their approach to the other Arabs is geared more to the idea of maintaining hegemony than of effecting a pan-Arab federation.

The "Egypt-first" syndrome is a powerful force, and is in large measure the product of Anglo-Egyptian relations from 1875 to 1954. As an ideology it was expressed in the doctrine of pharaonism. More importantly, however, it is a native predisposition of the Egyptian people. The Sudanese to some extent share the Nilotic frame of reference, but when called upon in 1955 to decide the question of the Sudan's future, they opted in favor of independence. This sub-regionalism stems largely from the fact that the Sudan is a meeting place of Arab and black Africa, the source of a distinctive Sudanese identity.

The nation-building process was similar in the Fertile Crescent, though more fragmented than in the Nile Valley. In an area where Syrian nationalism and the idea of a possible Fertile Crescent federation were the dominant political themes immediately following World War I, the partition of the region into five mandated territories under British and French administration was a severe disappointment to most of the indigenous population, with the exception of some of the Lebanese Christian community. The mandate system fostered the development of sub-regional national entities which became increasingly distinct from each other because of differing administrative influences.

In the British sphere, Iraq became a nominally self-governing monarchy under King Faisal in 1930; Transjordan was created as a puppet emirate under his brother, Abdullah, in 1921. Palestine was a unique case in that the mandate text called for the establishment of a "Jewish national home" and set up a Jewish Agency under the auspices of the Zionist Organization to assist the British administration in achieving this goal. Though the Balfour Declaration of November 2, 1917, had specified that the creation of a Jewish national home in Palestine should not prejudice the civil and religious rights of the existing non-Jewish communities, there was actually a secret Anglo-Zionist understanding that the country would be transformed into a Jewish state.[9] This set the Palestinian Arabs on a separate and ultimately tragic course which forced them to adopt an artificial sub-regional frame of reference.

9. Doreen Ingrams, *Palestine Papers, 1917–1922* (New York: Braziller, 1973), pp. 140–46.

The French kept tighter control over their mandates in Syria (northern Syria) and Lebanon. But they encouraged the development of republican rather than monarchial institutions and rejected the Zionist claim to southern Lebanon. On the other hand, the French encountered more opposition to their rule in Syria than did the British in Iraq and Transjordan. An insurrection spread throughout Syria in 1925–26, largely in response to the French practice of carving up the country into separate administrative districts, part of a divide-and-rule policy. Though it was brought under control with some difficulty, the mandatory authorities faced a continuing opposition from that time forward. The National Bloc emerged as the dominant party in the struggle for self-rule, but as in the case of Egypt, a compromise was reached in a treaty which was initialed in 1936. The treaty would have established the independence of Syria in exchange for military rights granted to France, but the French government never ratified it. During World War II, however, both Syria and Lebanon finally achieved full sovereignty.

French occupation of the Maghreb had started with the conquest of Algeria in 1830. Tunisia came under French rule in 1881 and Morocco in 1912. The settlement of French nationals in these countries posed the special problem of an entrenched *colon* class, whose interests were given priority by the administrative authorities.[10] It also made it increasingly likely that the occupation would continue indefinitely. Maghrebi intellectuals had been influenced by the *salafiyya* movement, and in the early twentieth century nationalist parties such as the Destour in Tunisia began to form. Allal al-Fasi, leader of the Moroccan Istiqlal Party, combined the idea of Islamic reform with a doctrine of Maghreb unity, but by and large the liberation struggle in North Africa was compartmentalized and isolated from parallel movements in Egypt and the Arab east. Though Morocco and Tunisia finally achieved independence in the mid-1950s, the Algerians became involved in a lengthy and bitter war with France which lasted until 1962. The idea of Maghreb unity still has some currency as a theoretical ideal, but the divergence of government in the three countries perpetuates their sub-regional orientation to the extent that any merger seems unlikely in the foreseeable future.

In the Arabian Peninsula, the nation-building process was slower and more traditional in character than in the other three basic regions of the Arab world. The most important development was the formation in the mid-1920s of the Kingdom of Saudi Arabia, following the victory in 1919 of the Saud family of Riyadh against the Meccan Hashimites. But the

10. Hourani, *Arabic Thought*, pp. 361–62.

new kingdom remained relatively isolated and ultraconservative until well after World War II, and it played only a minor role in inter-Arab affairs. The enormous oil wealth of Saudi Arabia and the innovative policies of King Faisal, however, transformed the country into a primary actor in the Arab system.

Aden and the Gulf sheikhdoms remained under British aegis until they became independent in the 1960s and early 1970s. The former eventually became the Marxist-oriented People's Democratic Republic of Yemen (PDRY, or South Yemen), whereas the latter retained their traditional pattern of princely family rule. Finally, Yemen was perhaps the most archaic of all the Arabian states, ruled until 1962 by a despotic imamate. The republican regime which followed was confronted for the first six years with a protracted civil war, in which Egypt and Saudi Arabia became involved as patrons to the republican rulers and the royalist counterrevolutionaries, respectively. Though the republic survived, Yemen entered a new phase in the 1970s, with the question of its relationship to South Yemen as the major issue.

The nation-building process throughout the Arab world became a major factor in the development and perpetuation of strong regional predispositions. Though the *salafiyya* movement and the Arab Awakening were ecumenical in scope and gave currency to the pan-Arab idea, it was difficult for countries caught up in localized struggles for emancipation to give more than theoretical consideration to operating in terms of a transregional nationalist ideology. Beyond this was the fact that regional political elites became the dominant class in societies where most people were essentially parochial and had very narrow concepts of loyalty and identity. Another factor was the natural tendency of the newly emerging ruling groups—whether dynasties or oligarchies—to preserve the existing political structure for the sake of protecting the bases of their own power. Even when these elites were in principle opposed to the artificial subregional fragmentation imposed by European powers, as was the case in the Fertile Crescent, they became increasingly disinclined to forward unionist alternatives for fear of the personal disadvantages that a change in the territorial status quo might entail.

The drift of Arab politics in the formative phase, therefore, was toward particularism rather than universalism. But this did not mean that broader approaches to nationalism had been entirely eclipsed. The new generation which came of age in the 1930s produced a political opposition to what was perceived as the class orientation of the earlier nationalists and the compromises they had made with the foreign powers. This led to the formation of doctrinal parties (*ahzab al-aqaid*), such as the Ahali group in Iraq (1931), the Syrian Social Nationalist Party in Lebanon (1932), and the Baath Party in Syria (1943).

The Ahali group was primarily concerned with promoting a comprehensive program of sociopolitical reform in Iraq, including genuine parliamentary democracy and the protection of personal civil rights. The Syrian Social Nationalist Party (SSNP), founded by Antun Saadeh, concentrated on popularizing an elaborate doctrine of Syrian nationalism, which asserted that a nation embracing the entire Fertile Crescent and including Kuwait and Cyprus had existed since ancient times and should be reconstructed in the present.[11] The party was also reformist in the sense that it called for the subordination of petty interests to the welfare of the Syrian nation and sought to engender a patriotic public philosophy. It continued to be active after the execution of Saadeh in 1949, but it went into eclipse following an unsuccessful encounter with the Baathists in Syria in 1955.

The Baath Party (*Hizb al-Baath al-Arabi al-Ishtiraki*) was founded by the Syrian Christian, Michel Aflaq, in 1943. Much of its pan-Arab nationalist philosophy, however, reflects the thought of another Syrian, Sati al-Husri.[12] Al-Husri's doctrine of Arab nationalism holds that all those who speak Arabic comprise a nation. They also share a common history, but this is secondary to the linguistic bond. Islam helps to reinforce Arab national feeling because it also is deeply rooted in the language. But the nation cannot be based on Islam because of Islam's universalist character and the fact that non-Muslims are part of the Arab nation. Islam therefore can strengthen Arab national sentiment, but should be seen as a facet of national culture. Al-Husri also believed that individual Arabs could find fulfillment only in and through the Arab nation.

Michel Aflaq, though himself a Christian, regarded Islam as not only a revolutionary model for contemporary Arabs, but as the essence of Arab national culture.[13] The idea that Islam justified the redistribution of wealth was incorporated in Baathist ideology when Aflaq's party amalgamated with Akram Hourani's Socialist Party, at which point Arab socialism and pan-Arabism became inseparable components of the Baath doctrine. The basic assertion is that there is one Arab nation and that political virtue

11. See Labib Yamak, *The Syrian Social Nationalist Party* (Cambridge, Mass.: Harvard University Press, 1966).

12. See William Cleveland, *The Making of an Arab Nationalist: Ottomanism and Arabism in the Thought of Sati' al-Husri* (Princeton, N.J.: Princeton University Press, 1971).

13. Sylvia Haim, *Arab Nationalism: An Anthology* (Berkeley, Calif.: University of California Press, 1962), pp. 62–65; Hourani, *Arabic Thought*, p. 357.

stems from the bond between the Arab people and that nation. Explicitly rejected is the idea of loyalty to regional segments of the whole, an aspect of Baathist ideology that led to the confrontation with the SSNP in 1955.

Aside from a brief period in 1936 when the Ahali group participated in a coup in Iraq executed by Hikmat Suleiman and General Bekr Sidqi, none of these younger parties exercised substantial political influence until the Baath rose to power in Syria in the late 1950s. Their significance lies rather in the attempt they made to bridge the gap between the educated and largely Westernized ruling elites and the general populace.

In all cases where third-world societies engage in the modernization process, there is inevitably a problem of communication between the Westernized intelligentsia, which seeks to transform the social order, and the traditionally oriented masses, which are resistant to change and cling to established institutions. In the Arab world, the first generation of nationalist leaders were in most cases deeply committed to the doctrines and mentality of Western liberalism, in which they were schooled. Liberalism was also appropriate to their essentially middle-class orientation and vested interests. But when it became apparent that the policies they were pursuing were at variance with the broader interests of their societies, it was natural that new ideologies would be introduced.

The appeal of pan-Arabism and Arab socialism was that they challenged a status quo in which the majority of people had little stake. The most important group in the transition, and the one which championed the new doctrines, was the growing educated class just beneath the ruling elite. These were the people who had nothing to lose and everything to gain from a change in the system. And it was they who popularized broader concepts of national loyalty and destiny. But what was particularly instrumental in inaugurating the movement for Arab solidarity was the threat posed by the gathering momentum of Zionism in Palestine.

THE BEGINNINGS OF ARAB SOLIDARITY

In 1931 the Arab majority in Palestine began to recognize that it was in serious danger of either becoming a minority in its own country or being evicted entirely by the Zionist settlers. Following the outbreak of further Arab-Jewish violence in 1929, Great Britain dispatched the Shaw Commission and Sir John Hope Simpson to investigate the disturbances. In both cases, the reports cited the basic cause of unrest as excessive Jewish immigration, which posed a variety of threats, both political and economic, for the Arab community. The recommendations for more stringent restrictions on Jewish immigration were embodied in the Passfield White Paper of October 1930, which asserted that in the matter of Palestine "a double undertaking is involved, to the Jewish people on the one hand and the non-Jewish population of Palestine on the other." It also stated that "any hasty decision in regard to more unrestricted Jewish immigration is to be strongly deprecated."[14] But on February 13, 1931, the British prime minister, Ramsey MacDonald, repudiated the Passfield White Paper in an official letter to Dr. Chaim Weizman, head of the Zionist Organization. This resulted in a vast increase in the number of Jewish immigrants. As Dr. Weizmann put it in his autobiography, "It was under MacDonald's letter that Jewish immigration was permitted to reach figures like forty thousand for 1934 and sixty-two thousand for 1935, figures undreamed of in 1930."[15]

MacDonald's action set the stage for mounting tension between Arab and Jew in Palestine throughout the 1930s, culminating in a rebellion by the Arab community against British rule in 1936. On the occasion of an Islamic Congress meeting in Jerusalem in December 1931, the Arab nationalists of Syria and Palestine met to discuss the situation. They issued an Arab Covenant which asserted that the Arab lands "are a complete and indivisible whole" and that the single goal of all Arab countries should be independence and unity.[16] With regard to Palestine, they expressed opposition to Jewish immigration and land purchase, and called for a unitary Palestinian government based on an Arab majority.

By the time of the Palestinian Arab rebellion of 1936, a deep concern with the Arab-Zionist conflict in the British mandate had spread throughout the Arab world. In 1937 a Pan-Arab Congress convened in Bludan, Syria, near Damascus to discuss the Palestinian issue. The main purpose of this congress was to underline the interest of all Arabs in what was transpiring in Palestine.[17] It also affirmed the unity of the Arabs and emphasized the interreligious character of Arab nationalism. In 1938 an even larger gathering, the Inter-Parliamentary Congress of the Arab and Islamic Countries for the Defense of Palestine, convened in Cairo. The resolutions of this meeting called for the immediate cessation of Jewish

14. The ESCO Foundation for Palestine, Inc., *Palestine: A Study of Jewish, Arab, and British Policies* (New Haven, Conn.: Yale University Press, 1947) II: 648.

15. Chaim Weizmann, *Trial and Error: The Autobiography of Chaim Weizmann* (New York: Harper & Brothers, 1949), p. 335.

16. Ahmed M. Gomaa, *The Foundation of the League of Arab States: Wartime Diplomacy and Inter-Arab Politics, 1941–1945* (London: Longman, 1977), pp. 5–6.

17. Hourani, *Arabic Thought*, p. 293.

immigration and the establishment of Palestine as a united and self-governing Arab state.[18] Later the same year, the British government recognized the general concern of the Arab countries over the Palestine question and invited several of them to send delegates to a Round Table Conference on the matter in London.

By the end of the decade, a common interest in the Palestine problem had brought the Arab states together in an attempt to deal with what they perceived as a threat to all of them posed by Zionism. If imperialism was in an ebbing phase, Zionism certainly was not, and the idea of a Jewish state in their midst seemed to virtually all Arabs a prospect which endangered not only their security, but their sovereignty and the stability of the area as well. Yet it is significant that the first step toward a system of Arab solidarity was reactive rather than self-generated. And when the Arabs finally began to lay the foundations of a regional organization through which they could develop concrete modes of cooperation with each other, it was in response to a British initiative.

THE ARAB LEAGUE

Following the failure of Great Britain to bring about an Arab-Zionist reconciliation in Palestine at the London conference, the British government issued the White Paper of 1939, which placed severe restrictions on future Jewish immigration. An annual limit of fifteen thousand was established for the next five years, and following that, no further immigration would be permitted without the consent of the Palestinian Arabs. This marked the beginning of a new British policy in the Middle East, one geared to developing closer relations with the Arab world. On May 29, 1941, the British foreign minister, Anthony Eden, declared in his Mansion House speech that the British government thought it both natural and right that inter-Arab ties be strengthened and "will give their full support to any scheme that commands general approval."[19]

In response to the British initiative, Emir Abdullah of Transjordan began to champion a Greater Syria project designed to bring Syria, Lebanon, Palestine, and Transjordan together as a united country under his crown. Though he continued his efforts to gain support for the idea,

18. Gomaa, *League of Arab States*, pp. 45–48.
19. See text in George Kirk, *The Middle East in the War* (London: Oxford University Press, 1953), p. 334.

especially in Damascus, until 1947, he had little success. This was largely because of his connections with Great Britain and his monarchial ambitions, which doomed the plan to failure from the start. In 1942 Nuri al-Said, prime minister of Iraq, put forward a more comprehensive unification scheme, which envisioned the merger of the Greater Syrian components with special provisions safeguarding the Jewish community of Palestine and the Christians of Lebanon as the initial step in a broader federation. Then the united Syrian entity would merge with Iraq to form an Arab League, which other Arab states could join as they saw fit. But here again, the main problem was Nuri al-Said's British connections, not to mention the fact that the Hashimites no longer exercised their former role in Arab politics. As a result there was a general lack of favorable response to Nuri al-Said's plan, despite its merits as an idea.

The initiative then passed to the Egyptian prime minister, Mustafa al-Nahas Pasha. On February 24, 1943, Anthony Eden had issued a second statement expressing Britain's continuing support for Arab unity and emphasizing the importance of an Arab consensus.[20] Convinced that the unity question had become basic to the future of the Arab world, al-Nahas was anxious to see to it that Egypt would play the primary role in the creation of an inter-Arab system of cooperation. Therefore, on March 30, 1943, he made a statement before the Egyptian Senate in which he declared his abiding interest in Arab affairs and said he intended to consult with all of the Arab governments with a view to resolving differences of opinion.[21] The ultimate objective was to be the convention of an Arab Congress, which would arrive at decisions concerning a closer relationship among the Arab countries.

From July 1943 to February 1944 al-Nahas met with all the major Arab leaders, and discovered that there was general agreement on two points: the need for a cooperative Arab system, and the desire to preserve the existing structure of sovereignty.[22] Following some difficulty in achieving agreement on the proposed conference, al-Nahas did manage to convene a Preparatory Committee in Alexandria on September 25, 1944, with the prime ministers of Egypt, Iraq, Transjordan, Syria, and Lebanon in attendance initially, and joined a few days later by Saudi Arabian and Yemeni delegates. Finally, on October 7, the representatives of the seven countries agreed on a statement of intentions which became known as

20. Gomaa, *League of Arab States*, pp. 154–55.
21. Ibid., p. 161.
22. Ibid., pp. 161–90. The only exception was the continuing interest of Iraq and Transjordan in the Greater Syria and Fertile Crescent schemes.

the Alexandria Protocol.[23] The basic proposal was that an Arab League be formed by the independent Arab states to consolidate inter-Arab ties, coordinate political plans, protect the sovereignty of member states against aggression, and supervise the affairs of the Arab countries. It was also stipulated that member states were prohibited from adopting foreign policies prejudicial to the league or to each other.

Following a series of meetings by a Political Subsidiary Committee from February 14 to March 3, 1945, to draft the text of the Pact of the Arab League, the Preparatory Committee convened again on March 17. Then, on March 22, a General Arab Congress approved the final text, and the league was formally established on May 10.[24] The league was, in effect, a loose regional confederation. Although it did set up an institutional vehicle for cooperation in the political, economic, and cultural fields, it also preserved the sovereignty of the member states to the extent that it did not even include the restrictions on foreign policy suggested in the Alexandria Protocol. It was also in no sense a step toward Arab unity, though it did not bar the members from trying to broaden the scope of cooperation among themselves. The dominant theme throughout the negotiations and committee meetings leading to the formation of the Arab League had been to avoid any radical change in the existing political-territorial status quo. It was as if the founding members, aware of the fact that the postwar world would be based on regional organizations and that the idea of Arab unity had been popularized, set out deliberately to create an Arab system which did not in any substantial way threaten the vested interests of the respective regimes. Within that context, the league was viewed as a means of achieving mutually beneficial modes of cooperation, while at the same time maintaining the stability of the established political structure and creating the facade of a movement toward unity. In the final analysis, it represented the victory of regionalism over universalism in the dynamics of inter-Arab politics.

23. See text in ibid., pp. 272–74.
24. See text in ibid., pp. 295–301.

3

Initial Alignments

THE HASHIMITE AND SAUDI-EGYPTIAN BLOCS

THOUGH THE ARAB LEAGUE was intended to provide the institutional basis of a comprehensive system of inter-Arab cooperation, it actually became a vehicle through which latent rivalries were brought to the surface. The regional structure of the Arab world lay at the root of the emerging struggle for power. Given the geographic and historical divisions that separate the Fertile Crescent, the Arabian Peninsula, the Nile Valley, and the Maghreb into distinct societies with particular interests, it was inevitable that political tensions would develop among them. But the precipitating factors were the compartmentalization of Arab politics during the formative period and the existence of a diversified leadership with conflicting interests and goals.

The principal inter-Arab rivalry has always been that between the Fertile Crescent and Egypt. The competition for dominance between these two regions dates back to ancient times. But in its contemporary form, it began with the resistance of Egypt to the attempts of the Hashimite rulers in Transjordan and Iraq to lay the foundations of Fertile Crescent unity. When Emir Abdullah and Nuri al-Said introduced their respective unification schemes in the early 1940s, Egypt was confronted with the prospect of a powerful state to the immediate northeast which, if it ever materialized, would certainly produce a formidable rival for hegemony in the Arab world. Though neither plan made any headway, the idea of a Fertile Crescent nation had existed since the Syrian Congress in

1919 and had more recently been put forward in ideological terms by the Syrian Social Nationalist Party. Furthermore, most Arab nationalists regarded a Fertile Crescent accord as the natural foundation of the Arab nation, since it was in that region that the doctrine of unity had its deepest roots. Hence the possibility of a political change which would open the door to closer relations among Baghdad, Damascus, and Amman was an ever-present danger for the Egyptians. Their desire to prevent such an eventuality led directly to the formation of countervailing blocs within the Arab system.

Another factor in the equation was Saudi Arabia. The rise of the Saud family to power in the Peninsula had involved a bitter struggle against the Hashimites, who subsequently established themselves as rulers in Transjordan and Iraq and sought to extend their power throughout the Fertile Crescent. The Saudis therefore had an equal interest in opposing the designs of the Hashimites, which made them the natural allies of Egypt. Since there still existed a dynastic rivalry between the two families, the Saudis could not accept the construction of a powerful Hashimite state just to the north. Such a development would pose a threat to their own position in the Peninsula, and had to be prevented at all costs.

Soon after the formation of the league, then, two competitive blocs were established within the Arab system (see Appendix 3). The Hashimite states of Transjordan and Iraq concluded a Treaty of Brotherhood and Alliance on April 15, 1947. This was largely a cosmetic pact because of the conflicting ambitions of Abdullah and his nephew, Abd ul-Ilah, the regent of Iraq. Yet the treaty cemented relations between the two countries and made them partners in a Hashimite bloc. Egypt and Saudi Arabia, in the meantime, became tacit allies through their mutual antipathy to the Hashimites and their opposition to the evolution of closer ties within the Fertile Crescent.[1]

The balance of power lay with the remaining three founding members of the league. But Lebanon and Yemen did not play a significant role in inter-Arab relations at this stage. Lebanon had essentially withdrawn from the mainstream of Arab politics with the conclusion of the National Pact in 1943. By the terms of this arrangement, the Christian community had agreed to relinquish all political ties with the European powers and in exchange the Muslims had made a commitment not to seek the merger of Lebanon with any larger Arab entity. On the threshold of independence, therefore, Lebanon resumed its traditional status as an

1. George Lenczowski, *The Middle East in World Affairs*, 4th ed. (Ithaca, N.Y.: Cornell University Press, 1980), pp. 742–46.

105,641

LIBRARY
College of St. Francis
JOLIET, ILL.

atypical society with special guarantees and immunities. Yemen, which had barely been touched by the modernization trend, was even more isolated and did not figure in the political maneuvering that surrounded the Hashimite issue. So though Lebanon and Yemen were founding members of the league, neither had any influence on the balance of power. This left Syria as the focus of attention for the two competing blocs.

REVOLUTION IN SYRIA

Syria had achieved independence during World War II, formally in 1941 and actually in 1945, when the British intervened to secure the withdrawal of the French. But the political future of the country remained uncertain. The National Bloc, which had led the struggle for independence during the interwar period, had in many respects lost its credibility. But no significant opposition appeared on the scene until the formation of the People's Party in 1948 and the gradual emergence of the Baath. The People's Party, however, was more a group representing the middle-class interests of Aleppo and northern Syria than it was a progressive opposition, and the Baathists were still novices in the political arena. The movement for change thus shifted to the army, which attracted many from the new generation of young men who had grown impatient with the status quo.

The Homs military academy became a training ground for the politicization of future officers, especially in the aftermath of Syria's poor performance in the Palestine war of 1948. Colonel Husni Zaim, who had become chief of staff of the Syrian army just after the war in Palestine, became the central figure in a coup conspiracy in the early part of 1949. The conspirators seized power on March 30, and Husni Zaim became the first military dictator of the country.

The change of government set in motion a chain of events which focused largely on Syria's relationships with Iraq and Egypt.[2] Zaim's first move was to develop closer ties with Iraq. This was a natural policy to pursue inasmuch as the regime of Shukri al-Quwatli which had just been deposed had leaned toward Saudi Arabia and the anti-Hashimite bloc. It also seemed the best way of strengthening his hand in the forthcoming

2. See Patrick Seale, *The Struggle for Syria: A Study of Post-War Arab Politics, 1945-1958* (London: Oxford University Press, 1965), pp. 46-131.

armistice negotiations with Israel. But despite the discussions that followed on a possible Syrian-Iraqi alliance, Zaim had decided by mid-April in favor of a pro-Egyptian position, and made a secret visit to King Faruq on the twenty-first to formalize the relationship. The reasons behind this decision were complex, but mainly involved the fears of both Zaim and the Iraqis of the consequences which would attend the displeasure of Egypt and Saudi Arabia at the emergence of a Syrian-Iraqi accord. Also, Nuri al-Said had a particular dislike for Zaim's unorthodox and impulsive political style, and was hesitant to cement relations with Syria despite his special interest in the Fertile Crescent idea.

Aside from his own lack of a clear political ideology or program, it was the strained relationship with Iraq that ultimately brought about the downfall of Husni Zaim. The Iraqis secretly planned a second coup with the help of another Syrian colonel, Sami al-Hinnawi, and several other accomplices. Backed by armored units, they took Zaim into custody and executed him immediately. Al-Hinnawi then asked the renowned politician, Hashim al-Atassi, to form a government. The new cabinet was dominated by the People's Party, which had always favored close ties with Iraq, thus raising again the possibility of a movement in that direction. A number of overtures were made from both Damascus and Baghdad, but the unpopularity of Abd ul-Ilah and Nuri al-Said and the strong preference for republicanism in Syria led to a split on the question of union among the leading Syrian political personalities. On December 19, 1949, Colonel Adib al-Shishakli and Akram al-Hourani took control of the country in the third coup of the year.

Through a series of political maneuvers, al-Shishakli retained control of Syria until his downfall in February 1954. Though he did not assume the trappings of formal political leadership at first, he staged a second coup at the end of November 1951, after which he issued a military decree making him the official chief of state. A new constitution was drawn up during the first half of 1953, and on July 10 of that year it was approved by a popular referendum which at the same time elected al-Shishakli as president. All political opposition was prohibited as al-Shishakli's newly contrived Arab Liberation Movement was declared the sole party, representing the totality of social forces in the country.

Al-Shishakli's Arab policies were geared to the perpetuation of his own power in Syria. Having come to the political foreground on a platform opposed to the idea of union with Iraq, he naturally leaned toward the Egyptian-Saudi side of the bloc system. But, of course, the major consideration on his part was to maintain the status quo, as any change in the territorial structure would threaten the political position he had assumed. Despite his former connections with the Syrian Social Nationalist Party and his continuing association with some of its leaders, he gradually adopted a sloganistic pan-Arabism as the official policy of the Arab Liberation Movement.

It was already becoming the common practice of regimes which really wanted to preserve the status quo to pay lip service to the idea of Arab unity. This not only gave them a more respectable image, but diminished the likelihood of any change inasmuch as the very scope of pan-Arabism put it beyond the possibility of implementation. That is to say, the extravagant rhetoric of pan-Arabism was a convenient and facile cover for the practice of the narrowest kinds of regionalism and sub-regionalism. But this was also tragic in that it created a tradition of hypocrisy which became so standardized that it was virtually the only model of political behavior for future generations. Consequently, the Arab world has remained immature in this respect.

In diplomatic practice, al-Shishakli maintained particularly friendly relations with Egypt, Saudi Arabia, and Lebanon. He adhered to the Egyptian-sponsored Arab collective security pact, or Treaty of Joint Defense and Economic Cooperation, of April 1950 (see Appendix 8). The main Egyptian purpose in creating this ineffectual mutual security system was to contain Iraq and reaffirm the Arab League's principle of preserving the sovereignty of each member state.[3] Al-Shishakli's acquiescence was therefore symbolic of his continuing hostility toward Syria's eastern neighbor, though both Hashimite countries themselves eventually joined the pact.

As long as al-Shishakli remained the dictator of Syria, the Arab balance of power was tilted in favor of the Egyptian-Saudi bloc. But in 1953 the Syrian political situation began to change. The former parties became more assertive and the mood of the general public called for political liberalization. Finally, in February 1954, al-Shishakli was unseated by a military coup, after which he resigned and went into exile. A provisional military rule was set up, but it was clear that the country would quickly revert to parliamentary government, and elections were to take place the following September.

The most important result of the transition was the emergence of the ideological parties as a new force in Syrian politics. The Baath and the SSNP were the dominant groups, though the local Communists also played a role. Ultimately, this drift was to change radically Syria's rela-

3. Ibid., p. 91.

tions with the rest of the Arab world. But an equally significant development was the overthrow of the regime in Egypt in the summer of 1952.

REVOLUTION IN EGYPT

Egypt emerged from World War II in a state of mounting political unrest. Though al-Nahas had secured the country's hegemony over the new inter-Arab system, two more important issues remained unresolved. The first was a socioeconomic structure which left the vast majority of Egyptians impoverished, while the privileged landed class and urban bourgeoisie enjoyed all the benefits which an essentially corrupt status quo conferred upon them. The second was the continuing military presence of Great Britain, which qualified Egypt's sovereignty and restricted Egyptian attempts to seek an ultimate union with the Sudan.[4]

In the immediate postwar period, the Saadist Party, a splinter from the Wafd, was in power, but made little headway in dealing with either of these questions. The Wafd itself comprised the major opposition party. But far more radical groups questioned the very premises of the existing political system. These included the Muslim Brotherhood, the formerly fascist but now socialist Young Egypt organization, the Communists, and student nationalists. It was they who formed the basis of a drift toward revolutionary orientation at the grass roots.

In 1948 Egypt was drawn into the Palestine war, in which its forces proved themselves incapable of dealing successfully with the Israelis. This humiliation led to a growing concern over Egypt's future among some members of the officer corps, a development of primary political significance. In a few years, the military was to set the country on a new course.

The elections of January 1950 produced an overwhelming Wafdist majority, and al-Nahas once again assumed the premiership. The British military presence immediately became the major national issue, but al-Nahas was indecisive in his attempts to resolve it.[5] In November 1950 he formally requested Britain to leave the Canal Zone and the Sudan. The talks that ensued in 1951 resulted in a British proposal that Egypt participate in a Middle East Defense Command which would include the United

4. Lenczowski, *Middle East in World Affairs*, pp. 502–507.
5. Sydney Nettleton Fisher, *The Middle East: A History*, 3rd ed. (New York: Knopf, 1979), pp. 723–24.

Kingdom, the United States, France, and Turkey. In exchange, Britain would be willing to terminate the 1936 treaty and evacuate the Canal Zone. The popular reaction to this proposal was extremely negative, and in October 1951 al-Nahas was forced to abrogate unilaterally the Anglo-Egyptian treaty. By January 1952, however, the country had entered a stage of pronounced political agitation which included riots and demonstrations. King Faruq replaced al-Nahas with Ali Maher as prime minister, but on July 23 an army group known as the Free Officers and nominally headed by General Muhammad Nagib staged a military coup.

The new government of Egypt was initially a junta with a Revolutionary Command Council (RCC) as the ruling body. On June 18, 1953, a republic was proclaimed and Nagib became president and prime minister. But the real leader of the Free Officers was Lieutenant Colonel Gamal Abd al-Nasir. Following a disagreement with Nagib over the latter's desire to restore civilian government,[6] Abd al-Nasir became the de facto ruler on November 14, 1954, when Nagib was placed under house arrest. Actually, Abd al-Nasir had been the dominant political personality throughout most of 1954, and in October of that year had concluded an agreement with Great Britain which abrogated the 1936 treaty and set June 18, 1956, as the final date for the evacuation of British troops from Egypt.[7]

From this beginning, Abd al-Nasir's charisma quickly made him the most dramatic and challenging political leader in the entire Arab world. His policies ranged from extensive land reform and other domestic changes heralded as "Arab socialism" to the formulation of neutralism as the basis of Egypt's stance in foreign affairs. As he moved from the arms deal with the Soviet Union and Czechoslovakia in 1955 to the Suez crisis in 1956, his stature grew and for many Arabs he became a legendary hero. Of major concern here, however, are the Arab policies he adopted, which ultimately transformed the structure of the Arab system.

Though Abd al-Nasir always retained a strong sense of Egyptian patriotism, he also felt very deeply that Egypt's problems could not be separated from those of the rest of the Arab world. His experience as a combat officer in the Palestine war, related in his *Philosophy of the Revolution*,[8] convinced him that there was a connection between the conflict with Israel and the Arab struggle to remove all forms of Western control. Just as imperialism was a common problem, so was the establishment of an alien Jewish state at the center of the Arab world. But

---

6. Ibid., p. 727.
7. Ibid., p. 729.
8. Gamal Abdul Nasser, *Egypt's Liberation: The Philosophy of the Revolution* (Washington, D.C.: Public Affairs Press, 1955), pp. 94–105.

neither threat could be addressed without solidarity, a lesson which was painfully learned in the 1948 war. Hence, the Arab countries were in fact interdependent and had to work together despite regional differences.

Another theme that emerges from *The Philosophy of the Revolution* concerns Egypt's destiny.[9] Abd al-Nasir imagined a role wandering about in search of a hero, an allusion to Egypt's special position in the Arab, African, and Muslim worlds and to his own part in helping the country to assume its leadership responsibilities. In January 1954 Egypt's official foreign policy was announced to be one of promoting anti-imperialist blocs among Arabs, Africans, and Muslims. But it quickly became clear that the major concentration would be on Egypt's role in Arab affairs. Radio Cairo's special service, the Voice of the Arabs, was expanded and it proclaimed Egypt as the new champion of Arab unity and the vanguard in the struggle against imperialism.[10]

Just as Abd al-Nasir was shaping Egypt's pan-Arab policy, the Northern Tier alliance, which came to be referred to as the Baghdad Pact, was in the process of formation. On April 2, 1954, Turkey and Pakistan signed a mutual cooperation treaty which was generally regarded as the first link in a chain of containment to be built on the southern periphery of the Soviet Union. Then on February 24, 1955, Turkey and Iraq concluded a five-year defense pact at Baghdad. Great Britain, Pakistan, and Iran joined the alliance later in the year. Unofficially known as the Baghdad Pact, its actual title was the Pact of Mutual Cooperation.[11] Though the United States was not a member it was active in some of the committees, and Secretary of State John Foster Dulles had played a major role in organizing the alliance as a link between NATO and SEATO after it became evident that Abd al-Nasir was not interested in participating in an anti-Soviet Middle East defense system.

It was also during this period that the events leading to the Suez crisis were beginning to unfold. Just four days after Turkey and Iraq had signed the first instrument of the Baghdad Pact, the Israelis launched an attack on an Egyptian military installation in Gaza.[12] Abd al-Nasir regarded this as a sign that Israel was preparing for war, and turned to the United States for a token arms support delivery as an indication that Washington took some interest in Egypt's security. President Eisenhower described the requested amount as "peanuts," but Secretary Dulles was opposed to a favorable

9. Ibid., pp. 87–94, 109–114.
10. Seale, *Struggle for Syria*, p. 196.
11. See text in Jacob C. Hurewitz, *Diplomacy in the Near and Middle East: A Documentary Record, 1914–1956* (Princeton, N.J.: Van Nostrand, 1956), pp. 390–91.
12. Kennett Love, *Suez: The Twice-Fought War* (New York: McGraw-Hill, 1969), pp. 5–20.

American response. In the face of the forthcoming US denial, Abd al-Nasir concluded an arms agreement with Czechoslavakia, thus more definitively establishing his policy of neutralism. A year later, in response to Dulles's announcement that the United States had withdrawn its offer to help finance the High Dam project at Aswan, he nationalized the Suez Canal. The Sinai war followed in three months.[13]

Against the background of the Baghdad Pact and the Suez crisis, Abd al-Nasir's pan-Arabism gathered special meaning. The premise that Zionism was a facet of imperialism seemed borne out by events, especially the joint Anglo-French-Israeli operation against Egypt in October 1956. By contrast with Egypt's position, Iraq's complicity in the Baghdad Pact appeared to be the very epitome of treason. The mounting tension from February 1954 to October 1956 set in motion a wave of nationalist sentiment which swept through much of the Arab world and made Abd al-Nasir the popular hero of the politicized masses.

Coincident with the emergence of pan-Arabism as an ascendant doctrine was the political change taking place in Syria, which was still the key to the Arab balance of power. Al-Shishakli's fall in February 1954 led to new elections in late September and early October of that year. But the results produced no real majority. Out of 142 seats, 64 went to independents, 30 to the People's Party, 22 to the Baath, 19 to the National Party (formerly National Bloc), and the remaining 7 to the SSNP, the Communists, and two other smaller factions.[14] Consequently, Syria entered a period of uncertainty under a coalition government. But it was clear that the old parties had declined in popularity and that the Baath had made significant gains. The SSNP had only two seats in the assembly, but its members were eager to challenge the Baath and it was the conflict between the two that ultimately led to Syria's merger with Egypt.

THE UNITED ARAB REPUBLIC

The Syrian army continued to be a powerful political force behind the scenes, and many of the younger officers were deeply influenced by the resurgence of ideological nationalism in Egypt and the Fertile Crescent. In this case, however, the SSNP and the Baath were actively seeking recruits

13. Ibid., pp. 297–521.
14. Seale, *Struggle for Syria*, p. 182.

in the military during the period following al-Shishakli's deposition.[15] This set the two parties on a collision course, and the future of Syria's relationship with the rest of the Arab world lay in the balance.

On April 22, 1955, the leading pan-Arab army officer, Lieutenant Colonel Adnan al-Malki, was assassinated by a sergeant who was later identified as a member of the SSNP. The incident inspired a public outcry against the Syrian nationalists, who were thought to be plotting a military coup and to have had secret contacts with American officials. Most of the other parties rallied in support of the Baath, which played a leading role in the subsequent purge of the SSNP. At the trials which ensued, all of the SSNP leaders who had not fled were sentenced to long prison terms and the influence of the party in Syrian political life went into eclipse.[16]

The al-Malki affair led to a period in Syrian history when power rested largely with a number of army officers, some of whom were associated with the Baath. One of the most influential figures initially was Abd al-Hamid Sarraj, who as chief of military intelligence presided over what approximated a surrogate police-state operation under the aegis of the formal trappings of parliamentary rule, headed by President al-Quwatli.[17] On October 20, 1955, Syria concluded a military alliance with Egypt, a harbinger of the much closer relationship that was to follow over two years later. By June 1956 the Baath had joined the cabinet, securing the important ministries of Foreign Affairs and Economics. It was at this point that the idea of union with Egypt began to be discussed seriously. By 1957 the Baath stood as the most lively political force in the country against the background of Abd al-Nasir's skyrocketing popularity among the Syrians. But the Baath was still a small minority in the assembly, a fact which left its members disenchanted with the existing political system.

The development which most concerned the Baath was the political influence wielded by Khalid Baqdash, head of the Communist Party.[18] Though the Baath played a prominent role in the amorphous "progressive front" which was then dominant in Syrian politics, Khalid al-Azm and Baqdash also exercised a good deal of power in the clique, along with Sarraj (now pro-Baath) and others. Baqdash insisted on closer relations with the Soviet Union, but the Baath regarded such a step as contrary to the goal of Arab unity. It was for this reason that the Baath drafted a

15. Ibid., p. 240.
16. Ibid., p. 243.
17. Ibid., p. 245.
18. Ibid., pp. 315–17.

proposal for federation with Egypt.[19] The Communists were eager to block such a merger, counting on the hesitancy which Abd al-Nasir was already showing. Then the Baath went a step further and came out in favor of complete unity with Egypt. Finally, on January 12, 1958, a group of top army officers led by the chief of staff went to Cairo and informed Abd al-Nasir of their full support for union on conditions to be determined by Egypt.[20] The two governments formally proclaimed a merger on February 1, and the United Arab Republic was officially established three weeks later (see Appendix 9).

The UAR's political structure was based on the transformation of Egypt and Syria into provinces under a highly centralized national government. All parties were dissolved and a National Union was to take their place as the sole political association of the new state. The Syrian Baathists agreed to this because they assumed that they would become the guiding force in the National Union and play a major role in defining the political ideology of the UAR.[21] But Abd al-Nasir never conceived of the Baath as performing such a function, and the other Syrian political factions successfully prevented it from gaining more than a quarter of the Syrian seats in the National Union in the July 1959 elections.

In practice, the political system assured the overwhelming dominance of Abd al-Nasir in the leadership role and the preponderance of the Egyptian over the Syrian province. But the question of foreign policy was more complex. In theory, the UAR was the nucleus of the united Arab Nation of the future. Its principal raison d'être was to serve as vanguard of the Arab-unity movement. The Baath's understanding of this theory was purist and highly doctrinaire. For them, the union with Egypt had brought about a new dichotomy in the Arab world between those who cherished the national ideal and the reactionaries who preferred to maintain the status quo. But Abd al-Nasir, though a proponent of pan-Arabism, was far more pragmatic and as chief of state had to take into consideration the preservation of amicable relations with the established Arab regimes.

The discrepancy between these different views of foreign policy became evident in the months following the union. The destabilization of Lebanon in May and the revolution in Iraq on July 14, 1958, seemed to the Baath the beginning of a series of events that would ultimately bring all of the other Arab countries into the UAR. But then order was restored in Lebanon and the Iraqi revolutionary leader, General Abd al-Karim

19. Ibid., p. 318.
20. Ibid., p. 320.
21. Malcolm Kerr, *The Arab Cold War: Gamal 'Abd al-Nasir and His Rivals, 1958–1979*, 3rd ed. (New York: Oxford University Press, 1971), pp. 12–13.

Qasim, took a strong position against joining the union and jailed many Nasirite sympathizers in Iraq. Qasim's attitude was both a disappointment and an affront, but Abd al-Nasir could not meet this unexpected challenge without strengthening his hand within the whole Arab system. He therefore quickly shored up his relations with Jordan and Saudi Arabia, an action which the Baath found difficult to understand.[22]

The emergence of the UAR created an anomalous situation in the sense that although it united two Arab states committed to pan-Arabism and socialism, it did not radically alter the structure of the Arab system. The balance-of-power game still had to be played, and in this case it involved the unlikely alignment of the UAR, Jordan, and Saudi Arabia. Yet at the same time, Iraq and Jordan announced a federation in mid-February 1958 as an expression of Hashimite solidarity in response to the establishment of the UAR.[23] The plan called for unity in foreign policy, defense, education, and customs. It also provided for a federal parliament and an executive to be headed by the Iraqi king. But both Faisal II and King Husayn were to retain independent authority within their own realms, limiting the degree to which the two countries could really be integrated. In any event, the scheme was repudiated by the new regime which came to power in Iraq the following July.

The Iraqi-Jordanian federation gave the appearance of an emerging progressive-conservative dichotomy in the Arab system, but this was an illusion. Though the idea of ideological polarity had been introduced, the fabric of Arab interaction assumed a conglomerate form in which political affinities, pragmatic considerations, and rivalries played alternating roles, producing a kaleidoscopic pattern of changing relationships. A bizarre alignment which almost symbolized the blurring of clear lines of demarcation in inter-Arab politics was the adherence of the Yemeni monarchy to the UAR on March 8, 1958, through a newly created entity known as the United Arab States.

Perhaps the most important single factor in determining the course of the Arab system was the continuing influence of regional predispositions. In the final analysis, it was regionalism which destroyed the UAR and dominated inter-Arab politics thereafter. And eventually, ideology became far more a tool to serve particularist interests than a vehicle to challenge the status quo.

---

22. Ibid., pp. 18–19.
23. Majid Khadduri, *Independent Iraq, 1932–1958: A Study in Iraqi Politics* (New York: Oxford University Press, 1960), p. 345.

4

Breakdown of the Arab System

COLLAPSE OF THE UAR

METAPHORICALLY SPEAKING, the Arab world descended into an abyss of confusion and disappointment during the decade of the 1960s. It was a time of intense inter-Arab quarreling, disillusionment with reform ideologies and the quest for unity, and a humiliating defeat by Israel which enlarged the scope of the Palestine problem. This was particularly difficult for those who had shared in the rising expectations of the 1950s, and certainly the psychology of despair played a role in preparing the ground for the untoward events that followed. But the process started with the collapse of the UAR.

The Baath had dropped out of the political picture following Abd al-Nasir's diplomatic rapprochement with Jordan and Saudi Arabia. Abd al-Hamid Sarraj ran Syrian affairs thereafter with the help of the Egyptian marshal, Abd al-Hakim Amir. But the relationship between the two provinces progressively deteriorated, and in the summer of 1961 a group of Syrian army officers began planning the termination of the union. Then on September 28 they formally announced the secession of Syria.

The causes of the rupture were manifold.[1] One was the secondary role of the Syrians in the political system. Even their participation in the National Assembly was by Abd al-Nasir's appointment rather than by

---

1. George Lenczowski, *The Middle East in World Affairs*, 4th ed. (Ithaca, N.Y.: Cornell University Press, 1980), pp 545–49.

election, though the local committees of the National Union were determined by popular ballot. Equally important was the fact that the two economies were very different and that the merger created a disequilibrium in Syria which was disadvantageous to all levels of the bourgeois class. Both of these conditions were aggravated by the disproportionate size of the two provinces and the lack of any political force in Syria to match the overwhelming stature of Abd al-Nasir. But underlying these particulars were the cultural differences between the Syrians and Egyptians, a factor which those caught up in the quest for Arab unity seldom took time to examine.

Syria had promoted the union while in a state of political disintegration, and largely as a means of ameliorating that condition. Abd al-Nasir was right when he warned them that they had better get their own house in order before opting so precipitously for such a radical change.[2] Yet they were insistent. Two years later, the Baathists who had engineered the merger were politically inactive, and the conservative and Communist elements in the country were set to reestablish local sovereignty. Once this was accomplished, Syria entered a phase of strong emphasis on its separate identity.

After the secession, Syria reverted to the rule of the traditional politicians, who blamed Abd al-Nasir for aborting the union. A number of important army officers and most of the Baathists, however, were disturbed by what had occurred, despite the attempts of the government to appear still committed to the principles of pan-Arabism and progressive political practice. In reality, however, the new rulers had little interest in Arab unity and represented mainly the Syrian middle class.

Abd al-Nasir, in the meantime, tried to repair the damage that had been done to his own image in the aftermath of the split by reemphasizing his revolutionary zeal.[3] Condemning the regime in Damascus as reactionary, he declared that Egypt now stood alone as the only true champion of the Arab national ideal. He also broke diplomatic relations with Jordan and sharply criticized the government of Saudi Arabia. In this respect, he sought to foster a picture of inter-Arab politics as an encounter between Egypt as the citadel of pan-Arabism and Arab socialism on the one hand, and the host of other regimes as partisans of conservative, petty, and regional interests on the other. This helped to promote what was later to

2. Patrick Seale, *The Struggle for Syria: A Study of Post-War Arab Politics, 1945-1958* (London: Oxford University Press, 1965), p. 314; Malcolm Kerr, *The Arab Cold War: Gamal 'Abd al-Nasir and His Rivals, 1958-1970*, 3rd ed. (New York: Oxford University Press, 1971), p. 11.
3. Kerr, *Arab Cold War*, pp. 27-33.

prove an increasing tendency of Arab leaders who considered themselves "revolutionary" to fall back on slogans and generalities in their search to establish their own legitimacy. But it also gave rise to a practice of name-calling and recrimination as the standard way in which inimical regimes dealt with each other.

In the early part of 1963 the governments in Iraq and Syria came under new leadership, introducing yet another alteration in the Arab system. The Iraqi coup took place on February 8, and was executed by the Baath party of that country. Abd al-Karim Qasim, who had been unable to deal with either the problem of Kurdish separatism or the division of Iraq into Nasirite, Communist, and regional nationalist factions, was executed. Colonel Abd al-Salam Arif, a staunch Nasirite, became president; the Baathist General Ahmad Hasan al-Bakr assumed the post of prime minister. The new regime quickly expressed its solidarity with Abd al-Nasir and its commitment to pan-Arabism.

A month later, on March 8, 1963, the Syrian Baath took over easily in Damascus. Salah al-Din al-Bitar, one of the old Baath leaders, was appointed prime minister by the National Revolutionary Command Council. Syria's official policy was renunciation of secessionism and exploration of the possibilities of union with both Egypt and Iraq. Talks on the unity question followed immediately. But in the meantime, Abd al-Nasir's attention had been drawn to a new situation which had arisen in southern Arabia.

THE YEMEN WAR

A few months before the political changes in Iraq and Syria, Abd al-Nasir became embroiled in a bitter inter-Arab dispute over the future of Yemen. A traditionalist autocracy had prevailed in Yemen until the death of Imam Ahmad on September 19, 1962. His reformist son, Muhammad al-Badr, succeeded to the throne but was overthrown a week later by his own chief of staff, Colonel Abdullah al-Sallal. A republic was proclaimed, and it was clear that the group of officers who had executed the coup were pro-Nasir and intended to maintain close relations with Egypt. Imam al-Badr, however, had escaped to the mountains and organized a royalist resistance to the republican regime. At the same time, Egypt sent an expeditionary force to the port of Hudeida as a protective gesture toward the new government, while Saudi Arabia came to the aid of the royalists. So from the beginning, the Yemen war was more than a civil conflict. It was a stage on which the rivalry between Abd al-Nasir and the Saudis was acted out.[4]

During the ensuing years, the Egyptian military force in Yemen grew from about fifteen thousand troops in October 1962 to seventy thousand in the summer of 1965.[5] But they found it difficult to fight in the rugged mountain areas and suffered a number of reverses. Another problem was the hostility of many Yemenis who regarded the Egyptians as foreign invaders. Burdened also by the high cost of the war, Abd al-Nasir was forced to seek some kind of reconciliation with Saudi Arabia. The first attempt was an agreement with Crown Prince Faisal in October 1964 to work out a compromise between the warring Yemeni factions. But the conference they arranged at Erkwith in the Sudan failed because neither side was willing to moderate its position.[6]

The second try was initially more successful. On August 24, 1965, Abd al-Nasir concluded the Jidda Agreement[7] with Faisal, who had become king the previous November. The Saudis pledged to stop supplying the royalist forces on the understanding that Egyptian troops would be evacuated within a year. The future government of Yemen was to be decided by a plebiscite in November 1966, but the royalists and republicans would be brought together much earlier to decide upon an interim regime. A conference between the two sides was subsequently held at the Yemeni town of Harad in November 1965. But owing to the fact that neither had been consulted at the time of the Jidda Agreement, the proceedings broke down over the issue of whether or not the provisional state would be called a republic. Another factor in the stalemate may have been Abd al-Nasir's decision to stay in Yemen on the basis of reports that Great Britain was planning to withdraw from Aden,[8] a change in the regional situation that was confirmed in February 1966. In any event, after the announcement, he made it clear that Egyptian forces would remain. He was undoubtedly also influenced by King Faisal's promotion of the idea of an Islamic conference, viewed by some as a way of shoring up Saudi Arabia's diplomatic position throughout the Muslim world.[9]

In the course of trying to figure out the most advantageous policy for

---

4. See Dana Adams Schmidt, *Yemen: The Unknown War* (New York: Holt, Rinehart & Winston, 1968).

5. Yaacov Shimoni and Evyatar Levine, eds., *Political Dictionary of the Middle East in the Twentieth Century* (London: Weidenfeld & Nicolson, 1972), p. 427.

6. Ibid., p. 428.

7. Ibid.

8. Ibid.

9. Kerr, *Arab Cold War*, pp. 109–10.

Egypt in the Yemen conflict, Abd al-Nasir was often involved in manipulating the republican leadership. When pursuing a hard line, he generally supported the most uncompromising republican, Abdullah al-Sallal. But if it seemed more propitious to adopt a flexible position, he installed as leaders more moderate personalities such as Ahmad Muhammad Numan, Abd al-Rahman al-Iryani, and Mahmud al-Zubeiri. Hasan al-Amri, who was ideologically quite close to al-Sallal, was another alternative. During the mid-1960s, these men moved in and out of office constantly according to changes in Abd al-Nasir's policies, demonstrating the tenuous character of inter-Arab politics at the time.[10]

Ultimately, Egypt's involvement in Yemen was radically altered by the June 1967 war with Israel. At the Khartum Summit Conference in August of that year (see Appendix 10), Abd al-Nasir agreed with King Faisal to bring the Yemen war to an end. The evacuation of Egyptian troops began in October. Fighting continued among the Yemenis through 1968, but in 1969 the Saudis shifted their support from the royalists to al-Iryani and al-Amri, who had successfully appeased the Riyadh government. Finally, in May 1970, an agreement was reached between the republican and royalist leaders by which the latter were allowed to participate in the administration of the country. But Yemen remained a republic and members of the royal family were barred from holding office. Saudi Arabia recognized the newly formed and more moderate republican regime in July 1970. Following nearly eight years of conflict that had deeply affected the Arab system, Yemen returned to a normal though greatly changed way of life.

THE CAIRO NEGOTIATIONS AND ARAB SUMMITRY

During the 1960s there were two major attempts to counter the disintegration of the Arab system. The first was a conference in Cairo in the early spring of 1963 which brought Abd al-Nasir and the leaders of the Iraqi and Syrian Baath parties together to discuss the question of unity. The other was the beginning of talks at the highest level among the Arab states, inaugurated by the Cairo Summit in January 1964. Both efforts came to naught, but perhaps certain lessons were learned which were in some respects helpful at a future date.

10. Shimoni and Levine, *Political Dictionary*, pp. 426–27.

The Syrian coup on March 8, 1963, had been executed by General Ziyad al-Hariri, an officer without political connections. He had, however, kept the Baath informed of his activities, allowing them to take credit for the deposition of the secessionist regime. They then took charge and formed a coalition government with the other pan-Arab factions in Syria, which were largely Nasirite, especially the Arab Nationalist Movement (ANM). Though the Baath was the senior partner, it was essential for their own credibility to make an immediate step in the direction of close relations with Baathist Iraq and with Egypt. It was in this way that they became the sponsors of the Cairo negotiations on Arab unity, which were held from March 14 to April 14, 1963.[11]

The talks were conducted in several phases, in some instances only between Egypt and Syria, but more frequently including Iraq as well. Much of the dialogue involved an airing of complaints, particularly those of Abd al-Nasir against the past performance of the Syrian Baath, which he sharply criticized for leaving the UAR government in December 1959. It was clear that the Egyptian leader had a low opinion of the Baath and considered its members untrustworthy and naïve. He addressed them condescendingly and with a considerable degree of contempt. It was also evident that there were ideological and procedural differences between Abd al-Nasir and the Baath.

In the end, no agreement could be reached on the conditions under which a union of the three countries could be implemented. It was largely a question of where the ultimate power would lie in a situation involving political personalities who thought differently and did not trust each other. But another aspect of the encounter was an underlying Egyptianism on Abd al-Nasir's part that made the whole prospect of uniting with the principal Fertile Crescent states distasteful. This distaste and the naïveté of the Baathists precluded a successful outcome of the talks.

Following the Cairo negotiations, relations between the Syrian Baath and the Nasirite factions deteriorated. On July 18, 1963, the Nasirites tried unsuccessfully to stage a coup, after which the Baath assumed full control of the country under the leadership of Amin al-Hafiz. As this entailed a breakdown of Syrian-Egyptian relations, the Baathists turned to Iraq to explore the possibilities of a merger. The initial reaction in Baghdad was favorable, and on October 8 a military treaty was signed. The Baath party of Syria interpreted this as a step toward union and officially called for the unification of the two countries. But Arif balked at the prospect and in November he took charge of Iraqi politics without the

11. See Kerr, *Arab Cold War*, pp. 44–76.

participation of the Baath,[12] leaving Syria on bad terms with both Cairo and Baghdad.

The Arab system was now beset with intense quarreling among its members. Abd al-Nasir had styled himself the last defender of Arab nationalism in the aftermath of the Syrian secession from the UAR, though he had already demonstrated a distinct pragmatism in his dealings with the other Arab states. In this instance, his determination to project a revolutionary image of himself led him to break diplomatic relations with Jordan and to become involved in a prolonged struggle with Saudi Arabia in Yemen. But he was equally estranged from the ostensibly more progressive regimes, being at odds with Syria over the rupture while Iraq was reverting to its traditional isolation. Particularism was again ascendant in Arab affairs, though it was masked by posturing.

By the beginning of 1964, Abd al-Nasir realized that it was necessary for Egypt's welfare to counter this divisive trend. He therefore called for a meeting of Arab heads of state to discuss what should be done about the impending Israeli project to divert the waters of the Jordan River. This led to the convention of the first Arab summit at Cairo in January 1964.[13] The conference produced a degree of cooperation among the Arab states with regard to countermeasures against Israel and the setting up of a joint defense system under Egyptian direction. It also diminished the propaganda war that had developed among the Arabs, and stimulated further efforts to coordinate policy on the Israeli question and to seek an end to the Yemen war at subsequent summit conferences held at Alexandria in September 1964 and at Casablanca in September 1965.

The early phase of Arab summitry, however, did not result in more than a semblance of solidarity. By 1966 the system began to deteriorate again, with a corresponding shift in alignments (see Appendix 4). As relations became strained between Jordan and the newly formed Palestine Liberation Organization (PLO), a rupture developed between Abd al-Nasir and King Husayn. Jordan then drew closer to Saudi Arabia, and Egypt and Syria began to patch up their differences. On February 23, 1966, the older Syrian Baath leaders were ousted by other Baathists, who quickly sought a rapprochement with Abd-al-Nasir. Relations between the two countries were gradually restored, culminating in the signing of a mutual defense treaty on November 7, 1966.[14] Summitry was now

12. Lenczowski, *Middle East in World Affairs*, pp. 300–302.
13. Ibid., p. 753.
14. Fred Khouri, *The Arab-Israeli Dilemma*, 2nd ed. (Syracuse, N.Y.: Syracuse University Press, 1976), p. 233.

abandoned, and the illusion of a revolutionary-conservative rivalry was revived.

It was at this point that the Arab states were drawn into the events leading to the June 1967 war. Divided into hostile blocs, they were hardly prepared for such a challenge, and indeed the rhetoric that flowed from Damascus in particular had a lot to do with setting the stage for the conflict that followed.[15] But the war profoundly changed the foundering Arab system.

THE 1967 WAR AS A WATERSHED

The most important consequence of the June 1967 war was that it enlarged the scope of the Arab-Israeli conflict. Suddenly there was more at stake than the question of Palestinian rights and repatriation; there was also the issue of the occupied territories. Egypt had lost the entire Sinai Peninsula and Gaza; Syria was divested of the Golan Heights region; and the West Bank was seized from Jordan. Since all these territorial concessions were major and entailed the security problem of heightened vulnerability, each of the three countries gave highest priority to the recovery of the lands that had been taken.

The war also raised the question of whether the idea of a military solution to the problem of Israel was still valid. The overwhelming superiority of the Israeli forces had been demonstrated in the crushing defeat of the Arab armies, and Abd al-Nasir and King Husayn in particular began to think in terms of a political settlement based on a return of the occupied territories in exchange for a de facto recognition of Israel.[16]

This shift in Egyptian and Jordanian policy became evident at the Khartum Summit Conference at the end of August 1967 (see Appendix 10). Though the final resolution issued on September 1 recapitulated some of the older sloganism by expressing the determination of the Arab states not to recognize, negotiate, or make peace with Israel, it also envisioned united efforts "at the international diplomatic level to eliminate the consequences of aggression and to assure the withdrawal of Israeli

15. Charles W. Yost, "The Arab-Israeli War: How It Began," *Foreign Affairs*, January 1968, p. 305.
16. Kerr, *Arab Cold War*, p. 131.

forces."[17] This left the door open for the three states which had lost territory to pursue political avenues to recover it. It was mainly Abd al-Nasir and King Husayn who were interested in following this path, and it was reported that both were prepared to make concessions to Israel as part of an overall settlement.[18] In this respect Egypt and Jordan, which had patched up their differences on the eve of the war, now appeared as partners in an altered situation which required new policies.

The Khartum conference also produced a rapprochement between Egypt and Saudi Arabia. Not only was a settlement of the Yemen war agreed upon by Abd al-Nasir and King Faisal, but Saudi Arabia joined with Kuwait and Libya in offering substantial annual financial support to Egypt and Jordan.[19] What Abd al-Nasir had done was essentially to abandon the revolutionary role he had adopted after the breakup of the union with Syria in favor of a more regionally oriented policy of relating to other Arab states in terms of Egyptian national interests. This involved a change of priorities as far as the Palestinians were concerned and implicitly put him at odds with Syria and Iraq. He was able to conceal this to some extent by embarking on the war of attrition with Israel. The war actually started in 1968 though it did not become an official policy until April 1969.[20] Yet the war of attrition was really designed to make Israel's position in Sinai sufficiently untenable to force the Israelis to consider a negotiated settlement.

In any event, Abd al-Nasir's position became amply clear at the Rabat Summit Conference in December 1969 (see Appendix 13). Accusing the other Arab states of failing to assume their share of the responsibilities involved in the struggle against Israel, he walked out of the meeting when they responded with hesitation. Thus he put the other Arabs on notice that Egypt was reserving for itself the right to work out its own problems in its own way.[21] One manifestation of this unilateralism was his acceptance of the American peace initiative known as the Rogers plan the following summer, when it became clear that the war of attrition had not altered Israel's stance.

While this shift was taking place in Egyptian policy, a number of substantial changes were unfolding in the rest of the Arab world. In Iraq,

---

17. Khouri, *Arab-Israeli Dilemma*, p. 313.
18. Ibid.
19. Ibid.
20. Lawrence L. Whetten, *The Canal War: Four Power Conflict in the Middle East* (Cambridge, Mass.: MIT Press, 1974), p. 82.
21. Kerr, *Arab Cold War*, pp. 145–46.

Abd al-Salam Arif, who had siezed power from the Baath in November 1963, was killed in an air crash on April 16, 1966. His brother, Abd al-Rahman Arif, had then assumed power. But on July 17, 1968, Ahmad Hasan al-Bakr, a Baathist who had played a major role in the revolutions of 1958 and 1963, executed a coup against the second Arif and restored the Baath to power.[22] Meanwhile in Syria, on February 23, 1966, Hafiz al-Asad had led the military wing of the Baath in a successful coup against Amin al-Hafiz and the older Baathists. Initially Salah Jadid was the major personality in the new government, but between the spring of 1969 and November 1970, al-Asad established his own leadership.[23] His first step in inter-Arab politics was to mend relations with Egypt, and in 1971 Syria joined with Egypt and Libya in forming a loose confederation known as the Federation of Arab Republics. The most significant development of al-Asad's rule, however, was the breach with the Iraqi Baath, which became a bitter feud in the 1970s.

Another important change was the overthrow of King Idris in Libya by Muammar Qaddhafi and other army officers in September 1969.[24] Libya was proclaimed a republic and became active in inter-Arab politics. As an admirer of Abd al-Nasir, Qaddhafi was initially pro-Egyptian, though he balanced this with his uncompromising support of the Palestinians and his respect for those who opposed a dominanat Egyptian role in Libya. But he did bring the country into the Federation of Arab Republics.

In the Sudan, a leftist military coup was carried out in May 1969 under the leadership of General Muhammad Jafar Numeiri.[25] In October he became prime minister, and has ruled the country ever since. Numeiri tried to strike a political balance among conservatives, some of the splinter Communist factions, and the army, though after the abortive Communist-inspired coup in July 1971 he shifted more to the right and was elected president in a plebiscite. Though Numeiri identified himself as ideologically pan-Arab, he did not join the Federation of Arab Republics and made no move to alter the status of the Sudan.

Just after Egypt and Saudi Arabia agreed to bring an end to the Yemen war, a new Arab state was formed in the British Crown Colony of Aden and the adjoining Western and Eastern Aden Protectorates. In

---

22. Majid Khadduri, *Socialist Iraq: A Study in Iraqi Politics Since 1968* (Washington, D.C.: Middle East Institute, 1978), pp. 21–24.
23. Lenczowski, *Middle East in World Affairs*, 352–59.
24. Peter Mansfield, *The Arabs* (New York: Pelican Books, 1978), pp. 459–66.
25. Ibid., pp. 444–47.

February 1966, Great Britain had announced that it would withdraw from this area by 1968. Already, nationalist organizations dedicated to securing independence had been formed. The most important of these were the National Liberation Front (NLF) and the Front for the Liberation of South Yemen (FLOSY). Following a struggle for ascendancy between the two groups, the NLF emerged as the dominant party and entered into negotiations with the British in the early autumn of 1967. The country became independent on November 29, 1967, under the name of People's Republic of South Yemen.[26]

Though a government was formed under the presidency of Qahtan al-Shabi, the situation was unstable because of a factional split within the NLF. Finally, in June 1969, the extreme leftist wing seized power in a coup and formed a new regime under Muhammad Ali Haitham and Salim Rubayyi Ali. In November 1970 the name of the country was changed to People's Democratic Republic of Yemen (PDRY),[27] reflecting the Marxist-Leninist orientation that prevailed. Close relations were established with the Soviet Union and the People's Republic of China, but Saudi Arabia and the Sultanate of Oman were extremely hostile toward the PDRY. Abd al-Nasir was relatively friendly, but after his death in September 1970, Egypt and South Yemen began to drift apart.

Great Britain also relinquished its protectorates in the Persian Gulf area. Kuwait became independent in 1961, but it was not until 1970 and 1971 that Oman, the United Arab Emirates (UAE), Qatar, and Bahrain became self-governing. All of these states remained traditional and conservative and, with the exception of Kuwait, fashioned most of their foreign policies on the Saudi model.

During the course of these developments, the Arab League increased in membership. The Sudan and Libya had joined in 1956 and Tunisia and Morocco in 1958, the latter having established their independence from France in 1956. Kuwait entered the league in 1961 and Algeria followed in 1962, at the end of a bitter war with France. South Yemen was admitted in December 1967, bringing the total membership to fourteen at the end of the decade. In the early 1970s, Bahrain, Qatar, the UAE, Oman, and Mauritania also joined.

One of the most significant by-products of the 1967 war was the gradual emergence of the Palestine Liberation Organization as a political force in the Arab system. The PLO was created by the Arab states at the

26. Joseph J. Malone, *The Arab Lands of Western Asia* (Englewood Cliffs, N.J.: Prentice-Hall, 1973), p. 205.
27. Ibid., p. 209.

Cairo Summit Conference in 1964, and remained largely under their aegis until the June war. At that point it was reorganized and became independent under new leadership,[28] though Syria and Iraq sponsored the Saiqa and Arab Liberation Front (ALF) factions, respectively. At the Palestine National Council meeting in 1968 a manifesto was adopted, committing the PLO to armed struggle against Israel, and in February 1969 Yasir Arafat was elected chairman of the executive committee.

But these changes were attended by the fragmentation of the PLO into numerous moderate and radical factions. The largest single unit was the Movement of Palestinian Liberation (*Fatah*), which was led by Arafat and confined its ideology to the struggle for national liberation. The more radical groups, such as George Habash's Popular Front for the Liberation of Palestine (PFLP) and Nayif Hawatmeh's Popular Democratic Front for the Liberation of Palestine (PDFLP), envisioned the reestablishment of Arab sovereignty in Palestine as part of a larger revolutionary movement which sought to unseat many established regimes and alter the status quo in much of the Middle East area.

Despite these differences, however, all of the PLO groups were anti–status quo in the sense that they rejected a compromise settlement with Israel and had a much closer relationship with the Palestinian rank and file than any of the Arab states had with their own people. In this respect there was a latent conflict between the PLO and the Arab regimes which became increasingly apparent in the 1970s.

The June 1967 war irreversibly altered the structure and character of the Arab system, which had been in the process of disintegration since the beginning of the decade. By 1970 Egypt had abandoned revolutionism in favor of a working relationship with Jordan and Saudi Arabia. Syria under al-Asad was moving toward a rapprochement with Cairo, as was Qaddhafi's Libya. Iraq retained a revolutionary orientation but was still isolated from the main currents of inter-Arab politics. South Yemen was even more radical; North Yemen was drawing closer to Saudi Arabia. Of the other states that had joined the system, Morocco and the Gulf sheikhdoms were conservative, Tunisia and Mauritania moderate, and the Sudan and Algeria to the left. Finally, the PLO had become an entity in its own right and posed a challenge to virtually all of the Arab regimes in its basic rejection of the status quo.

It was in the context of these changes that the Arab system entered a

28. William Quandt, Fuad Jaber, and Ann Lesch, *The Politics of Palestinian Nationalism* (Berkeley, Calif.: University of California Press, 1973), pp. 52–93.

new era. The dominant theme of the 1970s was a spirit of pragmatism. And despite ideological differences and the formation of blocs and alignments, interaction among the Arab states was based on an increased awareness of the balance-of-power relationships in a situation where interdependence was a reality and the establishment of some form of solidarity a need.

5

The New Pragmatism

THE TRILATERAL ALLIANCE

THE CHANGES in the Arab system that were introduced by the 1967 war began to solidify after Abd al-Nasir's death in September 1970. For Egypt, the guidelines had been set by Abd al-Nasir's rapprochement with Jordan and Saudi Arabia, and by his decision to seek a negotiated settlement of the Arab-Israeli conflict geared to Egyptian national interests. The task of carrying these initiatives to their logical conclusion was left to his designated successor, Anwar al-Sadat.

By the summer of 1971, al-Sadat had overcome all challenges to his leadership and had begun to define Egypt's position in world politics. On May 27, 1971, he had concluded a treaty of friendship with the Soviet Union. But he remained wary of the Soviet connection and his concern must have seemed justified by the attempted Communist coup in the Sudan the following July. Increasingly, he was to steer Egypt away from the dependence on Moscow that had become so pronounced in the last year of Abd al-Nasir's rule. The main problem was that he needed continuing Russian military support to keep his bargaining position strong.

From the early part of 1971 to the October war two and a half years later, al-Sadat carefully orchestrated his dealings with all parties to the Middle East conflict. Against the background of a general shift in Arab opinion favoring a political settlement with Israel, he pursued a negotiated agreement through all avenues which became open to him. The first of these was the renewed attempt of UN Special Representative Gunnar Jarring to break the deadlock. On February 8, 1971, Jarring issued a memorandum to both the Egyptian and Israeli UN delegations. The basis of the proposal was that Egypt and Israel should resolve the problem of whether recognition or withdrawal ought to come first by committing themselves at the same time to an Israeli evacuation of the Sinai Peninsula and an Egyptian agreement to end belligerency and to recognize Israel's sovereignty within secure borders. Egypt accepted the Jarring memorandum in its entirety, specifically stating that under these conditions it would make peace with Israel. The Israelis, however, declined the suggested accord and said that they would "not withdraw to the pre-June 5, 1967, lines." Though this brought Jarring's second attempt at promoting a peaceful settlement of the conflict to an unsuccessful conclusion, it earned for Egypt the reputation of having a sincere interest in peace.

In response to these developments, the United States took the initiative. After Sadat proposed the reopening of the Suez Canal in April 1971, the Americans tried to promote a limited Egyptian-Israeli understanding that would eventually lead to a broader agreement. But Israel's refusal to endorse Sadat's position that an accord on the canal be considered a first step in the withdrawal from all the occupied territories prompted the United States to seek a mediator role in talks between Egypt and Israel. However, these efforts also failed because of the disparity in the two negotiating positions. It was also evident in late 1971 that the United States had succumbed to the political pressure being applied by the Jewish lobby, which was demonstrated by the substantial increase in American military and economic aid to Israel.[1]

At this point Sadat began to refer to 1971 as the "year of decision," possibly a hint that he was reserving the war option if all attempts to achieve a peaceful settlement came to naught.[2] But he did cooperate with the endeavors of the Organization of African Unity in the autumn of 1971 and of U.N. Secretary General Kurt Waldheim in early 1972 to find some common ground between Egypt and Israel. As neither produced positive results, however, he began to turn to other alternatives.

In the meantime, Hafiz al-Asad had firmly established his own leadership in Syria in November 1970. His pragmatic approach to inter-Arab politics became evident when he indicated an interest in developing an amicable relationship with Egypt. This led in 1971 to the formation of the Federation of Arab Republics by Egypt, Syria, and Libya. Then on

1. Agency for International Development, *US Overseas Loans and Grants, July 1, 1945 - June 30, 1974* (Washington, D.C.: AID, 1975).
2. Fred Khouri, *The Arab-Israeli Dilemma*, 2nd ed. (Syracuse, N.Y.: Syracuse University Press, 1976), p. 367.

March 8, 1972, al-Asad announced that he would accept Security Council Resolution 242 if Israel would agree to withdraw from all the occupied territories and to include the Palestinians in any final settlement of the conflict.[3] This brought Syria even closer to Egypt, which had endorsed the resolution much earlier.

The Federation of Arab Republics was really a loose confederation which preserved the sovereignty of the participating states. As such, it had virtually no impact on the Arab system. Troubled by its ineffectiveness, Qaddhafi explored the possibility of a genuine Egyptian-Libyan union. Reluctantly, al-Sadat agreed to move in this direction and on August 29, 1973, a unified state was proclaimed, though the merger was to take place in stages. Following the October war, in which Libya was not involved, relations between Qaddhafi and al-Sadat deteriorated rapidly, and the union never materialized. The Federation of Arab Republics was also gradually disbanded, although it remained important as the beginning of Egyptian-Syrian collaboration.

It was at this time that al-Sadat began to explore a more substantial working relationship with Saudi Arabia than the rapprochement with that country initiated by Abd al-Nasir. Ultimately he decided that the best way to do this was to circumscribe the formidable presence of the Soviet Union in Egypt. Such a move would have the added advantage of encouraging the United States to pressure Israel into adopting a more flexible attitude with regard to the occupied territories, and it might also force the Soviets to reconsider their policy of withholding shipments of more sophisticated weaponry to Egypt. Therefore, in a bold gesture he evicted a large portion of the Soviet military and technical staff from Egypt in the summer of 1972.

Though this action did not have the desired effect in terms of changing American policy, it did eventually prompt the Soviets to supply Egypt with the equipment necessary for a war option. A more important consequence was the formation of a tacit trilateral alliance among Egypt, Syria, and Saudi Arabia.[4] Al-Asad had already established a close relationship with Egypt, and now Saudi Arabia was drawn into the orbit of al-Sadat's policies. This new alignment rapidly became the dominant political bloc in the Arab system and led eventually to the October war (see Appendix 5).

The trilateral alliance was the product of the pragmatic trend in Arab politics that had begun to develop after the 1967 war. Both al-Sadat

---

3. Ibid.
4. See Fouad Ajami, "Stress in the Arab Triangle," *Foreign Policy*, Winter 1977–78.

and al-Asad, as the respective leaders of the largest and strongest confrontation states, were more concerned with coordinating efforts to recover the occupied territories than with ideological issues.[5] Accordingly, they made concerted attempts to enhance their relationship with most of the Arab states, especially with each other, regardless of political orientation. What al-Sadat and al-Asad shared was a disinclination to introduce a "revolutionary" dimension into their foreign policies, as their predecessors had done at various times. This made them particularly appealing to King Faisal of Saudi Arabia, who did not hesitate to extend financial aid to both countries and to cement relations with them.

Though the Federation of Arab Republics was the initial vehicle of Egyptian-Syrian collaboration, the trilateral alliance soon replaced it as the key grouping within the Arab system. The three countries had no formal agreement, but there was a clear understanding among them that they comprised a leadership bloc based on an "equitable imbalance" of assets.[6] Egypt was the most powerful of the Arab states militarily; Saudi Arabia was by far the wealthiest. Syria enjoyed a certain prestige because of its historical role in the Arab awakening, and this gave it a degree of political influence. Syria also had a respectable army and a reasonably viable economy.

As a team, the trilateral states were unmatched in inter-Arab politics. They remained the dominant force in the system from 1971 until al-Sadat concluded the interim Sinai agreement with Israel in September 1975. They continued to exert considerable influence until the alliance was disbanded two years later.

The three states had a permanent impact on Arab affairs, however, in that they were the principal architects of the new pragmatism. The theme which they introduced and which became the common mode of inter-Arab political practice stressed the primacy of state interests and the development of cooperative relationships among sovereign entities. The emphasis was on realpolitik and the achievement of mutually beneficial schemes of collaboration, rather than on such doctrines as pan-Arabism and Arab socialism. The advantages to be gained from Arab solidarity were fully appreciated, but it was equally clear that a united front could be created within the context of the established territorial-political status quo. In this respect, the trilateral states and others that adopted their style were less interested in the issue of Palestinian rights per se than they were

5. George Lenczowski, *The Middle East in World Affairs*, 4th ed. (Ithaca, N.Y.: Cornell University Press, 1980), pp. 356, 564.
6. Ajami, "Stress in the Arab Triangle," p. 91.

in regional stability and a negotiated settlement of the Arab-Israeli conflict.[7]

By 1973 al-Sadat had lost faith in the willingness of the United States to pressure Israel into a more flexible position on the occupied territories. Prominent Israelis were already saying publicly that the territories should be retained, and the government was sponsoring the establishment of Jewish settlements in them. As a final test, al-Sadat called for a Security Council discussion of the situation,[8] in part to see what the American stand would be. Following many weeks during which the stalemate was reviewed, a resolution designed to force Israel's hand with regard to the occupied territories and Palestinian rights was introduced by eight members of the Council. Though thirteen of the fifteen members voted for it and one abstained, the United States used its veto in late July 1973 on the ground that the resolution was one-sided.

Convinced that only the war option remained, al-Sadat joined with Syria and Saudi Arabia in completing plans for a campaign against Israeli positions in the Sinai and the Golan Heights. Preparations for the attack were carried out in meticulous detail and complete secrecy. But it was clearly understood that the war would be limited in scope and purpose. Its aim in al-Sadat's mind was to jolt Israel into starting the withdrawal process and to show the United States in particular that the Arabs were capable of taking effective action to end the "no war, no peace" stalemate. Though the campaign was only partially successful, Israel was caught off guard and when the cease-fire negotiations had been completed with the participation of the superpowers, Israeli forces were no longer stationed on the east bank of the Suez Canal.

The Egyptian-Syrian military action and the imposition of a temporary embargo by the Arab oil producers led to substantial changes in the international relations of the Arab-Israeli conflict. Security Council Resolution 338, passed on October 22, called for negotiations to implement Resolution 242 and led to the inconclusive Geneva Conference in December. Al-Asad officially accepted Resolution 242 when he endorsed Resolution 338, though Syria remained unhappy about the insubstantial gains it had made in the Golan Heights. Egypt's acquisitions were more significant, but Israel was still in control of most of the Sinai. What was most important, however, was that the war had greatly enhanced the diplomatic leverage of the Arabs in world politics. Also al-Sadat began to

---

7. Fouad Ajami, "The End of Pan-Arabism," *Foreign Affairs*, Winter 1978–79, p. 357.
8. Khouri, *Arab-Israeli Dilemma*, p. 369.

establish an entirely new relationship with the United States which was to have a far-reaching effect on all aspects of the overall conflict.

Al-Sadat had always felt that Egypt's long-range interests would best be served by a close relationship with the United States.[9] He had also always been far more an Egyptian nationalist than a pan-Arabist.[10] He therefore interpreted Egypt's successes in the October war as a license to pursue whatever policies he considered most advantageous for his country.[11] In cooperating with US Secretary of State Henry Kissinger's step-by-step diplomacy, he established a convergence of American and Egyptian interests which radically altered Egypt's position in the Arab system. He patiently endured Israel's behavior in the negotiations that took place over the following two years, and achieved a tactical victory when Kissinger himself became exasperated with Israel and launched the "reassessment" of US Middle East policy in the spring of 1975.[12]

The policies which al-Sadat pursued after 1973 are best understood in terms of his relationship to the new Egyptian middle class. Whereas the old bourgeoisie of Abd al-Nasir's era regarded Israel as an obstacle to its natural markets in the Arab east, the entrepreneurs of the 1970s came to regard the Arab-Israeli conflict as obsolete.[13] They saw many economic advantages in close cooperation and joint ventures with both Israeli and American businessmen, and therefore favored a negotiated settlement with Israel and a tacit alliance with the United States. Hence the course of al-Sadat's policies was in compliance with the specific interests of this class, which held the greatest influence in Egyptian society.

Al-Sadat's diplomacy in the aftermath of the October war introduced a certain tension within the Arab system which was to become more complicated with time. The initial situation found Egypt, Syria, and Saudi Arabia disposed to seek a negotiated political settlement of the conflict which would include conditional recognition of Israel's sovereignty. But the trilateral states were not alone in this. The majority of Arab governments were of like mind, and there was a shift in Palestinian thinking which favored a political rather than a military approach to the problem. On February 19, 1974, Fatah, Saiqa, and the PDFLP concurred on the

9. Anwar El-Sadat, *In Search of Identity: An Autobiography* (New York: Harper & Row, 1978), pp. 146–47, 300–301.
10. *L'Orient* (Beirut), January 28, 1954. In an interview conducted by the French daily, al-Sadat asserted that he was first of all an Egyptian nationalist.
11. Ajami, "End of Pan-Arabism," p. 358.
12. Edward Sheehan, *The Arabs, Israelis, and Kissinger* (New York: Reader's Digest Press, 1976), pp. 159–65.
13. Walid Kazziha, *Palestine in the Arab Dilemma* (New York: Barnes & Noble, 1979), pp. 87–97.

principle of establishing Palestinian sovereignty in any part of the West Bank and Gaza relinquished by Israel.[14]

Iraq, Libya, South Yemen, and several of the radical Palestinian factions were adamantly opposed to the idea of a political solution, which they assumed would necessarily involve extensive compromises with Israel and the "imperialist" powers. In October 1974, Iraq, the PFLP, the PFLP-GC (General Command), the ALF, and the PSF (Popular Struggle Front) formed a loosely organized association known as the Rejection Front (*Jabhat al-Rafd*),[15] to which Libya and South Yemen later adhered. The main position of this group was that a reconvened Geneva conference would be counterproductive to Arab and Palestinian interests and should be avoided at all costs. That same month the PFLP resigned from the PLO Executive Committee to underline the extent of its opposition to the new trend in the mainstream of the Palestinian movement.

The emergence of the Rejection Front appeared to recreate the old revolutionary-conservative dichotomy. But in reality, much of the Arab world was moving away from doctrinaire ideologies and gravitating toward a pragmatic approach to political problems and a reassertion of regional interests and prerogatives. Yet there was a fine line between what was acceptable in practice and what should be considered going too far. For despite the resurgence of realism and regionalism, there was an awareness that the search for a political solution would require a closing of ranks among the Arabs. It would hardly be possible to emerge successfully from a negotiating process which included Israel and the United States if there were disagreement among the Arabs as to the perimeters of acceptable conditions. There was therefore an increased emphasis on the importance of solidarity, and the existence of a rejectionist position served in some respects to define the dividing line between real compromise and political finesse.

The issue was first brought into focus when Egypt concluded the interim Sinai agreement (Sinai II) with Israel under Secretary Kissinger's auspices on September 1, 1975. The agreement secured Israel's evacuation of the Abu Rudeis oil fields and its withdrawal beyond the Mitla and Gidi passes. But it did not make any connection between the adjustments in Sinai and either the other occupied territories or the Palestinian question. It was already beginning to appear that Egypt was pursuing a path that would ultimately lead to a separate peace with Israel. And in the meantime, Kissinger's step-by-step efforts ground to a halt. This confronted the

---

14. Khouri, *Arab-Israeli Dilemma*, p. 374.

15. Muhammad Y. Muslih, "Moderates and Rejectionists within the Palestine Liberation Organization," *Middle East Journal*, Spring 1976, pp. 127–28, 134.

Arab system with the problem of internal divisiveness and set in motion a search to reestablish solidarity. But at this stage, attention was drawn to the enhanced role of the PLO and to the crisis in Lebanon.

THE ROLE OF THE PLO

The PLO's ascent to prominence in the Arab system began with the reorganization of the movement under new leadership following the 1967 war. On March 21, 1968, Palestinian and Jordanian forces inflicted heavy losses on an Israeli column which was trying to destroy guerrilla bases at the Karameh refugee camp east of the Jordan River. This incident had a galvanizing effect and produced a marked increase in Palestinian political and military activity. Meeting in Cairo in July 1968, the Palestine National Council adopted a National Charter which called for the liberation of Palestine by armed struggle (see Appendix 11). During the ensuing two years the PLO became increasingly assertive in inter-Arab politics, soliciting financial support from the wealthier states and extending its bases of operation in Jordan and Lebanon. Ultimately this led to the bloody confrontation between the Jordanian army and the guerrillas in September 1970, and then to the termination of the Palestinian military presence in Jordan during the summer of 1971.

The PLO subsequently concentrated on building up its position in Lebanon, though in principle the extent of guerrilla activity in the south was restricted by the Cairo Agreement of November 3, 1969 (see Appendix 12). From the autumn of 1971 to the October 1973 war, the Palestinians were in disarray. Lacking a clearly defined political direction or methodology, they often expressed their frustrations through hijackings and terrorist activities which did little to help their cause. Equally counterproductive was the fragmentation of the movement into a plethora of moderate and radical groups, a development that deprived the PLO of cohesiveness and unified leadership.

After the October war, however, the PLO made substantial headway in expanding its political influence within the Arab system. The first major step in this direction was the recognition by all of the Arab states at the Rabat Summit Conference in October 1974 that the PLO was the sole legitimate representative of the Palestinian people (see Appendix 14). With its status firmly established, the PLO became intensely involved in the give-and-take of inter-Arab politics and on September 9, 1976, it was admitted to membership in the Arab League.

The relationship between the Palestinians and the Arab states has always been paradoxical and surrounded by contradictions. As Walid Kazziha has pointed out, "Historically . . . the Palestinian problem has been subject to the political fluctuations of the Arab political scene."[16] More specifically, "As far as the Arab regimes are concerned, the Palestinian cause is, and has been, a pawn of inter-Arab rivalry. Whenever inter-Arab conflict is intensified, the Palestinian problem gains prominence, but once the Arab leaders make peace with each other even for a short time, the Palestinian cause is brushed under the carpet."[17]

Kazziha's interpretation needs to be tempered by a recognition that virtually all Arabs are genuinely concerned by the eviction of the Palestinians from their homeland and the transformation of the country into a Jewish state. But he is correct in his observation that "state boundaries and national sovereignty became sacred elements in the life of the separate Arab entities . . . most of the Arab governing elites realized that they had a lot to lose if they allowed regional boundaries to disappear and new political elites sponsoring the cause of unity to emerge."[18] That is, the Arab regimes were beneficiaries of the established territorial status quo in the sense that their own authority was based on it.

The Palestinians, on the other hand, had no stake whatsoever in the existing political structure. They were committed either to the transformation of Israel into a "secular democratic state" or to the creation of an independent Palestinian entity in the West Bank and Gaza. Furthermore, both of these alternatives potentially entailed broader territorial implications, such as the inclusion of Jordan in any new dispensation. Added to this was the fact that the PLO frequently violated the sovereignty of Arab states by carrying on the armed struggle against Israel from inside their borders without consideration of the repercussions this might have. The leftist commando groups, moreover, openly proclaimed that one of their objectives was to topple many of the Arab regimes.

Another source of tension between the PLO and the Arab states relates to differences in political style. Most Arab governments are ruled by elites which monopolize the foundations of power. These include dynasties, charismatic leaders, military juntas, and party cliques. Gener-

16. Kazziha, *Palestine in the Arab Dilemma*, p. 15.
17. Ibid., p. 17.
18. Ibid., pp. 36–37.

ally, the rulers have a paternalistic orientation in the way they relate to the masses. For example, President Sadat sometimes referred to himself as "*rabb al-usrah*" (head of the family). In virtually all cases, however, there is little if any diffusion of power to the grass roots.

Though there may be some parallels to this kind of political practice among the organized Palestinian groups, there is a strong emphasis in the movement on popular armed resistance. As Kazziha points out, this "does not only invite the open and active participation of the Arab masses, but also establishes under certain conditions a new basis of political legitimacy, one which is based on massive violence and revolutionary activity."[19] In this respect, the Palestinian hierarchy narrowed the gap between itself and the masses and created a more democratic and egalitarian atmosphere within the movement than exists in most Arab countries. At any rate, Palestinian leaders and their constituents consciously believe that they have a unique political orientation and that they are giving the Arab world an example of genuine democracy. Ahmad Sidqi al-Dajani, a prominent PLO statesman, feels that the Palestinians have revived the early Islamic institution of the *shura*, in which acclaimed tribal dignitaries collectively discussed policies and made decisions.[20]

The degree to which the internal political practices of the PLO differ from those of the Arab states is a moot point. What is important is that many Arab regimes perceive the PLO as a potentially destabilizing influence within their own countries, and that the PLO is suspicious of the established authorities. As pointed out in Chapter 4, a latent conflict exists between the PLO and many of the Arab governments. But it became clear in the 1970s that there was a degree of interdependence. This is why, in Kazziha's words, one of the major questions raised in the aftermath of the October war "was precisely concerned with defining the relationship between the Palestinian Resistance Movement and the Arab governments and peoples."[21]

Particular friction has been generated by the attempts of several Arab regimes to exercise a degree of control over the PLO. At various times and in different ways Jordan, Syria, Iraq, and Libya tried to do this. Following the eviction of the Palestinian commandos from Jordan in the summer of 1971, King Husayn sought to establish himself as the legal representative of the Palestinian people. On March 15, 1972, he proposed a plan to create a federated state comprising Transjordan and the West

19. Ibid., p. 36.
20. Based on an interview with Ahmad Sidqi al-Dajani in Beirut in May 1980.
21. Kazziha, *Palestine in the Arab Dilemma*, p. 15.

Bank as two autonomous regions under his own crown.[22] But this was adamantly opposed by the PLO, which prevailed upon Egypt and other Arab states to reject the idea. Ultimately, King Husayn went along with the Arab consensus in recognizing the PLO as the sole legitimate representative of the people at the Rabat summit in October 1974.

President al-Asad attempted to bring the Palestinian movement under his own aegis, partly through the Syrian client faction, Saiqa, and also by means of the dominant position in Lebanon which Syria attained in 1976. But in early 1977, al-Asad agreed to accept a virtual Palestinian sovereignty in parts of southern Lebanon, thus ending his efforts to direct the activities of the PLO in that region. Syria continues, however, to influence the Palestinians, who look to Damascus as a champion of their cause and who could not maintain their position in Lebanon without Syrian consent.

The friction between Iraq and the PLO developed out of Iraq's objections to the position taken by Fatah, Saiqa, and the PDFLP on February 19, 1974, favoring a sovereign state in part of Palestine. On March 20, 1977, the Palestine National Council, which had been meeting in Cairo, endorsed this idea by a large majority, asserting in its declaration the right of the Palestinian people to establish "their independent national state on their national soil" (see Appendix 17). At this point Iraq joined its radical PLO allies in condemning the ministate concept and together they embarked on a terrorist campaign designed to force the mainstream of the PLO to abandon the new policy. This led to the assassination of several Palestinian representatives, such as Said Hammami, who was killed in London in January 1978. But following the first Baghdad conference Iraq discontinued these practices and acknowledged the right of the PLO to decide its own destiny.

Since Qaddhafi's accession to power in 1969, Libya has been among the most ardent supporters of the Palestinian cause. After the October war, Qaddhafi increasingly adhered to the hard line and considered himself heir to Abd al-Nasir's legacy. He associated with the Rejection Front after it was formed in October 1974 and later joined other alliances directed against Egypt. But like Iraq, he opposed the moderate platform which accepted the principle of a West Bank–Gaza state. Ultimately Qaddhafi's relationship with the PLO leadership deteriorated, and in December 1979 he sharply condemned Arafat and others for compromising the goals of the movement. Four months later a reconciliation was achieved, but the

22. Lenczowski, *Middle East in World Affairs*, p. 496.

contrast between Qaddhafi's purist idealism and the PLO's practicality left a residue of latent hostility between them.

The primary disadvantage of the PLO in its dealings with the Arab states is that it cannot operate without their support. This situation is particularly difficult given the underlying conflict of interests that exists. But the PLO also enjoys certain assets in the politics of the Arab system. Foremost among these is that Arab regimes gain prestige and enhance their own legitimacy by openly backing the Palestinian movement. After the PLO entered the mainstream of inter-Arab politics in October 1974, its leaders become increasingly adept at diplomatic maneuvering. As Jonathan Randal has put it, "Arafat skillfully shifts with the changing winds of Arab politics, taking advantage of the differences among the various Arab regimes to preserve the relatively autonomous position of the PLO."[23] In this respect, Arafat manages to keep the regimes slightly off balance, as they seek to preserve a favorable image with respect to the Palestine question in their competitive and often uncertain relationship with each other.

Arafat has also enhanced the PLO's bargaining power by assuming the role of interlocutor in some of the disputes that have arisen in the course of the complex interaction among the Arab countries. Equally important is the pragmatism that has come to characterize his style. Not only is it in keeping with the whole tenor of the system, but it has allowed him to make limited gains while putting most of the Arab governments at ease. His decision to support the ministate concept is a particular case in point.

The basis of the PLO's realism is its recognition that it has to deal with the Arab states diplomatically and to function on two levels—the ideal and the pragmatic. Although constantly seeking to gain maximum support for its own aims, it also understands that there is a diversity of interests in the Arab world and that it has to adopt a give-and-take policy.[24] Abd al-Nasir once distinguished between the concepts of "unity of ranks" (*wahdat al-saff*), and "unity of purpose" (*wahdat al hadaf*). The former referred to the common practice among Arab states of pursuing their own interests while trying to cooperate with the other members of the league. The latter was based on the idea that all the Arabs should work as a team to achieve such common objectives as the return of the occupied territories and the establishment of a Palestinian state. Though a number of Arab regimes claim to adhere to the principle of unity of purpose,

23. Jonathan Randal, "PLO's Armed-Struggle Rhetoric Muted by Pragmatic Politicking," *Washington Post*, March 2, 1980.
24. Based on an interview with Ahmad Sidqi al-Dajani in Beirut in May 1980.

virtually all of them actually operate in terms of unity of ranks. The PLO takes the position that it is necessary to achieve a balance between the two. For though the unity-of-purpose concept most closely approximates its own aspirations, it cannot force Arab regimes to adopt policies which run counter to the national interests of their own countries.

There is some opposition within Palestinian ranks to the pragmatic style of Arafat and Fatah. A number of radical factions still reject the idea of accommodating the interests of the Arab regimes and trying to define minimum goals. Also, many West Bank Palestinians cannot understand why the PLO feels it is necessary to be so flexible. The National Guidance Committee (*Lajnat al-Tawjih al-Watani*), which is charged with maintaining the solidarity of the West Bank constituency, tries to preserve the link between these Palestinians and the PLO. But since both confront very different sets of circumstances, it is understandable that they do not see the common challenge in the same way.

Despite some dissent, the PLO shared the new pragmatism of the 1970s, while preserving certain unique traits in its own internal political orientation. Its flexibility allowed it to maximize its assets and to assume a more powerful role in the Arab system than would otherwise have been possible. But it remained vulnerable to unpredictable dislocations in the balance of power, and its involvement in the Lebanese civil war put it in the middle of a complicated inter-Arab crossfire.

CRISIS IN LEBANON

The Lebanese civil war, which began in April 1975, was the product of several explosive ingredients. The major underlying cause was the established political system in Lebanon, which was based on a delicate balance of sectarian interests rather than on an integrated national model. Despite the brief destabilization in 1958, the balance was maintained from 1945 to 1970. But the system became dysfunctional in the ensuing years because it perpetuated the myth of Christian preponderance in the context of an actual Muslim majority. Aside from the general Muslim grievances, the most alienated group was the Shiite community, which was rapidly becoming the largest single sectarian element while exercising the least influence and suffering the disabilities of proletarianization. Yet another source of friction was the latent conflict between an affluent middle class and a relatively impoverished populace.

It was against the background of these untoward developments that the Palestinian commandos were expanding their presence in Lebanon, especially in the aftermath of their eviction from Jordan. The Cairo Agreement of 1969 had stated that "Palestinians residing in Lebanon are to be allowed to take part in the Palestinian Revolution through Armed Struggle while acting in conformity with Lebanese security and sovereignty" (see Appendix 12). But in practice the PLO tended to interpret the accord as giving it a free hand to carry on its paramilitary activities against Israel from southern Lebanon, rather than as a set of conditions under which it could operate on the soil of a sovereign state in which it had no authority.

Despite the impending clash of Lebanese and Palestinian claims to various prerogatives in Lebanon, the PLO became closely allied with the National Progressive Front, which was formed under the leadership of Kamal Jumblat in the late 1960s. This group represented a coalition of the left and the Arab-nationalist Sunni middle class.[25] As such, it was naturally sympathetic to the Palestinian cause and was prepared to assist the PLO in using Lebanon as a base of operations. The guerrillas also developed close ties with the Shiite community, and thus became an integral part of the Lebanese political landscape. But it was this circumstance that put them on a collision course with the Maronites, who were building up their own paramilitary capacity through the militant Phalange organization.

The festering situation in Lebanon, with its combination of Arab and regional nationalists, Muslims, Druze, Christians, and Palestinians, became a focal point of inter-Arab tension when the animosity between the two hostile camps escalated into a full-scale civil war in April 1975. The most intensely involved Arab state was Syria, though Egypt, Saudi Arabia, Jordan, Iraq, and Libya were also drawn into the conflict in terms of what they perceived as their own national interests. While the immediate parties were fighting over the issue of whether the Lebanese status quo would be maintained or altered, the external states were concerned with the ways in which the outcome would affect the Arab balance of power.

Syria's intervention in Lebanon was prompted by the notion of a "special role" that Damascus was assumed to occupy in Lebanese affairs and by a number of security considerations. Though Syria had accepted the establishment of an independent Lebanon and entertained no expansionist designs on its territory, the fragmentation of Greater Syria by Great Britain and France after World War I had never been accepted. Also,

25. Kazziha, *Palestine in the Arab Dilemma*, p. 46.

Syria and Lebanon shared the common experience of French administration in the interwar period and were linked economically. Significantly, they did not even consider it necessary to set up normal diplomatic relations because of their mutual affinity.[26] Syria regarded itself as the senior partner in a sub-regional entity that included Lebanon and reserved the right of intervention in the event of any dramatic change in the status quo.

From the beginning of the civil war until the end of 1975, Syria's involvement was minimal and was restricted to supplying the Muslim-Palestinian alliance and attempting to serve as mediator.[27] By January 1976, however, al-Asad had decided to assume a more prominent role. The Maronites had begun a campaign to partition the country, an eventuality which al-Asad regarded as intolerable. Indeed, the principal aim of Syrian policy throughout the crisis was to prevent the disintegration of Lebanon or a radical change in its existing system of government.[28] The main concern was that destabilization based on a violent collapse of the sectarian balance could stimulate reverberations in Syria. Since President al-Asad's ruling clique was itself drawn largely from the Alawite minority, the regime was particularly sensitive to this possibility. Hence the Lebanese crisis had substantial implications for Syrian security.

Another security problem was the uncertain impact the civil war might have on Syria's relations with Israel. The major danger was that Israel would use the conflict as an excuse to occupy southern Lebanon up to the Litani River, a development which would increase the vulnerability of Damascus in the event of war with Israel. There was also the possibility that the Israelis might point to the disorder in Lebanon to discredit the PLO's concept of a secular democratic Palestine.[29]

The Syrian intervention in early 1976 was initially designed to engineer a political settlement by introducing a reform proposal. Al-Asad's plan, which was presented to President Frangieh on February 15, called for the perpetuation of the sectarian, or confessional, political system but with some modification of the Christian preponderance.[30] This was accepted by the Maronites and their allies but strongly opposed by Jumblat

---

26. Itamar Rabinovich, "The Limits of Military Power: Syria's Role," in P. Edward Haley and Lewis W. Snider, eds., *Lebanon in Crisis: Participants and Issues* (Syracuse, N.Y.: Syracuse University Press, 1979), p. 56.

27. Ibid., p. 60.

28. Adeed Dawisha, "Syria in Lebanon—Assad's Vietnam?" *Foreign Policy*, Winter 1978–79, pp. 139–41.

29. Ibid., pp. 137–38.

30. Rabinovich, "Limits of Military Power," p. 62.

and the Muslim-PLO coalition, who favored a radical change in the system based on secularization. By early spring the tide had turned in the fighting and the Christians were thrown on the defensive. Faced with a marked alteration of the status quo, al-Asad decided to send large numbers of Syrian troops into the country. But in this case it was to prevent the Muslim-PLO side from gaining the upper hand and laying the foundations of a transformed Lebanon.

Syria's actions, both political and military, aroused the concern of its principal Arab rivals—Egypt, Iraq, and Libya.[31] Al-Sadat had maintained a relatively low profile with regard to the Lebanese crisis until Syria began to become actively involved in the autumn of 1975. This was also a time of tension between Cairo and Damascus because of Syria's objections to Sinai II. In October al-Sadat convened a meeting of Arab foreign ministers in Cairo to discuss the problem, but it had little effect because Syria, the PLO, and Libya did not attend. He subsequently called for nonintervention in the conflict by the Arab states, an indirect criticism of Syria.[32] As al-Asad adopted an increasingly active role in Lebanon, Egypt became more specific in its condemnations of Syria and tried to take advantage of the rupture between Damascus and the PLO in the spring of 1976 by posing as the champion of the Palestinians.

Egypt's major aims were to prevent the crisis from escalating into an Arab-Israeli confrontation, to avoid the transformation of Lebanon advocated by the Muslim-PLO coalition, and to keep Syria from establishing a dominant position both in the country as a whole and with regard to the PLO.[33] Inasmuch as Cairo and Damascus were in accord on the first two of these goals, the friction that developed between them was really over the issue of Syrian hegemony in Lebanon. The Egyptians had traditionally opposed all attempts to establish a greater degree of unity in the Fertile Crescent, and al-Asad's actions seemed to represent a move in that direction. Al-Sadat did not threaten to become involved militarily, but he sought to contain al-Asad's intervention by applying political pressure within the Arab system.

Iraq was equally opposed to the role Syria was playing. The rival branch of the Baath Party which ruled in Baghdad was especially sensitive to the balance-of-power situation within the Fertile Crescent, which was tilted in al-Asad's favor when he decided to take an active part in the

31. Ibid., p. 63.
32. Mohammed Mughisuddin, "Egypt," in P. Edward Haley and Lewis W. Snider, eds., *Lebanon in Crisis: Participants and Issues* (Syracuse, N.Y.: Syracuse University Press, 1979), p. 142.
33. Ibid., p. 138.

Lebanese crisis. Following the change in al-Asad's tactics which brought him to support the Christian militias in the spring of 1976, the Iraqis severely condemned Syria while supporting the Muslim-PLO alliance in Lebanon and encouraging opposition to al-Asad's policies within his own country.[34]

Libya was the third country to take strong issue with the Syrian intrusion in the Lebanese civil war. Qaddhafi's attention had been drawn to the crisis by the combination of issues that were at stake. He was sympathetic with those who wanted to change the status quo in a situation which appeared to give Christians the advantage over Muslims and to favor the interests of the rich over those of the poor.[35] He also felt that another issue implicit in the conflict was the ideological clash between pan-Arabism and parochial nationalism. For this reason, he encouraged the Muslim-PLO bloc to continue its struggle and gave it material support. But as in the case of Egypt and Iraq, there was no question of direct Libyan military involvement.

The challenge of these three Arab states to al-Asad's Lebanese adventure set up a countervailing force to the Syrian intervention which had an impact on the politics of the Arab system. To buttress his own position, al-Asad sought the support of Jordan, which also favored preserving a moderately reformed status quo in Lebanon but did not share the rivalistic attitudes toward Syria which were so apparent in Egypt and Iraq. King Husayn responded positively and served as an intermediary between Syria and various factions in Lebanon, particularly the Maronite followers of Camille Chamun and the Shiites under the leadership of Kamal Asaad.[36] He also approved the changes in the Lebanese system proposed by Syria and backed Hafiz al-Asad in his decision to intervene militarily to prevent the Muslim-PLO coalition from imposing its own alternative. Beyond this, King Husayn reassured Washington that the Syrian intervention did not imply any threat to Israel and redeployed his forces to assist Syria in the event of an Iraqi attempt to attack from the east. In these respects King Husayn allied himself with al-Asad in his undertaking, largely because a Muslim-PLO victory in Lebanon might isolate Jordan in its immediate regional situation and also preclude the possibility of a rapprochement between Amman and the PLO. In the long run, he looked to a solution to

---

34. Rabinovich, "Limits of Military Power," p. 65.
35. Walid Khalidi, *Conflict and Violence in Lebanon: Confrontation in the Middle East* (Cambridge, Mass.: Harvard Center for International Affairs, 1979), pp. 85–86.
36. Paul Jureidini and Ronald McLaurin, "The Hashimite Kingdom of Jordan," in P. Edward Haley and Lewis W. Snider, eds., *Lebanon in Crisis: Participants and Issues* (Syracuse, N.Y.: Syracuse University Press, 1979), pp. 156–58.

the crisis that would be imposed by the surrounding Arab states. Al-Asad, on the other hand, saw the alliance with Jordan as a stepping-stone in a broader scheme which envisioned a federation of Syria, Lebanon, Jordan, and the West Bank as a regional system under Syrian hegemony.[37]

Saudi Arabia was also gradually drawn into the inter-Arab confrontation brought on by the crisis in Lebanon. During the initial phase of the civil war the Saudis were relatively uninvolved. Their major concern was to ease the tension that had developed between Egypt and Syria over the stalled American peace initiative.[38] In mid-April 1975 they convened a trilateral conference in Riyadh which was partially successful in effecting a reconciliation. But the conclusion of the interim Sinai agreement by Egypt and Israel the following September revived the Asad-Sadat rivalry, while the fighting in Lebanon became more intense.

In the ensuing months the Saudis became increasingly concerned over the situation in Lebanon and its repercussions. Their attempts to revive the trilateral alliance had failed and they were suspicious of the intentions of Damascus, especially with regard to al-Asad's plan for a Greater Syrian federation.[39] But the Riyadh government was as opposed as the Syrians and the Egyptians to a dramatic change in the Lebanese system and to the prospect of a leftist victory in the civil war. They were also anxious to prevent the conflict from precipitating a broader Arab-Israeli confrontation. Thus they took a strong position in favor of a settlement imposed by all the Arab states acting in concert, rather than unilateral interventions by particular countries.

When the fighting escalated and the Christians perpetrated a particularly bloody assault on the Muslims in early December 1975, the Saudis terminated their tacit support of the Christian side, which favored the status quo. Another reason for this move was the liaison the Christians had established with the Israelis, who had begun to become involved in the Lebanese crisis. Though the Syrians turned against the Muslim-PLO coalition in the spring of 1976, Saudi Arabia backed the Syrian intervention as the only plausible solution to the problem. But the key to linking Syria's intervention to a pan-Arab peace initiative remained a reconciliation between Damascus and Cairo.

In the spring of 1976 the Saudis tried to organize a meeting in Riyadh of the prime ministers of Syria, Egypt, Saudi Arabia, and Kuwait.

---

37. Rabinovich, "Limits of Military Power," p. 69.
38. M. Graeme Bannerman, "Saudi Arabia," in P. Edward Haley and Lewis W. Snider, eds., *Lebanon in Crisis: Participants and Issues* (Syracuse, N.Y.: Syracuse University Press, 1979), pp. 118–20.
39. Ibid., p. 123.

But this endeavor failed because al-Asad and al-Sadat could not resolve their differences over Sinai II.[40] Gradually, however, al-Asad began to favor the idea of a broader Arab role in the Lebanese crisis. Aside from the fact that Syria was relatively isolated within the Arab system, there was mounting domestic unrest and the government was economically pressed. Also, Lebanon had been virtually partitioned, with the Syrians in control of the east, the Christians established in a centrally located enclave based on Junieh, and the Muslims and Palestinians dominant in the Tripoli area, West Beirut, the southern coastal region, and parts of Mount Lebanon. Because of the explosive and unpredictable nature of this fragmentation, the Israelis had become involved in the crisis beginning with a raid into southern Lebanon in December 1975. This was meant to be a warning not only to the PLO, but to Damascus as well. Israel made it clear that it would not tolerate a Syrian military presence beyond an undefined "red line," thought by many to be the Litani River. Finally, the fighting in Lebanon intensified markedly in the spring and summer of 1976, and al-Asad became more receptive to the mediating role the Saudis were trying to play. Ultimately this led to the Riyadh mini-summit in October 1976, a meeting which marked a triumph for Saudi diplomacy (see Appendix 15).

The crisis in Lebanon involved a number of substantive ideological issues. The inequities of a corrupt confessional system, the continuing dominance of a minority sectarian grouping, exploitation of the poor, and the right of Palestinians to self-determination were perhaps the major ones. But most of the Arab states which were drawn into the conflict based their policies on pragmatic considerations. This was particularly clear in the case of Egypt, Syria, and Saudi Arabia, the architects of the new pragmatism who were at pains to preserve their tacit trilateral alliance. By the autumn of 1976 these countries recognized that they had to end the civil war in Lebanon and to establish solidarity among the Arabs to meet the challenge posed by the prospect of a negotiated settlement of the Arab-Israeli conflict. During the following year their major preoccupation was the search for a united front.

THE SEARCH FOR SOLIDARITY

During the years immediately following the October war, most of the Arab states recognized that an era of armed conflict with Israel had given way to one in which the major theme would be diplomatic maneuvering.

40. Ibid., p. 128.

This made it essential for the Arabs to close ranks so that they could undertake the political task before them as a coordinated bloc. Otherwise they could never hope to achieve even their minimum requirements in a settlement involving negotiations with Israel, the United States, and perhaps other powers.

Saudi Arabia had taken the initiative with its attempts to reconcile the differences between Egypt and Syria. These differences originated with al-Sadat's decision not to pursue the campaign in Sinai after pushing the Israelis back from the Suez Canal. This had allowed the Israelis to concentrate on the northern front, resulting in a disastrous defeat of Syrian forces in that sector. Furthermore, the disengagement agreement with Israel on May 29, 1974, to which al-Asad had to accede, left Syria with the minor gain of an insubstantial strip of land including the virtually destroyed city of Quneitra in the Golan Heights.

The interim Sinai agreement of September 1, 1975, led to a further deterioration in relations between Cairo and Damascus. Since it took no account of the situation in the Golan Heights, many Syrians interpreted it as a further step in what seemed to them an overall betrayal by Egypt. The relationship between the two countries reached its nadir in June 1976, when the respective ambassadors were recalled. This heightened the concern in Riyadh and led to Saudi efforts to resolve both the Lebanese problem and the Egyptian-Syrian rupture. Ultimately they forwarded the idea of an inter-Arab conference to mediate the conflict in Lebanon, a step designed to have the added advantage of reconciling Saudi Arabia's two partners in the trilateral alliance.

By the end of September 1976, the Syrian forces had gained the upper hand in the military confrontation in Lebanon and al-Asad was in a position to impose his own settlement. He decided, however, that the inter-Arab solution which Saudi Arabia was beginning to sponsor was a more propitious course in terms of Syria's broader interests in the Arab system. Since al-Sadat had already committed himself to this procedure, the Saudis succeeded in convening a preliminary meeting in Riyadh on October 16–18 (see Appendix 15). The mini-summit was attended by King Khalid, the sheikh of Kuwait, Yasir Arafat, and the presidents of Egypt, Syria, and Lebanon. The particulars of a cease-fire and the guidelines for a settlement were discussed. But equally important was the decision to end the inter-Arab quarreling that had surrounded the conflict for the sake of reestablishing solidarity and enabling the Arab states to play a constructive role in bringing an end to the civil strife in Lebanon.[41] A week later an

41. Colin Legum and Haim Shaked, *Arab Relations in the Middle East: The Road to Realignment* (New York: Holmes & Meier, 1979), p. 2.

Arab summit conference met in Cairo, with all members of the Arab League participating (see Appendix 16). The summit endorsed the resolutions of the Riyadh conference and set up a fund to support an Arab peacekeeping force in Lebanon.

Aside from taking positive action to end the Lebanese civil war, the Riyadh and Cairo meetings had the intended effect of bringing about a rapprochement between Egypt and Syria. The ambassadors were reinstated and on December 18–21, 1976, al-Asad went to Cairo to discuss relations between the two countries.[42] A communiqué issued at the end of the visit affirmed the bonds of friendship between Egypt and Syria and a joint determination to pursue a political solution to the Arab-Israeli conflict consistent with the Arab position on the rights and prerogatives of the PLO. It was also at this time that al-Sadat and al-Asad agreed to form a Joint Political Command. But though this was formally announced on February 4, 1977,[43] it was never more than a declaration of intention.

Another aspect of the rapprochement between al-Sadat and al-Asad was Egypt's recognition of Syria's role as the dominant mediating party in Lebanon. Though the Syrian troops were now considered the major contingent of an Arab League peacekeeping force, they were really in charge of maintaining order and deterring renewed hostilities. But Syria fell short of gaining control over the PLO. In a confrontation between them in February 1977, the PLO was able to establish its power to exercise authority in parts of southern Lebanon. Al-Sadat had always opposed Syria's attempts to subordinate the Palestinian movement, and was undoubtedly relieved by this turn of events.

Though Egypt and Syria continued to consult each other through the summer of 1977 and the trilateral alliance was reconstructed at a meeting of al-Sadat, al-Asad, and King Khalid in Riyadh on May 19, their relationship slowly began to deteriorate once again.[44] When Secretary of State Cyrus Vance visited Cairo on August 2, 1977, al-Sadat proposed that the United States play a role in making preliminary preparations for the convention of a second Geneva conference. But he had not consulted al-Asad about this, and the Syrian leader opposed the idea when Vance arrived in Damascus to discuss it with him. Underlying the differences between Egypt and Syria was al-Asad's suspicion that al-Sadat was prepared to go much further than Syria in quest of a negotiated settlement.

While Egyptian-Syrian relations were proceeding on this tenuous course, both countries were actively seeking closer relations with their

---

42. Ibid., p. 5.
43. *New York Times*, February 5, 1977.
44. Legum and Shaked, *Arab Relations*, pp. 6–7.

southern neighbors. Syria and Jordan had started a rapprochement in 1975, when they set up a Joint Supreme Leadership Council and took steps toward economic integration.[45] Jordan subsequently supported Syria's intervention in Lebanon, and al-Asad kept King Husayn well informed of the proceedings at the Riyadh mini-summit in October 1976. But Husayn made it clear that he was not interested in a federation that would in any way compromise Jordan's soveriegnty.

Beyond the friendship with Syria, Jordan also established closer ties with Egypt and the PLO. After the Arab League intervention in the Lebanese civil war, King Husayn made two visits to Cairo.[46] At the first, on January 13–15, 1977, al-Sadat and Husayn spoke of the importance of solidarity among the confrontation states, which was interpreted to mean that although Egypt welcomed closer ties with Jordan, it also accepted the developing cordiality between Syria and Jordan.

King Husayn's relations with the PLO had been very strained since the confrontations of 1970 and 1971, which had resulted in the eviction of Palestinian troops from Jordanian territory. The situation improved slightly when the king accepted the resolutions of the 1974 Rabat summit proclaiming the PLO to be the sole legitimate representative of the Palestinian people. Subsequently, the trilateral states had sought a comprehensive Jordanian-Palestinian rapprochement to strengthen the Arab bargaining position in any forthcoming negotiations toward a settlement of the overall conflict. Their efforts were rewarded when King Husayn and Arafat met for the first time in seven years at an Arab-African conference on March 8, 1977.[47] This was the beginning of a reconciliation which was approached very cautiously at first, but which later became more substantial.

Aside from his preoccupation with restoring amity with al-Asad and maintaining cordiality with King Husayn, al-Sadat was anxious during this period to strengthen his ties with the Sudan. This was largely because of the friction that had developed between Egypt and Libya. Qaddhafi had strongly opposed al-Sadat's handling of the October war, and became an active partner in the Rejection Front. He also sided with al-Asad in the Egyptian-Syrian quarrel of 1975–76. When this quarrel subsided at the Riyadh minisummit, which left Libya, Algeria, and Iraq very much on the periphery of mainstream inter-Arab politics, Qaddhafi began to mount a campaign against Egypt. This included stirring up opposition to al-Sadat

45. Ibid., p. 8.
46. Ibid., pp. 11–12.
47. *New York Times*, March 9, 1977.

among Egyptian Islamic fundamentalist groups. He had earlier meddled in internal Sudanese affairs, leading to a joint defense agreement between Egypt and the Sudan on July 15, 1976.[48]

In the wake of Qaddhafi's new offensive in early 1977, Cairo and Khartum drew even closer together. On February 28, 1977, the Sudan joined the Egyptian-Syrian Joint Political Command,[49] and in the following months the two countries closely coordinated their economic activities and mutual defense arrangements amid talk of federation. In late October 1977 the idea of Egyptian-Sudanese union was discussed at a joint session of the respective parliaments convened in Cairo, though both al-Sadat and Numeiri showed their awareness of the problems involved in such a merger.[50] Meanwhile, open fighting had broken out between Egypt and Libya in July 1977, a rupture which brought even Arafat into a mediating role.[51] A cease-fire came into effect at the end of the month, but Egyptian-Libyan relations remained mutually hostile.

Syria's conflict with Iraq was roughly parallel to the Egyptian-Libyan dispute. The Baath Party in Baghdad, which had come to power in 1968 under the leadership of Ahmad Hasan al-Bakr, considered itself an authentic representative of the original Baathist ideology and regarded the policies of al-Asad as a flagrant compromise of those principles. The Iraqis took particular exception to al-Asad's acceptance of the cease-fire after the October war and to the Golan Heights disengagement agreement of May 1974. They also opposed his involvement in Lebanon, not to mention his maneuverings within the Arab system.[52] In the period after the Riyadh mini-summit, Iraq had become a committed enemy of Syria but remained isolated in inter-Arab politics except for its participation in the Rejection Front.

During these shifts in the relations among the Arab states, Saudi Arabia maintained its role as a stabilizing power and tried to promote a greater degree of harmony and cooperation. Aside from its close contacts with the confrontation states, including financial aid to them, and its continuing participation in the trilateral alliance, Saudi Arabia sought to preserve a low profile while maintaining a degree of influence over the course of events. Above all, the Saudis felt circumstances had thrust upon them a responsibility to protect the Arab world from divisiveness and to

48. Legum and Shaked, *Arab Relations*, p. 19.
49. *New York Times*, March 1, 1977.
50. *The Economist*, October 29, 1977.
51. *New York Times*, July 24, 1977.
52. Legum and Shaked, *Arab Relations*, pp. 14–15.

play their own part in preventing the Soviet Union from extending its power in the area. Though basically not interested in pan-Arabism, they regarded solidarity as vital to the future of the Arab states.

The Riyadh mini-summit inaugurated a series of attempts by various regimes to establish closer ties among the Arab states, either bilaterally or as a bloc. The search for solidarity continued for a year, but the results were minimal. By the autumn of 1977 it was clear that the Saudi efforts to revitalize the sagging trilateral alliance had failed, since Egypt and Syria seemed on an irreversible collision course. Furthermore, relations between Egypt and Libya became very strained, and the Iraqi-Syrian rivalry which had followed al-Asad's rise to power was severely aggravated by Syria's involvement in the Lebanese civil war.

One of the most significant developments of this period was the inclination of regimes to form bilateral pacts in the absence of substantial solidarity in the Arab system as a whole. Arrangements between Syria and Jordan, Egypt and Jordan, Egypt and the Sudan, and the PLO and Jordan were products of this trend. Some of the agreements turned out to be quite transitory, and others were either uncertain or superficial. But the practice remained rather constant. Given the perennial unpredictability of inter-Arab politics and the tensions introduced into the system by the Lebanese crisis and the delicate negotiating climate that prevailed after the October war, most governments sought security in small alignments or bilateral accords. Saudi Arabia continued to be concerned with the broader solidarity question, which was quite natural in the light of the diverse ramifications of Saudi relations with the other Arab states and with major powers outside the area. But the majority of Arab regimes came to conduct their foreign affairs in terms of relatively narrow alliances, often based on the need to counter other blocs perceived to be potentially threatening.

The arithmetic of the Arab balance of power became essentially parochial, and the focus of pragmatic concern was manipulation of the different assets available in an interdependent but fluid system. Another dimension was the greater degree of Israeli inflexibility under the Begin government and the lack of consistency in the Carter administration's Middle East policies. It was against this background that al-Sadat suddenly decided to pursue a unilateral course in dealing with the Arab-Israeli impasse. This action destabilized the Arab system, and a new pattern of alignments developed in response to it. The overall effect of the changes that ensued was a polarization of inter-Arab politics. But the polarization itself proved fluid and not without some tendency toward establishing a common front to meet the Egyptian challenge.

6

Polarization

THE ARAB-EGYPTIAN CONFRONTATION

O N NOVEMBER 16, 1977, al-Sadat went to Damascus to inform President al-Asad that he was planning an official state visit to Israel. He did not come to consult the Syrian leader, but simply to inform him that Egypt was about to launch its own unilateral peace initiative. Three days later, al-Sadat arrived in Jerusalem and addressed the Knesset as a first step in an attempt to break the impasse that had left the Arab-Israeli conflict unresolved for decades.

This dramatic move had a profound impact on inter-Arab politics. The system was already drifting toward polarization because of the deterioration of Egyptian-Syrian relations and the conclusion of bilateral accords in response to the failure of attempts to establish a united Arab position on the Middle East conflict. Iraq, several of the radical PLO organizations, Libya, and South Yemen had been in opposition to Egypt since the formation of the loosely organized but nevertheless durable Rejection Front three years earlier. Now Syria, Algeria, and the mainstream PLO were drawn in the direction of the rejectionist camp, whereas the more conservative and moderate states either supported al-Sadat or refused to take sides against him.

Al-Sadat's decision to go to Jerusalem without consulting other members of the league or even his partners in the trilateral alliance split the Arab system into several blocs with differing positions on the new thrust of Egyptian policy (see Appendix 6). The Sudan, Morocco, Oman,

73

and Tunisia expressed immediate support for the initiative,[1] forming the *Jabhat al-Qabul* (Front of Support), though Tunisia soon adopted a neutral position in order to maintain good relations with its anti-Sadat neighbors—Libya and Algeria. Saudi Arabia and Jordan, both concerned by the divisive effect the step would undoubtedly have on inter-Arab relations, adopted a cautionary stance. The Saudis declared that al-Sadat had placed the Arab world in a "precarious position" and asserted that "any move with regard to a settlement must be within the framework of Arab unity."[2] A Jordanian statement warned that "the gravest danger that threatens the Arab world lies in its falling prey to inter-Arab disputes, dissentions, and divisions,"[3] and King Husayn called on Arab leaders to "unify ranks and prevent a destructive division"[4] over al-Sadat's visit. Though not openly attacking al-Sadat, it was clear that these states at least disapproved of his failure to undertake some consultation with other Arab leaders before the action. But once it had been done, their first priority was to prevent an unmanageable split in Arab ranks.

At the other extreme, a new anti-Egyptian bloc was created, with Syria playing a leading role. At a meeting held in Tripoli, Libya, on December 2–5, 1977, Syria, South Yemen, Algeria, Libya, and the PLO proper formed the Front of Steadfastness and Confrontation (*Jabhat al-Samud wa al-Tasadi*). Iraq was also present but decided not to join the bloc because its resolutions were not radical enough. These resolutions called for a freezing of diplomatic relations with Egypt, consideration of a proposal to move the Arab League headquarters away from Cairo, boycott of Egyptian companies engaged in trade with Israel, and the conclusion of a mutual security pact among the five members of the Front.[5] A number of Western observers felt that Syria's role in the bloc was designed to soften the rejectionist camp and to put an end to its own isolation within the Arab system.[6] But Iraq's position was more equivocal. The real reason for its refusal to join was a disinclination to be associated with Syria. This involved not only an objection to Syria's endorsement of the principle of a negotiated settlement, but a tactical maneuver to avoid further estrangement from Egypt in the context of a reshuffling of inter-Arab alignments.[7]

---

1. *New York Times*, November 19, 1977.
2. Ibid.
3. *New York Times*, November 20, 1977.
4. *New York Times*, November 29, 1977.
5. *The Economist*, December 10, 1977.
6. Ibid.; *Time*, December 12, 1977.
7. *The Economist*, December 10, 1977.

The remaining Arab countries gravitated toward a neutral position. During the early months of 1978, the Gulf sheikhdoms, North Yemen, Somalia, Djibouti, Tunisia, and Mauritania became part of a group that included Saudi Arabia and Jordan. Lebanon was also tacitly one of this bloc, though it hesitated to take a position contrary to Syria's. Known collectively as the "silent" states (*Jabhat al-Samt*), these countries were hesitant to adopt an official stand against Egypt though they disapproved of al-Sadat's visit because of the rupture it had caused in inter-Arab politics. They were all particularly sensitive to the problem of their own respective weaknesses, and therefore stressed the importance of maintaining solidarity and avoiding friction in a situation of interdependence.

On March 28, 1978, seventeen of the foreign ministers who collectively make up the Council of the Arab League created the Arab Solidarity Committee (*Lajnat al-Tadhamun al-Arabi*) to counter the divisive currents within the Arab system. The committee was headed by the Sudan, then in the chair of the league, and included Saudi Arabia, Kuwait, the UAE, Jordan, North Yemen, and the Arab League Secretariat. But in part because the Sudan had sided with Egypt in the dispute over al-Sadat's visit to Jerusalem, its efforts were ineffective and produced no concrete results.

Egypt responded very negatively to the opposition that was forming. It did not recognize any substantive difference between the Steadfastness and Rejection fronts and considered the former an unholy alliance which was not really related to the Arab-Israeli conflict and offered no constructive alternative to al-Sadat's policy. In its view, Egypt had made the greatest sacrifices in the struggle against Israel and had developed an imaginative political finesse based on taking calculated risks while remaining entirely consistent. Unlike most other Arab states, it avoided sloganism and simplistic generalizations. Implicit in much of Cairo's policies, however, were an "Egypt-first" orientation and a sense of superiority. Virtually all of the Arab states were regarded as unsophisticated, naïve, or immature. Nevertheless Sadat was careful to preserve a working relationship particularly with Saudi Arabia.[8]

The Egyptian-Israeli talks in early 1978 revealed sharp differences between the two parties and ultimately led to another impasse. In the middle of the year, the United States mounted an initiative of its own with President Carter's proposal that al-Sadat and Begin meet with him in an attempt to define areas of agreement. The subsequent Camp David accords, signed in September 1978, created a new storm in the Arab world

---

8. The observations in this paragraph are based on interviews at the Egyptian Foreign Ministry in Cairo in June 1978.

because they left much ambiguity as to the degree to which the prospective Egyptian-Israeli treaty would be linked to the future of the other occupied territories and the Palestinians.

Saudi Arabia's reaction to the accords was guarded at first. The Saudis declared that "what has been reached at Camp David cannot be considered a final acceptable formula for peace," and specified that it "did not make absolutely clear Israel's intention to withdraw from all the Arab territories it occupies, including Jerusalem."[9] They also attacked the accords for not giving the Palestinians the right to set up their own state and for ignoring the PLO. Yet the Saudis also maintained that they did not have the right to interfere with the efforts of any state to regain its territories whether through armed struggle or peaceful means, unless this clashed with higher Arab interests. The dilemma was that whereas the Saudis were strongly opposed to what Egypt had done to disrupt Arab solidarity, they were afraid to risk the fall of al-Sadat and the possible radicalization of Egypt if support were withdrawn. Thus, in the immediate post–Camp David period, Saudi Arabia became the leader of a bloc of Arab countries which sought to prevent the isolation of Egypt.

King Husayn, on the other hand, reacted with dismay to al-Sadat's apparent willingness to conclude a separate peace with Israel. He disavowed any "legal or ethical commitment" to the accords,[10] and following consultations with Arafat, Qaddhafi, and al-Asad, he resisted the efforts of Washington and Cairo to involve him in the negotiating process. Ultimately Husayn's image was greatly enhanced throughout much of the Arab world, and especially in those countries which had been strongly critical of his policies.

King Husayn's position marked the beginning of a shift among the "silent" states in the direction of the platform originally adopted by the Steadfastness Front. At the Baghdad Summit Conference (Baghdad I) in early November 1978 (see Appendix 18), Saudi Arabia and its allies initially indicated that they would not condemn or isolate Egypt. But when al-Sadat refused to receive a delegation of high-ranking emissaries from the conference or to accept a $5 billion annual grant offer,[11] Saudi-Egyptian relations began to chill. The summit ended with an agreement that if Egypt concluded a separate peace, it would be expelled from the league and a boycott would be imposed on Egyptian companies doing business with Israel.[12] Later in the month, al-Sadat shunned a conciliatory message

9. Anthony McDermott, "Sadat and the Arabs," *Middle East International*, October 1978.
10. Ibid.
11. *Washington Post*, November 5, 1978.
12. *Washington Post*, November 6, 1978.

from Crown Prince Fahd because Saudi Arabia had adhered to the summit agreement.[13] Then, in early December, he accused the Saudis of inadvertently cooperating with the Soviet Union by failing to back the Camp David accords.[14] The Saudis maintained that they had done their best to defend Egypt from the radical Arabs and would not cut off financial support. "No matter what happens," they said, "our relations with Egypt will remain the same." Nevertheless they made it clear that the extent of future aid would depend largely on the degree to which al-Sadat succeeded in linking the prospective treaty with Israel to an overall settlement.

One of the most important developments that followed the signing of the Camp David accords was a rapprochement between Iraq and Syria, and Iraq's assumption of a leadership role in inter-Arab politics. Iraq began its entry into the mainstream of Arab affairs just before Baghdad I. When President al-Asad suggested a Syrian-Iraqi meeting to discuss the problems confronting the Arabs in the aftermath of Camp David and the improvement of relations between the two countries, Iraq sent its information minister, Tariq Aziz, to Damascus to ascertain how serious al-Asad was in making the proposal.[15] Subsequently al-Asad was invited to Baghdad for talks, and on October 26, 1978, Iraq and Syria announced that they had shelved their differences and would work toward a "full military union" against Israel.

The Iraqi-Syrian rapprochement was stimulated by several common concerns. Mutual opposition to the course of Egyptian policy was the most obvious. But equally important was the reaction of both countries to the increasing military involvement of Israel in southern Lebanon and a feeling that it was vital to stress the secular role of the Baath Party in maintaining a religious balance in the Fertile Crescent, which seemed threatened by the resurgence of Shiite political agitation in Iran.[16] The fall of the shah and the establishment of Khomeini's Islamic republic not only posed the possibility of a revived sectarianism in Iraq and Syria, but put in question the continuity of the improvement in relations between Iraq and Iran which had taken place in the last years of the shah's regime.

In January 1979, Iraq's Saddam Husayn and al-Asad met in Damascus to consider federation. They envisaged an initial merger of the respective foreign, defense, and information ministries as a step toward

13. *Washington Post*, December 9, 1978.
14. *Time*, December 11, 1978.
15. Robert Stephens, "Union in the Fertile Crescent," *Middle East International*, March 2, 1979.
16. Ibid.

the future creation of a united state.[17] By mid-June, however, the project had not advanced beyond the stage of a joint political command, far short of the anticipated federation scheme.[18] The budding Baghdad-Damascus axis was virtually aborted by the purges in Iraq and Saddam Husayn's assumption of the presidency from Hasan al-Bakr in July 1979. Though purges were directed against a group which tried to circumscribe Saddam Husayn's monopoly of power, Syria was accused of having been involved in the plot, and negotiations on the proposed union came to a halt.

The idea of Iraqi-Syrian unity is logical in terms of geographic and economic affinities, but it had always been opposed by Egypt because such a state would have rivaled Egypt for hegemony in the Arab world. Once al-Sadat had withdrawn his country from the Arab system, however, it was natural that Iraq and Syria gravitated toward each other, and at the time this was regarded by some observers as the most important recent development in inter-Arab politics.[19] Certainly, with a combined population of twenty million, a respectable Soviet-armed military establishment, and the oil resources of Iraq, a union between the two would have had a major impact on the Arab system. But aside from Iraq's larger population and greater wealth, the major problem was the question of control. A merger would have brought to the surface an implicit power struggle between al-Asad and Saddam Husayn and between the rival factions of the Baath Party and their respective bureaucracies, which still mistrusted each other.[20]

Another obstacle to Iraqi-Syrian union was the fact that the two regimes based their power on minority elements with which they were identified. The ruling elite in Damascus is largely drawn from the Alawite sect, a branch of Shiite Islam with a geographic center in the Latakia region. Similarly, the leadership in Baghdad is mainly comprised of Arab Sunnis, who represent about twenty percent of the total population, and many of the top echelon come from Takrit. Though both regimes have a broad following in their respective countries, the tendency to particularism diminishes their capacity to foster a transnational unification project.

While Iraq was trying to change its relationship with Syria, it was also establishing a leadership role in inter-Arab politics. The Iraqi rulers realized that in order to fill the vacuum created by the withdrawal of Egypt from the Arab system, it was essential to adopt a politically centrist

17. *Washington Post*, January 30, 1979.
18. Nikolaos van Dam, "Union in the Fertile Crescent," *Middle East International*, July 20, 1979.
19. Michael Hudson, "Peace Treaty through Arab Eyes," *Washington Star*, April 1, 1979.
20. van Dam, "Union in the Fertile Crescent."

position.[21] As hosts at the Baghdad conferences it was natural for them to do so, and at the first meeting in November 1978 they stood between the Steadfastness Front and the moderates, emphasizing a "minimum" agreement.

At the meeting of Arab foreign and economy ministers (Baghdad II) held in Baghdad in late March 1979 (see Appendix 19), Iraq adroitly avoided a split between the Steadfastness and moderate factions by working closely with Syria and Saudi Arabia. Relations with Syria had been improving for some time, and on February 5, 1979, Iraq and Saudi Arabia announced they would sign an agreement for cooperation on internal security. It was felt by some that this might be a harbinger of a formal mutual security pact in the strategic and oil-rich Gulf area.[22] In other respects Iraq had become an active force in the Gulf, using the leverage of a disguised threat of subversion or assassination to push the states of the region into openly opposing the Egyptian-Israeli treaty.[23]

In any event, Saddam Husayn was able to get the participants at Baghdad II to adopt a substantive resolution and to avoid what he had called "paper resolutions."[24] He was facilitated by a considerable change in Iraq's image. Its formerly intransigent position had been tempered by the events in Iran and the fear of Communist influence, which was heightened by the coup in Afghanistan. Iraq's crackdown on local Communists and its mediation role in a war which had broken out between the two Yemens were manifestations of this change in policy.

When it became evident in early March that Egypt was headed toward a separate peace with Israel, the reconstruction of the Arab system which had started after Camp David became more clearly defined. While Iraq had been moving away from the hard line of the Rejection Front since Baghdad I and closer to the Steadfastness position, now the conservative states were drifting even more sharply from the right in that direction than in the previous autumn. On March 15, 1979, Saudi Arabia and Jordan reacted angrily to the U.S. role in promoting the Egyptian-Israeli peace agreement,[25] and on March 19 Saudi Arabia declared its official opposition to the prospective treaty if it failed to include all of Israel's Arab adversaries and provide guarantees of self-determination and statehood for the Palestinians.[26]

21. Edward Mortimer, "Sadat's Arab Critics: An Agreed Minimum," *Middle East International*, December 1978.
22. *New York Times*, February 8, 1979.
23. *Washington Post*, April 26, 1979.
24. *Washington Post*, March 28, 1979.
25. *Washington Post*, March 16, 1979.
26. *Washington Post*, March 20, 1979.

The treaty was signed on March 26, and the linkage was considered inadequate by most Arab states. Aside from Egypt, only the Sudan, Oman, and Djibouti were not represented at the second Baghdad conference which convened three days later. Saudi Arabia initially seemed disinclined to go beyond the sanctions agreed to at Baghdad I. But Iraq and Syria ultimately persuaded the Saudis to take a stronger position, and the meeting ended on March 31 with a resolution to impose a total boycott on Egypt, recall ambassadors immediately, and sever diplomatic relations within one month. The next day it was decided to suspend Egypt from the Arab League and to transfer the league's headquarters to Tunis. It was also agreed that all economic aid, technical assistance, loans, and oil exports to Egypt would be terminated.[27]

Although Saudi Arabia hesitated to immediately cancel subsidies already committed to Egypt, its intention to abide by the spirit of Baghdad II seemed assured when the Arabian Gulf Organization for Development in Egypt, supported by Saudi Arabia, Kuwait, Qatar, and the UAE, was disbanded on April 26.[28] The aid from similar organizations was also discontinued, and on May 14 Saudi Defense Minister Sultan announced that the Cairo-based Arab arms industry was to be liquidated.[29]

In response to Saudi Arabia's increasingly hard line, al-Sadat accused the Saudis on May 1 of paying other Arab states to sever diplomatic relations with Egypt.[30] A significant development in this connection was the reported diminution of Crown Prince Fahd's role in the decision-making process. Prince Fahd had been identified as a proponent of moderate policies and a champion of close ties with the United States. But in the spring of 1979 he appeared to be yielding some of his power to other members of the royal family who questioned the US-Saudi relationship because of Washington's sponsorship of the Egyptian-Israeli treaty.[31] At any rate, Saudi Arabia did not try to conceal its annoyance at American policy at that time.[32]

Al-Sadat's decision to pursue a unilateral course in quest of an agreement with Israel led to Egypt's isolation from the political arena in which it had played a dominant role since 1945. Though this may prove

27. *Washington Post*, April 1 and 2, 1979.
28. *Washington Post*, April 27, 1979.
29. *Washington Post*, May 15, 1979.
30. *Washington Post*, May 2, 1979.
31. *Washington Post*, April 15, 1979.
32. Karen Elliott House, "The Anger in Saudi Arabia," *Wall Street Journal*, June 11, 1979; *Washington Post*, April 15, 1979.

temporary, the structure of inter-Arab politics was altered by al-Sadat's policies. One result was the polarization of the Arab system. Though a considerable degree of consensus was achieved at the two Baghdad conferences, there were basic differences in the extent and character of the opposition to Egypt. Ultimately, competitive alignments and rivalistic feuding began to emerge against a fluid and volatile background.

THE IRAQI-SAUDI-JORDANIAN AXIS

The most important development to emerge from the shifts in the Arab balance of power brought on by al-Sadat's unilateralism was the formation of an Iraqi-Saudi-Jordanian axis (see Appendix 7). Iraq played the key role in creating the new alignment, partly because Saddam Husayn had achieved good rapport with the two monarchies at the Baghdad conferences. But the main reason for the Iraqi initiative was the need that was felt in Baghdad for a complete reorientation of foreign policy in the light of substantial changes that were unfolding in the Middle East. The major dislocations that had taken place were the Islamic revolution in Iran, the Egyptian-Israeli peace treaty, and the deterioration of Iraqi-Soviet relations.

Iraq and Iran had been on relatively good terms with each other since an agreement settling the differences between the two countries was concluded at an OPEC meeting in Algiers on March 6, 1975, followed by a treaty signed in June.[33] The advent of the Islamic Republic of Iran after the departure of the shah and the fall of the Bakhtiar government on February 11, 1979, however, confronted Baghdad with an entirely different and potentially dangerous situation. The combination of a charismatic religious leader backed by a volatile populace in predominantly Shiite Iran and a secular Baathist Sunni ruler in an Iraq which was at least fifty-five percent Shiite raised the possibility that Khomeini would have a political impact on his western neighbor. Among those arrested in the summer 1979 purges were Shiites who occupied high positions within the Baath Party itself. Before the year was out, Iraqi fears were substantiated. An underground Shiite organization known as *al-Dawah al-Islamiyya* (The Islamic Call) had been formed with Iranian support and became a

33. See text in Majid Khadduri, *Socialist Iraq: A Study in Iraqi Politics since 1968* (Washington, D.C.: Middle East Institute, 1978), pp. 245–60.

focus of anti-government agitation. In 1980 this led to the expulsion of 35,000 Shiites, supposedly of Iranian origin.[34] Despite a degree of sectarian restlessness in the south, the heavily Shiite poorer classes have derived enormous benefit from Saddam Husayn's policies. More menacing were the territorial claims of the new leaders in Iran. In September 1979, for example, Ayatollah Rouhani said that Bahrain should be annexed and that the revolution should be exported to the entire Gulf region.[35] Considering Iraq's vulnerability in the Gulf, the regime became particularly sensitive to such provocations.

Al-Sadat's rapid movement in the direction of a separate peace with Israel was another factor in the reorientation of Iraqi foreign policy. The course of Egyptian diplomacy was particularly repugnant to the Baghdad regime, which had traditionally given highest priority to the welfare of the Arabs as a community.[36] This predisposition made it at the same time tolerant of moderate states which remained committed to the basic Arab causes and adamantly opposed to anything that suggested abandoning those causes on behalf of regional or parochial interests. It was the pure Egyptianism of al-Sadat's policies that Baghdad found unacceptable and unforgivable.

Beyond the question of ideological transgression, Saddam Husayn responded to al-Sadat's actions in terms of the changes they introduced in the Arab balance of power. With the impending isolation of Egypt, Iraq was in many respects the logical candidate to assume the leadership of the Arab system.[37] It had all the attributes to play such a role—a sophisticated manpower capacity, a well-equipped military establishment, and a high level of revenue from petroleum reserves which may be second only to those of Saudi Arabia. The Baghdad government, eager to end its isolation within the Arab system, seized the opportunity open to it without hesitation. As noted earlier, Saddam Husayn moderated his policies so that he could direct the opposition to al-Sadat at the Baghdad conferences. In so doing, he laid the foundations of Iraqi hegemony in inter-Arab politics.

The deterioration of Iraqi-Soviet relations was the third development that helped to alter Iraq's policies in such a way as to make Saddam Husayn the principal architect of the emerging leadership axis in the Arab

34. Adeed Dawisha, "Iraq: The West's Opportunity," *Foreign Policy*, Winter 1980–81, p. 142.
35. Ibid., pp. 145–46.
36. Claudia Wright, "Iraq: New Power in the Middle East," *Foreign Affairs*, Winter, 1979–80, pp. 273–75.
37. Dawisha, "Iraq," p. 139.

world. The 1972 treaty of friendship between Iraq and the Soviet Union had enhanced the former's military potential. But Baghdad was determined to prevent this from making it a Soviet client. Furthermore, the Baath was willing to accept the local Communist Party as a junior partner in the political process, but not in a more powerful role. The dynamics of this situation led initially to a diminution of Iraqi Communist influence. Saddam Husayn's first move came in 1978, when he executed twenty-one Communists and arrested others who were implicated in an alleged attempt to infiltrate the armed forces. After a similar purge in April 1979, the Iraqi Communists went into hiding.[38]

Of greater concern to the Baghdad regime was the general pattern of Soviet activities in the Middle East as a whole. The advent of a pro-Moscow government in Afghanistan in April 1978, the Soviet influence in South Yemen, and the Soviets' backing of Ethiopia in the war with Somalia over the Ogaden region were alarming in that they suggested an encirclement strategy and a potential threat to broader Arab interests. The Soviet invasion of Afghanistan on December 27, 1979, further confirmed such apprehensions. These events undermined the relatively close relationship that had existed between Baghdad and Moscow since 1972, and shaped the future course of Iraq's role in the Arab system.

Saudi Arabia shared all of Iraq's concerns. The Riyadh government had taken a special interest in promoting and preserving a harmonious relationship among the Arab states because it viewed this as essential to its own security and to the long-range interests of the Arabs as a bloc. In a sense the Saudis considered themselves the guardians of Arab solidarity, and thus they were troubled by the divisive impact of Egyptian policy. They were drawn to al-Sadat by his pro-American and anti-Soviet position, but could not tolerate his apparent disregard for the interests of the Palestinians and the other Arab states. This led to a certain ambivalence in their attitude toward Cairo, though it did not prevent them from adhering to the consensus achieved at the Baghdad conferences.

The Saudis were also disturbed by the revolution in Iran. As was the case with many Arab states, the "combination of Iranian expansionism and Islamic radicalism" caught them off balance.[39] The fact that a reigning monarch was unseated by a broadly based popular movement was particularly unsettling, since the ruling family in Riyadh was anxious to preserve its own legitimacy. Another problem was the possible impact of the

---

38. Ibid., p. 138.
39. Claudia Wright, "Implications of the Iraq-Iran War," *Foreign Affairs*, Winter 1980–81, p. 283.

Iranian revolution on the large number of foreign workers in Saudi Arabia, estimated to comprise forty-three percent of the entire labor force.[40] Furthermore, many of those working in the oil fields all along the eastern coast of the Arabian Peninsula are Shiites, a circumstance which increases the security vulnerability of this sensitive region. There was also a strong flavor of radical fundamentalism in the seizure of Mecca's Grand Mosque in November 1979, and one-third of those who were later executed were non-Saudi Arabs.[41] All of these particulars left the Saudis in a defensive posture toward the dramatic change of government in Teheran.

Riyadh's perception of the Soviet Union's machinations throughout the Middle East was similar to that of the Iraqis. From a Saudi perspective, the major Soviet aim in the area is to gain control of the vast Arabian petroleum reserves. The means employed to achieve this goal is a methodical encirclement of the oil fields through subversion and revolution, which by the end of the 1970s left the Soviets with a dominant position in Afghanistan, South Yemen, Ethiopia, and Libya. The Saudis were therefore very receptive to the idea of regional pacts designed to meet the challenge of Russian expansionism.

One of the most important considerations in Saudi Arabia's move toward a close affiliation with Iraq was the desire not to be at odds with the radical forces in the fluid Middle East situation. At Baghdad II the Saudis moved sharply toward accommodating the regimes which had strongly opposed al-Sadat. It was also suggested that the Saudi leaders believed they could offset the danger from the left by putting themselves at the head of an anti-Sadat movement.[42] In order to dispel any misunderstandings about the Riyadh government's stand on the Palestinian issue, Foreign Minister Saud al-Faisal made it clear on October 4, 1979, that "any interpretation of our position that says we do not support a Palestinian state is erroneous."[43]

A further manifestation of this general theme in official Saudi policy was the stand on Israel's declaration in the summer of 1980 that Jerusalem was the eternal capital of the Jewish state. Reacting angily to this statement, Crown Prince Fahd announced in August that a *jihad*, or Islamic holy war, should now be considered. He also warned the Western powers that if they accepted the Israeli position, Saudi Arabia and other Arab countries would break diplomatic relations with them.

---

40. David Ottaway, "Saudis Cast Wary Eye on Foreign Workers," *Washington Post*, March 4, 1981.
41. Ibid.
42. *The Economist*, March 24, 1979.
43. *Washington Post*, October 5, 1979.

At the same time, Riyadh joined with Kuwait in continuing to supply the Sudan with petroleum despite Numeiri's relatively amicable relationship with Egypt, a decision thought to be based on the possibility of a future Sudanese role in achieving a reconciliation between Egypt and the other Arab states.[44] Above all, the Saudis are determined to minimize divisions in the Arab system, while protecting themselves from disruptive forces in their own country and throughout the Middle East.

King Husayn's policies developed along a parallel course. His reaction to Camp David and al-Sadat's subsequent moves was unambiguous and openly critical from the start, and he frequently sought to buttress Arab solidarity in the strained atmosphere that surrounded the polarization trend. He was perhaps less concerned about the change of government in Iran than Iraq and Saudi Arabia because there was no significant Shiite element in his own country. But he was certainly sensitive to the anti-monarchist aspect of the revolution and the repercussions it might have in other parts of the area. His relations with the Soviet Union were correct but cool, and his major concern in this regard was the uncertain linkage between Moscow and the regimes in Baghdad and Damascus.

The general concurrence of Iraqi, Saudi, and Jordanian interests in the aftermath of these dislocations provided the basis of the emerging Iraqi-Saudi-Jordanian axis. In January 1979 the Iraqi interior minister and other prominent Baathists visited Saudi Arabia to discuss "common security interests."[45] Then in early February, the two countries announced that they were going to conclude an agreement on internal security, with the possibility that this would lead to a larger mutual defense pact in the Gulf.[46] The foreign minister of Oman was advocating at this time a treaty with neighboring states "to ward off aggression or subversion financed by a foreign power," indicating the general receptivity of the sheikhdoms to such an arrangement. In any event, Iraqi military representatives concluded the details of a coordinated defense agreement with Saudi Arabia the following summer and autumn.[47] Just after Ayatollah Rouhani made his remark about annexing Bahrain in September, Saddam Husayn also assured the other Gulf states that he would protect them from Iranian designs by sending his defense minister on a visit to all of them. By late 1979 a virtual alliance existed between Iraq and Saudi Arabia, with the sheikhdoms as junior partners. North Yemen was also entering the orbit of

---

44. *New York Times*, June 22, 1979.
45. Dawisha, "Iraq," p. 145.
46. *New York Times*, February 8, 1979.
47. Wright, "Iraq: New Power," p. 259.

Saddam Husayn's policies because of the effective role he had played in ending the war with South Yemen earlier in the year.

An Iraqi-Jordanian rapprochement was developed during this same period. It was part of Saddam Husayn's "policy of calculated flexibility,"[48] designed to build as many supportive ties as possible in the Arab world. In August 1979 King Husayn called on Iraq and Saudi Arabia to work with Jordan and Syria on a joint military plan to deal more effectively with the transfer of Israeli forces from the Egyptian front to the northern and eastern borders with Syria and Jordan.[49] Interpreting this as an invitation for Iraq to develop a closer relationship with Jordan, Saddam Husayn received King Husayn in Baghdad in October 1979 to discuss various aspects of a comprehensive peace settlement.[50] Then in early 1980, the Jordanian monarch described Iraq as "the backbone of the Arab struggle," cementing the new ties between Amman and Baghdad and further defining the blossoming Iraqi-Saudi-Jordanian axis.

King Husayn's own interest in participating in such an alignment came partly from admiration for the role Iraq had played in coordinating the Arab opposition to al-Sadat. He was also impressed by Saddam Husayn's other attempts to maintain solidarity within the Arab system and by his resistance to Soviet overtures in Afghanistan, Ethiopia, and South Yemen. Yet another reason for King Husayn's policy was his desire to prevent any further consideration of an exclusive Iraqi-Syrian merger, which could lead to a dominant Baathist role in the Fertile Crescent and a consequent eclipse of Jordanian political influence in the region.

At the same time, King Husayn believed that Syrian-Iraqi cooperation would provide better protection than a conflict situation between them. Though the Iraqi-Jordanian rapprochement was not well received in Damascus and relations between Jordan and Syria were strained by al-Asad's suspicion that the Jordanian branch of the Muslim Brotherhood had assisted its Syrian counterpart in its activities against the regime, Prime Minister Abd al-Hamid Sharaf made it clear in May 1980 that Jordan would not tolerate any agitation against Syria.[51] In general, King Husayn was anxious to maintain good relations with Syria, despite the new Iraqi connection. This was in part because he thought it was important to sponsor a coherent Arab peace program designed to offer a con-

48. Jonathan Randal, "Iraq Shelves Area Ambitions to Focus on Internal Strife," *Washington Post*, May 4, 1980.
49. *Jerusalem Post*, August 19–25, 1979.
50. *Time*, November 12, 1979.
51. Based on an interview at the Syrian Foreign Ministry in Damascus in May 1980.

structive alternative to al-Sadat's policies, a position he had tried to encourage in trips to Iraq, Syria, and Saudi Arabia.[52] Nevertheless the interest in preserving a working relationship with Syria did not obstruct the close ties Jordan was in the process of establishing with Iraq and Saudi Arabia.

The Iraqi-Saudi-Jordanian axis became an increasingly viable bloc in 1980 and 1981. On February 8, 1980, Saddam Husayn proposed a National Covenant (see Appendix 20), which was designed to suggest the principles upon which inter-Arab cooperation should be based. The two most important guidelines in this document were a ban on the use of force in disputes between Arab states and a doctrine of neutralism which precluded commitments to either superpower. The covenant not only enhanced Saddam Husayn's leadership role, but further ensured the hegemony of the Iraqi-Saudi-Jordanian axis. Aside from its broad applicability, it was specifically intended to prevent North Yemen from becoming dependent on Soviet military assistance.[53] As an inducement, Iraq offered the Sanaa government $300 million in financial aid and technical help in training its troops. Baghdad also sought to organize a collective effort to liberate South Yemen from its own Soviet-backed Marxist regime, demonstrating an interventionist dimension in Saddam Husayn's policies.

The National Covenant was directed against the extension of US power in the Middle East as well. In June 1980 Iraqi officials met with Sultan Qabus bin Said of Oman in an attempt to discourage him from providing the United States with bases and other naval facilities.[54] The alternative proposed was a mutual defense pact among the Arab states of the Gulf region, a measure directed against Iranian expansionism which would make an American naval presence redundant.

This type of security arrangement became the basis on which the new trilateral alliance headed by Iraq established its leadership in the Arab system. In May 1980 King Husayn and the crown prince of Kuwait went to Baghdad for consultations. Representatives of the UAE came later for the same purpose. The most important of such official talks, however, was the visit of Saddam Husayn to Riyadh on August 5, 1980,[55] the first time an Iraqi chief of state had been in the Saudi capital since the 1958 revolution. The discussions were supposed to have centered on Israel's

52. *Washington Post*, October 29, 1979. See also Joseph Kraft, "Road to Nowhere in the Mideast," *Washington Post*, April 17, 1980; and *Washington Post*, April 25, 1980.
53. Dawisha, "Iraq,"pp. 137–38.
54. *New York Times*, June 22, 1980.
55. Wright, "Implications," pp. 181–82.

annexation of Jerusalem, but they were mainly concerned with Iran. At their conclusion, the Saudis had committed themselves to support Iraq in the event of a war with Iran, a development which seemed increasingly likely.

Saddam Husayn enjoyed the same kind of backing from Jordan, which also played an important political function for the axis. By early 1981 King Husayn had assumed the role of spokesman for the Arab states opposed to the Camp David peace process.[56] But this involved more than simply articulating the objectives of the Arab majority. It also included a specific mandate from Iraq and Saudi Arabia to seek to induce the Reagan administration to adopt a new peace formula which would bring the PLO into the negotiating process. In exchange for this and related services, King Husayn receives an annual subsidy of approximately $1 billion from Baghdad and Riyadh.

The Iraqi-Saudi-Jordanian axis has become the focus of a powerful and carefully orchestrated alignment within the Arab system. It has brought the southeastern flank of the Fertile Crescent together with all of the Arabian Peninsula except South Yemen, and its influence extends to the west as well. But it has also inadvertently contributed to the polarization tendency. The moderation of Saddam Husayn's policies inevitably led to a rupture with the radical Palestinian organizations which had taken refuge in Iraq. In May 1980 the PFLP and the PDFLP were expelled from the country because they had openly accused the president of having rightist leanings.[57]

The Iraqi-Syrian unification project was also aborted by Iraq's changed position in the Arab system. The scheme not only threatened the leadership role which Saddam Husayn had been constructing for himself,[58] but it was not well received in either Riyadh or Amman. Though it had remained a dead letter since the summer of 1979, it was not until a year later that serious friction developed between the two countries. In August 1980 the Iraqis expelled the Syrian diplomatic mission in Baghdad, following which the Iraq mission in Damascus suffered the same fate.[59] Though both Iraq and Syria refuse to allow a deterioration of their relationship to sink below a certain level owing to their continuing interdependence, the estrangement led in this case to a countervailing alignment made up of Syria and Libya, backed by the Soviet Union.

56. David Ottaway, "Hussein Assumes New Role as Spokesman for Arabs," *Washington Post*, February 19, 1981.
57. *New York Times*, June 22, 1980.
58. Dawisha, "Iraq," p. 141.
59. Wright, "Implications," p. 284.

THE SYRIAN-LIBYAN COUNTER-AXIS

The opposition to the Iraqi-Saudi-Jordanian axis began with the mounting internal dissent against al-Asad's regime. Though the Syrian president retained control of the army, the Sunni majority became increasingly alienated by the dominance of the Alawite rulers. The Muslim Brotherhood, especially active in the north of the country, eventually reached the point of open insurrection with the murder of seventy cadets, mostly Alawite, at a military academy near Aleppo in June 1979.[60] The tension between al-Asad and his adversaries intensified and ultimately led to an assassination attempt on his own life in June 1980, followed by repressive measures on the part of the authorities.[61] By March 1981 the situation had degenerated to such an extent that a special unit of the Syrian army was assigned to carry out a punitive campaign in the anti-Asad city of Hama,[62] and a further confrontation occurred in the same place in February 1982. These untoward developments were further complicated by the general state of disarray in the Syrian economy.

Al-Asad tried to quell the domestic unrest by combining steps toward political and economic liberalization with a tightening of internal security.[63] But the opposition did not really diminish, a fact which made the regime all the more anxious to shore up its tenuous international position. Aside from the collapse of the unity talks with Iraq, Syria was excluded from the Iraqi-Saudi-Jordanian axis and did not accrue many advantages from its pratication in the Steadfastness Front. Al-Asad therefore found himself in a situation of relative isolation. His peacekeeping role in Lebanon had led to confrontation with the Christian militias and did not produce rewards commensurate with the costs of maintaining a large military force in the country. These circumstances made him receptive to new affiliations which might provide him with greater international viability.

While al-Asad was trying to strengthen his hand at home and abroad, Muammar Qaddhafi was leading Libya into a series of provocative African adventures. Libyan-Tunisian relations had been strained since 1974, when Habib Bourguiba refused to implement a projected merger to which he had agreed with Qaddhafi. A further deterioration

60. *Washington Post*, February 19, 1980.
61. Jonathan Randal, "Under Assad, Syria Survives Trials, but Loses Prestige," *Washington Post*, February 20, 1981.
62. *Washington Post*, March 17, 1981.
63. *Washington Post*, February 16, 1980.

occurred later in the decade because of Libya's active support of the Polisario guerrillas at a time when Tunisia favored the Moroccan side in the Western Sahara conflict. Finally, in late January 1980, Qaddhafi tried unsuccessfully to stage an insurrection in the Tunisian town of Gafsa,[64] inaugurating a new trend in Libyan policy characterized by opportunistic intervention in neighboring African states. Though Algeria also backed the Polisario Front in Western Sahara, it reacted negatively to the Gafsa incident and decided to act as protector of Tunisia against Libyan machinations.[65] Algeria was also troubled by Qaddhafi's increasing arms supplies to the Western Saharan guerrillas because this tended to undercut its own leverage with the Polisario movement.[66]

Qaddhafi next turned to Chad, where his intervention was far more extensive and had much broader implications. Chad had been beset by intermittent civil war since it became independent from France in 1961. Qaddhafi became interested in the country in 1975, when he annexed a strip of Chadian territory adjoining his southern borders.[67] This interest grew over the following few years as it became clear that Chad, like neighboring Niger, was rich in uranium. Qaddhafi was therefore prompted to intervene when the civil war started up again in March 1980.

The warring factions were headed at this stage by President Goukouni Oueddei and Defense Minister Hissène Habré. In December Qaddhafi became involved in the conflict by sending in troops to support Oueddei, whom he wanted to use as a surrogate in his larger plan aimed at establishing a Saharan Islamic empire under Libyan control in central Africa. Some 4,000 Libyan troops assisted Oueddei in securing the capital, Ndjamena, on December 15,[68] and Qaddhafi also created a "Pan African Legion" made up of Libyans, other Arabs, and black Africans to help him in his broader designs.[69]

Qaddhafi's Chadian adventure antagonized all the neighboring countries. The black African states of Senegal, Gambia, Ghana, Niger, Equatorial Guinea, and Nigeria either expelled the Libyan envoys or broke diplomatic relations entirely. The Arab countries of Egypt, the Sudan, Mauritania, and Tunisia did likewise. These actions came in response to Qaddhafi's announcement on January 6, 1981, that a merger had

64. *Time*, February 11, 1980.
65. *Washington Post*, February 12, 1980.
66. John Cooley, "The Libyan Menace," *Foreign Policy*, Spring 1981, p. 91.
67. *Washington Post*, January 7, 1981.
68. *Washington Post*, January 8, 1981.
69. *Washington Post*, January 17, 1981.

been effected between Libya and Chad, a development perceived by all the surrounding states as a threat to their own sovereignty. Egypt and the Sudan were particularly concerned, as they saw the Libyan move to the south as a step to make Chad a staging ground for a subsequent intervention in the Sudan. It was for this reason that al-Sadat and Numeiri had backed Habré in the civil war. In 1976 Qaddafi had attempted to overthrow the Sudanese government, and the Chadian episode seemed to be yet another chapter in the same campaign. At the end of March 1981, Numeiri concluded that he was essentially "at war" with Qaddafi.[70] But in November Qaddafi agreed to evacuate his troops so that an OAU peacekeeping force could attempt to pacify the civil war.

The significance of these events was that they led to a Libyan isolation within the Arab system comparable to that of Syria. It is not surprising, therefore, that these two states were drawn to each other, especially since they had been associates in the Steadfastness Front. On September 1, 1980, Qaddafi delivered a speech in Tripoli in which he called for immediate union with Syria.[71] The next day al-Asad announced his approval of the proposal, and on September 8 he arrived in Tripoli to confirm the accord.[72] Then on September 10, a joint Syrian-Libyan declaration on the formation of a unitary state was issued (see Appendix 21). Though the merger was official, the approach to integration was cautious and it remains to be seen whether it will ever amount to more than an attempt by both countries to deal with their common problem of isolation by creating the appearance of a close relationship.

The Syrian-Libyan union did, however, establish a counter-axis aimed at offsetting the power and influence of the tacit Iraqi-Saudi-Jordanian alliance. A significant dimension of the new entente was its close links with the USSR. On October 8, 1980, Syria concluded a treaty of friendship and cooperation with the Soviet Union, after having resisted Moscow's overtures throughout the 1970s. But as al-Asad found himself increasingly isolated in inter-Arab politics, he strengthened his ties with the Soviets and finally agreed to the treaty.

Libya had enjoyed a close relationship with Moscow since 1972 and had concluded a number of accords on technical assistance and arms supply thereafter. With the advent of Qaddafi's African adventure in 1980, this Soviet support intensified. As of March 1981, Western intelligence sources estimated that some 5,000 Soviet-bloc and Cuban military

---

70. *Washington Post*, April 1, 1981.
71. *Washington Post*, September 2, 1980.
72. *Washington Post*, September 3 and 9, 1980.

and technical advisors were assisting Qaddhafi and that $12 billion in mostly Soviet weaponry was at his disposal.[73] In exchange, Libya supplies the Warsaw Pact countries with oil at favorable prices.

The Soviet connection gives the Syrian-Libyan counter-axis a source of strength, though it does not match the Iraqi-Saudi-Jordanian grouping. But the two blocs came into confrontation over the issue of Iraq's war against Iran. Though there was no armed conflict between the blocs, the new polarization of the Arab system became more distinct.

THE IRAQ-IRAN WAR

On September 22, 1980, Saddam Husayn ordered his air force to strike deep inside Iran against air bases, thus launching the Iraq-Iran war. Relations between the two countries had deteriorated rapidly in 1979 when it became clear that the ayatollahs were trying to export their revolution across the Gulf and that they had an interest in reviving the old Iranian claim to Bahrain. Saddam Husayn was quick to reassure the sheikhdoms of this protective role. Then, during the first half of 1980, he began border raids along the Iranian frontiers and assisted Bakhtiar in his campaign against the regime by transmitting his broadcasts from Iraq. This more aggressive Iraqi policy was prompted by the fall of Bazargan's government in November 1979 and the inability of Bani Sadr to control the fundamentalist forces in the country. It was also based on the perception that Iran was in a state of internal anarchy and was relatively weak militarily.[74]

Another reason for Saddam Husayn's decision to adopt the war option was to enhance his leadership role in the Arab world.[75] This aspect of his policy was successful in the sense that he obtained support for the undertaking on his visit to Riyadh in August 1980 and later won the backing of Jordan, Kuwait, Qatar, the UAE, North Yemen, Tunisia, and Morocco.[76] King Husayn was particularly emphatic in his endorsement of the Iraqi venture, and called for a unified Arab stand to help Iraq in "defending its dear homeland and national soil." Though Saddam Hu-

73. *Washington Post*, March 10, 1981.
74. Wright, "Implications," pp. 279–80.
75. Jim Hoagland, "Saddam's Gamble: Oil and Power or a Noose," *Washington Post*, September 28, 1980.
76. *Washington Post*, September 25 and 30, 1980.

sayn had initiated the war, his supporters considered his quest for full control of the Shatt al-Arab River and liberation of the formerly Arab-held islands in the Strait of Hormuz to represent valid irredentist claims. Even al-Sadat supplied Iraq with Soviet military equipment, though this may have been partly designed to decrease Egypt's isolation within the Arab system.

Syria and Libya, on the other hand, adamantly opposed Saddam Husayn's campaign and reportedly gave military assistance to Iran.[77] Qaddhafi's open support for Iran, coupled with his sharp criticism of the Saudis for accepting a protective American role in the Gulf, led Saudi Arabia to break diplomatic relations with Libya on October 28, 1980.[78] Normal relations were restored, however, on December 31, 1981. Though the Syrian-Libyan opposition did not measurably impede the Iraqi assault, the tenacity of Iranian resistance confounded Saddam Husayn and raised the problem of possible internal dissent and a loss of ground in terms of his inter-Arab leadership aspirations. This led him to depict the war in exaggerated terminology as a struggle against "infidel Persians," who had traditionally been adversaries of the Arabs.[79] In this respect, the power the Iraqi leader had established in the Arab system became particularly vulnerable. By early 1982 the war had turned in Iran's favor, prompting Jordan to send a volunteer force to support the Iraqi troops.

The Iraqi-Saudi-Jordanian axis and the Syrian-Libyan entente reached a point of confrontation in connection with the summit conference scheduled to meet in Amman at the end of November 1980. Fearing Iraqi dominance at such a meeting, al-Asad sought the cooperation of his Steadfastness Front partners in forcing a postponement.[80] The other Arab states, however, decided to convene the summit as planned. Syria then proceeded to organize a boycott, and though Algeria and the PLO initially hesitated, they finally joined Syria, Lebanon, Libya, and South Yemen in refusing to attend the conference.[81]

Though the summit convened in Amman on November 25, it only underlined the polarization between the two blocs. King Husayn made a point of sharply criticizing Syria and Libya for backing Iran in the war, and the summit expressed its support for the Iraqi side. When the meeting ended on November 27, al-Asad mobilized 247,000 troops along the Jordanian border, in response to which King Husayn deployed 57,000 of

77. *Washington Post*, October 8, 1980.
78. *Washington Post*, October 29, 1980.
79. *Washington Post*, November 11, 1980.
80. *Washington Post*, November 21, 1980.
81. *Washington Post*, November 26, 1980.

his own armed forces northward to meet the Syrian challenge.[82] Ultimately this proved to be a passing military confrontation. Following Saudi mediation efforts and King Husayn's assertion that he was "open to all reasonable suggestions for resolving this pointless dispute," al-Asad began withdrawing his troops from the Jordanian border in early December.[83] Also instrumental in defusing the situation was the summit's call for a peaceful resolution of the Iraq-Iran war and the fact that both Syria and Jordan wanted to avoid open hostilities for the sake of preventing a more serious fragmentation of inter-Arab relations than already existed.

The friction between Syria and Jordan did not subside, however, with the ending of this incident. In February 1981 Jordan accused Syria of kidnapping one of its top diplomats in Beirut and instigating a plot to assassinate Prime Minister Mudar Badran.[84] Though Damascus denied these allegations, the Jordanians were convinced that al-Asad had decided to set in motion a terrorist campaign to destabilize King Husayn's government. This apprehension was further encouraged when the Syrian information minister, Ahmad Iskander, issued a warning that the Damascus regime would "punish" Jordanian leaders for promoting internal disorder in Syria in 1980.[85]

The Iraq-Iran war exacerbated the polarization of the Arab system which had commenced with al-Sadat's trip to Jerusalem in November 1977. Though a degree of solidarity had been established by the Arab majority opposed to Egyptian policy at the Baghdad conferences, the formation of the Iraqi-Saudi-Jordanian axis and the countervailing Syrian-Libyan entente formalized a split which became particularly intense when Saddam Husayn launched his campaign against Iran. This left the system in a state of disarray and lacking in any positive direction appropriate to the broader interests of the Arabs as a regional affiliation. A paradoxical outcome of these developments, however, was that the Iraq-Iran war opened the door to a possible rapprochement between Egypt and Saudi Arabia.[86] This arose in part from the break in relations between the Saudis and the Libyan regime, which was on especially bad terms with al-Sadat. The most significant aspect of this turn of events is that it could ultimately bring Egypt back into the Arab system. But this depends entirely on Mubarak's ability to modify the policies Sadat pursued in recent years.

82. *Washington Post*, November 28, 1980.
83. *Washington Post*, December 3 and 4, 1980.
84. *Washington Post*, February 14, 1981.
85. *Washington Post*, February 15, 1981.
86. *Washington Post*, November 4, 1980.

THE PLO AT BAY

The division of the Arab world into two antagonistic blocs was particularly detrimental to the PLO.[87] Though Arafat had become adept during the years since the October war at keeping the Arab states off balance and playing one faction off against the other, the polarization process and the Iraq-Iran war established a certain rigidity within the system which made this decidedly more difficult. The reduced political leverage of the PLO became apparent when Arafat sought to reassert his independence by adopting a relatively neutral position in the Iraqi-Syrian feud over Saddam Husayn's war. His preference was a postponement of the summit until the antagonism between the rival camps had subsided. But after this failed, he succumbed to al-Asad's pressure and reluctantly agreed to boycott the 1980 Amman summit meeting.

Syria's power over the PLO was also evident in Lebanon. Al-Asad's Arab Deterrent Force retained a large measure of control over the territorial status quo, despite the recurring friction among the various factions involved in the conflict. By keeping the PLO forces within a narrow corridor between Beirut and a point below Tyre, he was able to limit their military options and prevent them from challenging or qualifying Syrian military supremacy in the country.

Another problem confronting the Palestinians is the animosity that has developed between them and the Lebanese. The Palestinians, for their part, are generally contemptuous of the Lebanese, while the latter are convinced that the PLO is intent on "implantation" now that there is very little left in the way of genuine state authority.[88] The concept of implantation assumes that the Palestinians are in the process of establishing sovereignty in southern Lebanon as part of what is seen as an American plan to resolve the Middle East dilemma by settling them there permanently, though there is nothing to substantiate such a claim.

The Lebanese Shiites, most of whom are from the south or have roots there, have reacted with particular hostility. Eventually they formed a paramilitary organization known as *Amal* (Hope) to prevent the Palestinians from actually trying to set up a state in that locale.[89] Meanwhile the Israelis and their Lebanese surrogates under the command of Major

87. Loren Jenkins, "War, Arab Feuding Leave Arafat, PLO in Disarray," *Washington Post*, December 14, 1980.
88. William Claiborne and Jonathan Randal, "Palestinians Struggle to Keep Last Redoubt," *Washington Post*, March 17, 1981.
89. Ibid.

Haddad have constantly attempted to restrict or retaliate against all PLO military actions. The result has been that ever since the Israeli invasion of Lebanon in March 1978, the Palestinians have been on the defensive in the one region where they have some authority and freedom of movement.

Given the changing character of inter-Arab politics, it seems unlikely that the PLO will lose its resilience and viability, or that it will return to its former condition of extreme vulnerability. Its leaders are sophisticated statesmen and it enjoys political assets in the Arab system, although it remains necessary to utilize these with skill and caution. Militarily, the PLO is reasonably well armed and strongly motivated. Despite its limited offensive capacity, it is able with Syrian support to sustain itself against almost any Israeli attack except an all-out war.[90]

Nevertheless the PLO's position in the Arab system has been undermined by polarization and by the Iraq-Iran war. The problem is that it depends on different kinds of support from each of the two blocs currently in conflict, and cannot afford to take sides on a long-term basis. But once the war is resolved, the animosities may subside and give way to a climate in which the PLO can regain its equilibrium and pursue its goals in a productive and positive way.

90. Ibid.

7

Regional Disputes

WESTERN SAHARA

THE CONFLICT THAT arose among Western Sahara's three neighbors—Algeria, Mauritania, and Morocco—over their rival claims to the territory was a by-product of Spanish policy. In the last years of Spain's colonial rule over what had been known as Spanish Sahara, the Madrid government had tried to prevent an accord on the future disposition of the region by encouraging the ambitions of each of these Maghreb countries at the expense of the other two.[1] This led especially to friction in Morocco's relations with both Algeria and Mauritania in the early and mid-1960s.

After 1967, however, they began to temper their differences. On September 14, 1970, King Hasan and Presidents Mukhtar Ould Daddah and Houari Boumedienne agreed on a common strategy to bring about the decolonization of Western Sahara. But despite further attempts to coordinate policy in 1972 and 1973, the common opposition to continued Spanish rule did not resolve the underlying conflict of interests. By 1974 Algeria, Mauritania, and Morocco were again operating independently of each other on the issue.[2]

Following the breakdown of Spanish-Moroccan talks later in 1974, however, Morocco and Mauritania concluded a secret accord on the

---

1. Pauline Lalutte, "Sahara: Notes toward an Analysis," *The Struggle for Sahara* (Washington, D.C.: Middle East Research and Information Project, 1976), p. 10.
2. John Mercer, *Spanish Sahara* (London: Allen & Unwin, 1976), pp. 238–39.

partition of Western Sahara, with the northern sector assigned to the former and the southern third to the latter. This action was based on the conviction of both countries that they had legitimate territorial claims to the region, and on their concern over the pospect of a separate state appearing if the plebiscite proposed by Franco were held. Algeria had no irredentist claims of its own but adamantly opposed the partition scheme and supported the Popular Front for the Liberation of Saguia al-Hamra and Rio de Oro (Polisario), which had emerged as the dominant organization in the Saharan independence movement. This became the crux of the ensuing problem, since the essence of the Polisario position was resistance to the annexation policies of Morocco and Mauritania.

The opening gambit of what was to become a war involving several Arab countries was King Hasan's Green March of November 1975, in which some 300,000 Moroccan volunteers staged a peaceful invasion of Western Sahara. As this was endorsed by Mauritania, Spain finally yielded to the partition proposal and transferred authority over the region to the two Maghreb states on February 28, 1976. Morocco thereby established its sovereignty over the northern sector, rich in phosphate, and Mauritania gained control of the south with its iron ore deposits and fishing coasts.[3]

At the same time that Spain relinquished Western Sahara to Morocco and Mauritania, the Polisario Front proclaimed the creation of a Saharan Arab Democratic Republic (SADR). Though its forces numbered only about 800 at first, by mid-1978 they had risen to approximately 5,000.[4] Training and equipment were supplied mainly by Algeria, Libya, and Syria. The general strategy of the Polisario Front was a war of attrition based on guerrilla operations against Moroccan positions and more concentrated attacks on Mauritania aimed at terminating its involvement in the conflict. But as the war escalated, Morocco committed 30,000 troops to the struggle against the guerrillas and stationed 9,000 more in Mauritania. In response Algeria and Libya increased their support for the Polisario Front, converting what had begun as a relatively small encounter into a much broader inter-Arab confrontation.

In 1979 the situation began to change. The new government which had come to power in Mauritania under Mustafa Ould Salek the previous year reiterated its commitment to the joint defense pact with Morocco, but also stated that it was not opposed to a referendum in the Mauritanian-controlled sector of Western Sahara. This was followed by an agreement

3. I. William Zartman, *Conflict in the Sahara*, Problem Paper 19 (Washington, D.C.: Middle East Institute, 1979), p. 5.
4. David Price, *The Western Sahara* (Beverly Hills, Calif.: Sage, 1979), p. 28.

between Ould Salek and King Hasan that the 9,000 Moroccan soldiers stationed in Mauritania would be withdrawn by March 1979, a condition the guerrillas had been demanding. Then in August, Mauritania concluded a peace treaty with the Polisario Front, which was able to strengthen its position in the south and launch successful raids into Moroccan territory.[5]

King Hasan was prompted by this turn of events to seek military aid from Egypt, and al-Sadat complied by sending shipments of armaments, ammunition, and spare parts.[6] Morocco was thereby inclined to resume the pro-Egyptian stance it had adopted before Baghdad II, but for al-Sadat it meant being drawn into the widening Western Sahara controversy. The significance of both developments is that they demonstrate the repercussions a geographically limited regional dispute can have on the patterns of division and alignment within the Arab system as a whole.

Though Mauritania came closer to Egypt in the aftermath of the Mauritanian-Polisario rapprochement, Algeria did not alter its position on Western Sahara under the new leadership of Chadli Benjedid following the death of Boumedienne in December 1979. As a member of the Steadfastness Front, Algeria had been relatively radical in political orientation since the end of 1977 and had played the major role in supporting the Polisario guerrillas, a circumstance which brought it on several occasions to the brink of war with Morocco.

Algeria's relations with Libya were relatively cordial. In 1976 the two countries agreed to defend each other's territory if one were attacked, and the Algerians backed Libya in its various encounters with Egypt. At the same time, Algeria was particularly cautious about Qaddhafi's impulsive and dramatic African adventures and chose not to become involved in them as a partner. On the contrary, it became Tunisia's protector from Lybian machinations and sought to maintain its own special influence with the Polisario guerrillas in light of Qaddhafi's attempt to establish himself as the primary patron.

King Hasan was left isolated in the immediate area by the Mauritanian step. But besides the help he enlisted from Egypt, he also enjoys the support of the Gulf states and Jordan. Saudi Arabia not only set up a joint Moroccan-Saudi investment company with a capital of $50 million in August 1977, but has provided generous subsidies for arms purchases as well.[7] Tunisia, though a relatively weak state in terms of wealth and military power, is also fundamentally supportive of Morocco. This is a

---

5. John Gretton, "Hassan's Last Trump," *Middle East International*, September 14, 1979.
6. Ibid.; *Washington Post*, October 8, 1979.
7. Price, *Western Sahara*, p. 54.

significant factor in the equation inasmuch as Tunisia is an integral part of the Maghreb complex.

In April 1981 the dividing line in the Western Sahara dispute was further defined by the decision of Mauritania to shift from a position of neutrality to one of open support for the Polisario Front.[8] This, in effect, brought it into the tacit alliance that the guerrillas have with Algeria and Libya. It also raised a special problem for King Hasan, despite the increase in his forces to 50,000, in that the guerrillas now have the option of mounting operations against the Moroccan army from Mauritanian bases. Prompted by the suspicion of the new Mauritanian president, Khuna Ould Haidallah, that Morocco had tried to engineer a coup in Nouakchott in March, this change in policy was more than a superficial gesture. Mauritania made a point of promoting cordial relations with Qaddhafi by reopening the Libyan cultural center in the capital. Qaddhafi responded by suggesting a merger between Mauritania and the Polisario Front and a "revolutionary alliance" among these two, Algeria, and Libya. Though the leadership in Nouakchott did not endorse these proposals, it was clear that Mauritania was associating itself with this side in the dispute.

What has emerged from the continuing Western Sahara conflict is a microcosmic alignment of states within the broader structure of the already polarized Arab system. Backing the Polisario Front are Algeria, Libya, and Mauritania, with added approval expressed by Syria and South Yemen. Though there is no explicit alliance between these powers and the guerrillas, they either materially assist them or at least give moral support. The PLO and Iraq have remained essentially neutral because both have a particular disinclination to take sides in inter-Arab squabbles that do not directly involve them. Logically, however, they would favor the Polisario Front over Morocco.

King Hasan's sympathizers include Tunisia, Egypt, and the Sudan among the African Arab states, and Saudi Arabia, the Gulf sheikhdoms, and Jordan in the east. Once again there is no formal alliance, but rather a sense of common interests or identity. Egypt and Saudi Arabia have extended substantial military and economic assistance to Morocco and take particular exception to the adventurism of King Hasan's principal enemy—Libya's Qaddhafi. In this sense they are in collaboration with the Moroccan cause.

Like the crisis in Lebanon, the Western Sahara imbroglio has drawn many Arab states into a proliferating confrontation. Though not central to

8. John Cooley, "Morocco's Western Sahara War Expands as Mauritania Shifts Stand," *Washington Post*, April 26, 1981.

the politics of the Arab system, it has come to play an important role in the Arab balance of power because it further qualifies existing alignments and raises the level of tension. The degree to which it will affect inter-Arab politics will depend on the way the conflict is resolved.

NORTH AND SOUTH YEMEN

With the establishment of an independent state in the former British colony of Aden in 1967, the question of a union between this region and Yemen was raised for the first time. It has been considered and discussed as a serious and logical project ever since. The People's Democratic Republic of Yemen (PDRY) is geographically known as South Yemen and is an extension of Yemen proper. The latter is politically designated the Yemeni Arab Republic (YAR), but has been referred to as North Yemen since the British evacuation of Aden. The major obstacle to a merger is that the PDRY is ruled by a Marxist regime, whereas the YAR is a republic on the Western model.

The friction generated by this disparity in political orientation led to a virtual state of war between the two countries in late September 1972. Following Arab League mediation efforts, however, the warring parties concluded a unification agreement in Cairo on October 28.[9] The accord remained a dead letter until March 1976, when Saudi Arabia and South Yemen established diplomatic relations with each other. This opened the door to fresh discussions between the two Yemens because Sanaa's closeness to Riyadh during the years of tension between the Saudis and the Aden government had precluded any serious move to implement the 1972 agreement. It was the Saudi opposition to a merger of North Yemen, over which it exercised considerable influence, and pro-Soviet South Yemen which had kept the whole scheme dormant. But the thaw in Riyadh-Aden relations created an entirely new atmosphere.

At the end of 1976 the leaders of North and South Yemen, Ibrahim al-Hamdi and Salim Rubayyi Ali, acknowledged the common interests shared by their own states and Saudi Arabia, and expressed the hope that "rapid measures would be taken to unify the two parts of Yemen as a natural and necessary step. . . and as a strategic issue important to both

9. George Lenczowski, *The Middle East in World Affairs*, 4th ed. (Ithaca, N.Y.: Cornell University Press, 1980), p. 650.

countries."[10] They also agreed to form a unified delegation at international conferences and to represent each other's interests in countries where only one had a diplomatic mission.

The unification trend accelerated, and in mid-February 1977 the two leaders met again at the border town of Qataba. A joint communiqué issued after this meeting announced the establishment of a joint council composed of the respective ministers of defense, foreign affairs, trade, and planning. The council was to convene every six months alternately in Sanaa and Aden to discuss matters of mutual concern. Also at this time, a North-South Yemeni ministerial delegation began a tour of Saudi Arabia and the Gulf sheikhdoms to seek assistance in resolving their economic problems.[11] Though in the months following these accords, both al-Hamdi and Rubayyi Ali declared their intention to work toward unification, reports indicated a dispute between them over control of Purim Island in the strategic Bab al-Mandab Straits, which had been held by South Yemen since 1967.

Despite the friction over Purim Island, the leaders of the two Yemens met again in Sanaa on August 13–15, 1977. Rubayyi Ali later said that the visit "has given us the opportunity to review the affairs of our Yemeni people in both parts [and] to exchange views on the Arab and international situation."[12] During the following months, al-Hamdi continued to press for a closer relationship with South Yemen. He planned a trip to Aden in mid-October to pursue the unification talks. But two days before his expected arrival he was assassinated, presumably by individuals opposed to the developing rapprochement between the two Yemens.

The death of al-Hamdi temporarily ended the quest for a merger of North and South Yemen. His successor, Husayn al-Ghashmi, adopted a strong pro-Saudi position which precluded further attempts to forward the unity scheme. During the ensuing period, relations between the two countries oscillated between statements affirming friendship and expressions of hostility accompanied by border clashes. Then in late June 1978, al-Ghashmi himself was assassinated. This was followed by the deposition and execution of the South Yemeni leader, Rubayyi Ali.[13] The Arab League held the PDRY responsible for al-Ghashmi's death and decided to suspend political and economic relations with it.[14]

10. Colin Legum and Haim Shaked, eds., *Middle East Contemporary Survey, I: 1976–1977* (New York: Holmes & Meier, 1978), p. 660.
11. Ibid., p. 661.
12. Ibid.
13. *Time*, July 10, 1978.
14. *The Economist*, July 8, 1978.

Subsequently South Yemen accentuated its revolutionary orientation, both internally and beyond its own frontiers, leading to a situation of mounting border tension between the two Yemens. But the PDRY soon realized that it was in danger of becoming extremely isolated within the Arab system and resumed its earlier attempts to achieve a reconciliation with the YAR. On July 11, 1978, the South Yemeni foreign minister declared, "We have extended our hands and they remain extended to our brothers in Sanaa for dialogue on our various problems and their peaceful resolution."[15] Several days later the South Yemeni Presidential Council reiterated this call for a dialogue and asserted that it should be based on the elimination of propaganda, the withdrawal of troops from border areas, an end to all provocative acts, and the resumption of economic cooperation.

The PDRY also announced its willingness to allow an Arab League mission to investigate the situation on its frontiers with the YAR, pending the discontinuation of the boycott imposed after al-Ghashmi's assassination. But the relationship between the two Yemens remained highly volatile, with provocative troop and naval movements and accusations becoming common occurrences in the summer and autumn of 1978. Meanwhile an internal power struggle was taking place in South Yemen over the issues of unity with Sanaa and alignment with Moscow. This heightened the level of tension, and on February 24, 1979, a war broke out between the two countries.

The Arab League foreign ministers, with those of Iraq and Syria playing the leading role, immediately intervened to bring an end to the fighting.[16] The negotiations which followed were very successful. North and South Yemen agreed to terminate the war on March 16, and at the end of the month they set up a constitutional committee to draft a charter for a prospective unified state.[17] Subsequently both sides made some concessions to each other and agreed to avoid armed conflict and to promote economic cooperation. But a major obstacle to federation was the apprehension among many North Yemenis at the prospect of merging with a Marxist state.[18]

Despite this reluctance in some circles in Sanaa, the politics of the Yemeni dispute changed substantially with the conclusion of the 1979 war. Saudi Arabia was displeased with the Sanaa-Aden rapprochement,

---

15. Legum and Shaked, *Middle East Contemporary Survey, II: 1977–1978*, p. 663.
16. *New York Times*, March 5, 6, and 7, 1979.
17. *Washington Post*, March 17 and 31, 1979.
18. Fred Halliday, "Eleventh Hour for the Yemeni Union," *Middle East International*, August 3, 1979.

fearing that the Marxist South Yemenis might become the dominant political force in a unified state. Though relations between the Saudis and South Yemen had improved after Camp David, the strongly leftist leaning of the Aden regime after June 1978 was of concern to Riyadh. Also, it was clear that the PDRY wanted to see a diminution of Saudi influence in the YAR and that the attack in February 1979 was directed in part against Saudi Arabia.[19] An even more ominous development was the admission of the PDRY to the Warsaw Pact and the conclusion of a treaty of friendship and cooperation between South Yemen and the Soviet Union in October 1979.[20]

Another dimension of the political equation was the Sanaa-Moscow connection. During the second half of the 1970s the Soviet Union had been trying to establish a foothold in North Yemen, a tactic stiffly resisted by Saudi Arabia. For example, just after the Soviets had contributed to the expansion of the port of Hudayda in 1977, the Saudis used economic pressure to bring about a drastic cut in the size of the USSR mission in Sanaa.[21] Riyadh's influence notwithstanding, North Yemen was seriously interested in a closer relationship with the Russians. This was based partly on a fear of Soviet subversion engineered through Aden, and also on the desire to demonstrate a measure of independence from the Saudis. The fact that relations between Riyadh and Moscow seemed a little less chilly than usual in the late 1970s further encouraged the YAR to pursue such a course.

The Saudis were extremely displeased by the Soviet tilt of North Yemeni policy, especially after Sanaa began negotiating an arms supply agreement with Moscow in 1980, and they threatened to cut off their own aid program.[22] They also tried to induce the United States to sell military aircraft to the YAR by offering to pay for the transaction.[23]

The North Yemeni leader, Ali Abdullah Salih, was therefore faced with a choice between yielding to Saudi pressure or developing a closer relationship with the radical Arab states. He elected to follow the latter course,[24] leaving Saudi Arabia no alternative but to resort to its traditional role of cooperating with both the radical and conservative forces in

19. *The Economist*, March 10, 1979.
20. Nimrod Novik, *Between Two Yemens*, Paper 11 (Tel Aviv: Center for Strategic Studies, 1980), pp. 16–18.
21. Ibid., p. 6.
22. *Washington Post*, January 30 and February 20, 1980.
23. *The Economist*, March 10, 1979.
24. Novik, *Between Two Yemens*, p. 14.

inter-Arab politics in the hope of constructing a regional defense pact in the Arabian Peninsula:

The Yemeni dispute has contributed to the fluidity of the Arab system and to the polarization trend within it. The lack of political stability in the two Yemens is a major source of tension. The power struggle that started in the PDRY in late 1978 and continued for well over a year brought Abd al-Fattah Ismail to power by the end of 1979. But by April 1980, Ali Nasir Muhammad had replaced him, leaving the question of internal rivalry in the PDRY essentially unresolved. In North Yemen, President Salih's policies reflected a realization that Saudi Arabia and the West were more concerned with limiting radical influences than with helping the country establish its own political and economic viability. Though perhaps more stable than its southern neighbor, the YAR has experienced disruptions in the continuity of power and has mixed feelings about its relations with the superpowers and the Arab states.

Saudi Arabia took particular interest in the situation because of its concerns over domestic unrest and Soviet machinations in the entire Middle East from Afghanistan to the Maghreb. But Saudi policy was characterized by vacillation between the hard line and a more flexible accommodation of radical forces. Iraq assumed the role of interlocutor, not only to promote solidarity within the Arab system but also to assure its own leadership position. The impact of the whole episode, which is still unfolding, has been to sharpen the polarization trend in inter-Arab politics in much the same way as the Western Sahara controversy has done. Though a peripheral dispute, the conflict between the Yemens has broader implications for the Arab balance of power.

THE RED SEA AND THE HORN OF AFRICA

The Red Sea area and the Horn of Africa are predominantly Arab. Except for Ethiopia, all the littoral states of the Red Sea belong to the Arab League; and Somalia, which occupies the coastal sector of the Horn, was admitted to membership in February 1974. Consequently, international developments in the region affect the Arab balance of power.

The primary destabilizing factors during the past two decades have been the conflict between Ethiopia and Somalia and the involvement of the Soviet Union in the affairs of these two countries. Soon after the Somali

Republic was proclaimed in 1960, the Soviets started to supply Mogadishu with armaments and to send military assistance to the Eritrean liberation movement in Ethiopia. In exchange, Somalia provided the USSR with naval facilities at the port of Berbera, giving it an important strategic advantage in the Indian Ocean.

Moscow pursued this policy until the fall of Haile Selassie and the establishment of a Marxist regime in Addis Ababa in 1974. Though the Somali government was also very leftist, by 1976 the Soviets had decided that Ethiopia was a more important target. Gradually they shifted their support from Mogadishu to Addis Ababa, a change which became particularly sensitive after Somalia invaded the Ogaden region in 1977.

The Ogaden dispute originated in the decolonization of what was formerly British and Italian Somaliland. The Anglo-Abyssinian Treaty of 1897 transferred a large portion of Ogaden to Ethiopia, and this was reaffirmed by another treaty in 1954 after a short period of British administration following the liberation of Ethiopia from Italy in 1942.[25] Inasmuch as Ogaden is inhabited by Somali-speaking people, the establishment of an independent state in the former British and Italian colonies in 1960 fell short of achieving the unification of greater Somalia. Therefore, the irredentist claim to the Ogaden region became the major concern of the new Somali Republic. Ethiopia has always rejected this claim on the basis of the fact that a greater-Somalian state never existed as a sovereign entity in earlier history.[26]

The campaign launched by Somalia in 1977 made some headway initially, but was soon checked because of the extensive military assistance given Ethiopia by the Soviet Union and Cuba. At this stage Saudi Arabia began giving financial aid to President Muhammad Siad Barre of Somalia, and Egypt and the Sudan subsequently expressed their support of the Mogadishu regime. But most other Arab states remained uninvolved, though South Yemen was believed to have backed Ethiopia's Mengistu Haile Mariam. Nevertheless, King Khalid and President Numeiri played a major role in convening a conference in Taiz, North Yemen, on March 22–23, 1977, which brought the two Yemens, the Sudan, and Somalia together to discuss their common interests in the security of the Red Sea and Horn of Africa region.[27] Though the meeting had limited results, it marked a success in Riyadh's policies in the sense that it drew the attention

25. Abdulqawi Yusuf, "The Anglo-Abyssinian Treaty of 1897 and the Somali-Ethiopian Dispute," *Horn of Africa*, January–March 1980, p. 38.

26. Mesfin Wolde-Mariam, *Somalia: The Problem Child of Africa* (Addis Ababa: Artistic Press, 1977), p. 20.

27. *Washington Post*, March 24, 1977.

of the Arab states to the threat posed by the new relationship between Moscow and Addis Ababa. The primary goal of Saudi Arabia was to check Soviet moves by fostering a coordinated Arab resistance to them. Beyond this, Riyadh sought to enlist American support for Somalia, a policy which made some headway in mid-1980 through an agreement between Washington and Mogadishu which provided the United States with port facilities in Berbera to assist its naval operations in the Indian Ocean.[28] But when the Ethiopians gained the upper hand in the Ogaden fighting in November, the United States was very reluctant to offer substantial military assistance to the Somalis.[29]

The dispute between Somalia and Ethiopia over Ogaden was yet another regional controversy which influenced the politics of the Arab system. Though there was a considerable degree of Arab solidarity in support of the Somali side, Moscow's influence in South Yemen and also in Libya gave rise to an underlying incompatibility between these two Soviet-backed regimes and the rest of the Arab world. This raised the question whether their ultimate loyalty was to the Arabs as a community of nations or to radical ideologies which gave priority to the Soviet connection.

28. *Washington Post*, May 24, 1980.
29. Jay Ross, "Somalia Seeks Arms from Reluctant U.S.," *Washington Post*, November 25, 1980.

8

The Arab Dilemma

LEGITIMACY AND CONTINUITY

AT THE BEGINNING of this study, it was pointed out that the sociopolitical dynamics of the Arab world have for centuries been based on the interplay of universalist and particularist forces. This dichotomy springs from a common cultural heritage and historical experience on the one hand, and a diversity of regional predispositions and geographic circumstances on the other. The emergence of the Arab states in 1945 as an international sub-system did not alter this underlying reality. Rather, it bore witness to the continuity of history, a fact which remains fundamental to any clear understanding of contemporary inter-Arab relations.

During the early Islamic period, the Arabs created a vast empire which unified much of the Middle East. But the territories they controlled were so extensive that within two centuries a gradual process of fragmentation began to take place. Ultimately this led to the compartmentalization of the area into regional components under the sovereignty of separate and often rival dynasties. It was not until the rise of the Ottoman Empire in the fourteenth, fifteenth, and sixteenth centuries that large portions of the Middle East were once again brought together under the rule of an ecumenical imperium. But in this case, it was not Arab, but Turkish, and all traces of an Arab political identity were submerged in the Ottoman system.

In the nineteenth century, a modern Arab movement gradually began to develop. Its initial themes were both idealistic and ecumenical, since they were introduced by the *salafiyya* reformers in Egypt and the champions of the Arab Awakening in Greater Syria. Nevertheless, the fact that the Arab struggle for independence unfolded in fairly sharply defined geographic compartments gave rise to a regional orientation which remains powerful in the various societies of the contemporary Arab world. This dichotomy between a national resurgence formulated in universalistic terms and a nation-building process based on regional entities created a profound psychological dilemma which has perplexed twentiety-century Arabs and complicated their political evolution.

At the heart of the problem is the issue of ideological legitimacy. Though regionalism has often been classed with Zionism and imperialism as unacceptable, it has been the basic orientation of Arab politics for the past sixty years. This applies not only to the established regimes, but also to significant segments of society. A recent study conducted by Tawfiq Farah among students at Kuwait University indicated that a majority of the respondents had a sense of patriotic loyalty to the states of which they were citizens.[1] Though many may still cherish Arab unity as an idea and oppose the artificial boundaries that exist in such areas as the Fertile Crescent, the likelihood remains that most Arabs identify with a particular country.

Though the tendency to regional or sub-regional affiliation may engender some feelings of guilt over having betrayed a higher national ideal, particularism provides a sense of security in the context of the instability and dislocations that have plagued the Arabs since World War I. In times of uncertainty and disruption, it is natural for people to turn to those closest to them. In contemporary Arab society, this has not infrequently manifested itself in an almost tribal parochialism based on relatively narrow geographic, sectarian, or ethnic identities. The result has been a fragmented and fluid political structure in which shifting alignments and a high level of tension are common characteristics.

It is against this background that the Arab ruling elites seek to maintain power in their own constituencies and to preserve a degree of equilibrium within the system. Given twenty-two entities with varying types of governments, it is impossible to make generalizations which apply to all of them. But particularly in the case of those regimes that seek to project an image of ideological purity, there is a strong inclination to manipulate the issue of ecumenical as opposed to parochial nationalism as a way of legitimating domestic and foreign policies. When al-Shishakli

---

1. Cited in Fouad Ajami, "The End of Pan-Arabism," *Foreign Affairs*, Winter 1978–79, p. 364.

was ruler in Syria, for example, an official position in support of pan-Arabism masked an actual determination to protect the sovereignty of Syria and to contain all internal opposition to this policy. Abd al-Nasir was initially more sincere in his commitment to Arab unity, but after the collapse of the UAR, he gradually shifted his ground without ever renouncing pan-Arabism. By the time of his death, he was in essence an Egyptian nationalist, though he used the "revolutionary" image as a tactical device in inter-Arab politics.

The present regimes in Syria and Iraq are similarly oriented. Both espouse the Baathist doctrines of pan-Arabism and Arab socialism, but in practice they pursue policies geared to their own respective national interests. This has led some to assert that the classical Baath no longer exists.[2] The issue, however, is not one of adherence to a doctrine, but the discrepancy between professed ideals and actual policy. Inasmuch as regionalism and pragmatism have been the dominant themes in inter-Arab politics for the past decade, it would be unrealistic for Syria and Iraq to adopt a rigid pan-Arab position. The problem they face in terms of continuity at home and credibility abroad is their failure to clarify the way in which they have revised the original Baathist ideology and the reasons for doing so. Saddam Husayn has done this implicitly in the role he has assumed in inter-Arab politics since late 1978, but he has not been explicit about the implications of the changes he has introduced. Hafiz al-Asad, faced with mounting internal opposition and isolation within the Arab system, is for the moment without a specific policy and has resorted to spontaneous reactive measures.

The central issue in the legitimacy problem is the ability of Arab regimes to remain consistent with openly declared principles, and this in turn is the key to their continuity. In many cases the greatest barriers to such a political order are the inclination to monopolize power and the intolerance of opposition. Most Arab ruling elites are incapable of sharing the responsibilities of leadership with other sociopolitical entities within their respective societies. They are also hypersensitive to any kind of criticism and constantly try to project an image of themselves as perfect in every way. The ubiquitous portraits and adulation of the chiefs of state, the lengthy speeches that these men make to justify their policies, and the silencing of even constructive dissent reflect this dimension of Arab politics. It is also evident in inter-Arab relations. Aligned states treat each other as virtually faultless, whereas rivals are accused of a variety of offenses, mostly related to betrayal of noble Arab causes. Then, when

2. Ibid., p. 360.

shifts take place within the system, old enemies become new friends and vice versa. These *reversements des alliances*, which have been so common over the past thirty-six years, often require alterations of principles previously regarded as sacred, generating an inconsistency which helps to undermine the legitimacy of Arab regimes and to confront them with a problem of continuity. The cyclical nature of these interrelated phenomena is the basis of instability and constant realignment in the system.

An interesting example of the political dynamics involved in this process is the Syrian-Iraqi relationship. Though both countries are ruled by the Baath, they had been on extremely bad terms throughout most of the 1970s. Following Camp David, however, they achieved a rapprochement and began planning a federation. But by the summer of 1979 the project had become a dead letter, and a year later the two countries were once again at loggerheads. The merger of Syria and Iraq is both logical and possible. It is logical because they are the major states of a geographically natural country in the Fertile Crescent and because Egypt's decreased role in the Arab system has shifted the focus of the confrontation with Israel to that area. It is possible because it is sufficiently finite in scope to make it feasible.

But it is precisely the fact that a Syrian-Iraqi union could be implemented that made it so frightening to the respective regimes. Virtually all Arab ruling elites oppose substantive change in the territorial status quo because it would in one way or another curtail the power they enjoy. This is why they have always felt more comfortable with the vague and essentially unrealizable doctrine of pan-Arabism than with more specific projects of regional integration. One of the paradoxes of contemporary Arab politics is that pan-Arabism has been used as a tool to block any movement toward greater unity. More finite schemes, which are really the only viable basis of altering the compartmentalization of Arab society, are either suspect or undertaken with such inefficiency that they end in failure.

The concept of an "Arab Nation" has popular appeal because it is perceived as a panacea for all social and political problems. But both the generalization and its manipulation by ruling elites for political advantage have only perpetuated the existing divisions of the Arab world. The inability of the Syrian and Iraqi regimes to make any significant progress toward unification was a disservice to their constituencies because the artificial fragmentation of the Fertile Crescent is harmful to the long-range interests of the people who inhabit that region. Though it is possible to understand that the project was aborted by uncertainties as to where the ultimate power in a federated Syrian-Iraqi state would lie, it is also important to recognize that power by itself has no meaning in terms of broad social interests. Hence the questions of legitimacy and continuity are indissolubly linked to whatever comprises the common good. Social interests and political practice have to be integrated to produce a healthy situation.

It must also be pointed out that the legitimacy crisis which confronts the Arab world cannot be reduced to black-and-white categories. For example, many positive accomplishments have been made by the Syrian and Iraqi regimes. Though Iraq is now playing a particularly constructive role in inter-Arab politics, Syria also did so in the early and mid-1970s. Iraq has made notable strides in converting its petroleum revenues into development and social welfare projects, and it has been both generous and consistent in providing financial aid to other Arab states. The two countries do take into consideration the long-range interests of the Arabs as a bloc and have on various occasions given priority to those interests. It is also significant that the rulers in Damascus and Baghdad have remained in power for well over a decade.

Similarly, there are other regimes which have had less trouble with the problems of legitimacy and continuity than most, and which have contributed to stability and solidarity in the Arab system. The monarchies of Saudi Arabia and Jordan, which enjoy the greatest longevity of all the Arab states, have remained essentially consistent with their own principles and, especially in recent years, have assumed important positions of leadership. In the 1970s the Saudis developed a style of keeping a low profile while working actively to promote cooperation and to mediate inter-Arab disputes. Though sometimes overly cautious, their policies have helped to minimize friction and to foster a common Arab stand on the major issues at stake in the area. The biggest disappointment encountered by the Saudis in their endeavor to assume such a role was the collapse of the Fez Summit Conference on November 25, 1981. Though the meeting had been convened to consider Crown Prince Fahd's peace plan as an alternative to the Camp David process, there was strong opposition to it from virtually all the more radical Arab states and the PLO.

King Husayn of Jordan, whose reign has experienced turbulent periods, assumed a prominent role in Arab affairs after Camp David. His objections to Egyptian policies have been clearly articulated, and he currently acts as a spokesman for the largest bloc of Arab states as well as a coordinator of the Iraqi-Saudi-Jordanian axis. The immediate future of the Arab system depends in particular on the relationship that develops between King Husayn and his partners on the one hand, and the course of Egypt's policies on the other.

Any analysis of Arab politics should take into consideration the difficulties all third-world regimes encounter in their endeavors to modernize their countries and make them viable in a competitive and rapidly changing world. Though the European colonial powers may have provided some guidelines for political development, the nation-building process was impeded in the Middle East by the imposition of artificial boundaries and the restrictions that were placed on the evolution of self-determination. Though it is easy for Westerners to criticize the ineptitude of Arab politics, it is often forgotten that the West itself generated many of the area's problems.

DESTABILIZATION AND SECURITY

The Iranian revolution of January 1979 had profound implications for the entire Arab world. It left most Arab regimes in a state of shock because of its significance in terms of their own political difficulties. The primary question that it raised was the durability of existing authority,[3] a particularly sensitive subject in the majority of Arab states. The intensity of feeling which accompanied the emergence of fundamentalist Islam and of mass demonstrations in the streets as the dominant political forces in Iran not only challenged the status quo in virtually all Arab societies, but posed the possibility of destabilization throughout the Middle East. The very fact that the shah's regime, which had seemed so firmly entrenched, could be ousted with such rapidity was in itself unsettling. The way in which the legitimacy of the shah and his government was opened to question, and the claims of the new Iranian leaders to Arab territories in the Gulf region were even more disturbing.

The revolution in Iran had a particularly destabilizing effect on the Arab world because it came at a time when some regimes were faced with internal opposition, while the Arab system itself was becoming polarized. In a situation characterized by structural incoherence and political fluidity, the model of change in neighboring Iran was one of anarchy, with all its component images of gesticulating throngs and indignant mullahs interpreting social justice with simplistic intransigence. One does not have to exaggerate the power of Islamic fundamentalism to appreciate its appeal

3. *Washington Post*, January 31, 1979.

for impoverished masses, who see it as an alternative to political systems in which they have little stake.

Historically, Islamic tradition in the Middle East distinguished between the rule of law (*siyadat al-kanun*), based on inviolable principles of legitimacy and justice, and the rule of persons (*hukmat al-ashkhas*), based on the changing whims of rulers. Today there is a revived consciousness of the difference between justice (*adalah*) and corruption, and this has popularized the idea of bringing Islam back into politics. But one of the problems is that the fundamentalist leaders in Iran have provided a poor example of the rule of law. Much of their power is derived from crowds in the streets, which they manipulate through emotional appeal, and the constitution is more an instrument of authoritarianism than the basis of a consistent and equitable administrative system.

The events in Iran have confronted the Arabs with complex problems of internal and external security. The emerging competition among bourgeois, leftist, and Islamic fundamentalist camps for ascendancy, which has become implicit in the politics of the entire Middle East, has created an underlying tension in many Arab societies. Though this has not yet disrupted the functioning of established political processes, it has intensified the awareness of conflicting interests and posed the possibility of rifts in the social fabric. While trying to preserve the internal status quo, the Arab regimes are also preoccupied with their common concern that if one of them falls, the rest will face the same fate.[4] To some extent the recent alignments in the Arab system are based on the search for a way of consolidating forces to meet this security challenge.

The external security threat that developed in the aftermath of the fall of the shah is rooted in the aspirations of the new rulers in Teheran to export their revolution into the Arab area and to expand their power and influence in the Gulf. This brought them into confrontation with Iraq, Saudi Arabia, and the sheikhdoms in particular. The problem has been compounded for these countries by the intensified Soviet activity in the Middle East. The strong positions which Moscow established in Afghanistan, South Yemen, and Ethiopia in the late 1970s provided the framework of an encirclement strategy which left the eastern Arab world vulnerable and exposed to the politics of superpower confrontation.

Aside from the Iraqi-Saudi-Jordanian axis and Saddam Husayn's Iranian campaign, the most important recent security measure has been the formation of the Gulf Cooperation Council (*Majlis al-Taawun al-Khaliji*) on February 4, 1981, by Saudi Arabia, Kuwait, Bahrain, Qatar,

---

4. Walid Kazziha, *Palestine in the Arab Dilemma* (New York: Barnes & Noble, 1979), p. 68.

the UAE, and Oman.[5] Though officially aimed at the economic, administrative, and cultural integration of the members, this organization is essentially a mutual security pact in response to Iranian and Soviet machinations. Its greatest weakness is the absence of Iraq, which had earlier pledged to protect the sheikhdoms from Iranian aggression. The exclusion of Iraq reflects a degree of mistrust with which the Gulf states view the regime in Baghdad, despite the existence of common interests. But the establishment of the council shows a determination to work toward a comprehensive regional security system.

The destabilization of the Middle East and the security problems it has engendered have become major factors in the politics of the Arab system. This has led to an increased awareness in the established regimes of the need for closer links with the people over whom they rule. It has also made them more conscious of the mutual interdependence among them. Hence the alignments that have been formed during the past few years are more pragmatic in character than the earlier rivalries and ideological confrontations. Given the increasing skill in statecraft and diplomatic finesse, the result may well be a sounder balance of power in the Arab world.

SOURCES OF DISUNITY

The fundamental source of Arab disunity is regionalism, though the existence of distinct geographic entities does not necessarily preclude a harmonious relationship among them. Yet ever since the Arab system became operative in 1945, the member states have been involved in a series of intense rivalries over the question of leadership. The most prominent of these was the struggle for hegemony between Egypt and the Fertile Crescent, which has historical roots in ancient and medieval times. In the 1970s a variety of transregional alignments emerged because of the diffusion of assets and influence. But the competitive nature of inter-Arab politics remained unchanged.

The continued rivalry stems from the diversity of Arab political systems, the insecurity that arises from the constantly shifting structure of the balance of power, and the preoccupation with special interests. The very fact that the Arab states are ruled by varying forms of governments

5. *Al-Anba'* (Kuwait), May 23, 1981.

based on different ideological premises generates an underlying climate of friction which impels the established regimes to seek supportive allies. Though the alignments that have been formed often do not reflect political affinities among the partners, they provide a degree of security in the sense that they represent a combination of respective assets which serve common interests. In the case of the Egyptian-Syrian-Saudi alliance in the early 1970s and the Iraqi-Saudi-Jordanian axis that developed at the end of the decade, extremely important leadership positions were assumed by both blocs.

The main problem confronting such arrangements is continuity. The earlier trilateral grouping proved transitory and became relatively ineffective after 1975. The more recent alignment appears to rest on a solid foundation, but the exclusion of Iraq from the Gulf Cooperation Council reflects some tension between Baghdad and the Saudi-led security system. Also, a counter-axis was formed by Syria and Libya, and though it does not seem likely to pose a serious threat, the Jordanian-Syrian confrontation of late 1980 has not completely subsided and remains a potential source of conflict. The fluidity in inter-Arab politics intensifies the rivalries that exist at any given time because of the uncertainties that always surround the balance of power.

Preoccupation with special interests is a third source of disunity, and often it is associated with regional concerns. The whole course of al-Sadat's policies following the October war was geared to specifically Egyptian interests, especially in the economic sphere. Ultimately it led to a rupture between Cairo and the other Arab states, and later the Arab system itself became polarized on various levels. Similarly, the renewal of friction between Syria and Iraq after a brief rapprochement in the late 1970s was based on the conflicting interests of the two regimes. The PLO, despite its adeptness in diplomatic maneuvering, became so preoccupied with securing its position in Lebanon that it antagonized much of the indigenous population. Jonathan Randal has analyzed the PLO's main problem as its "incorrigible habit of alienating the few Arab societies in which Palestinians are allowed to move about freely. Most Lebanese feel they destroyed one state (Lebanon) to make their own."[6]

These are only a few examples of ways in which the priority given to special interests has contributed to breaches in the solidarity of the Arab system. Underlying much of the tension in inter-Arab politics, however, is a mutual lack of trust and a fear of sharing power. This partially explains the preference for alliances over transnational projects within regions. But

6. Jonathan Randal, "Obstacles Keep New Blood from PLO Leadership," *Washington Post*, March 3, 1980.

whereas the former are often temporary accommodations among sovereign entities, schemes of regional integration represent the only possibility of greater unity in the Arab world.

The respective Arab regimes perceive their relationship to the system as a whole in very different ways. Those in command of Cairo's foreign policy do not see the disagreement between Egypt and the other Arab countries as a matter of principle, but of style and methodology. Though they recognize that the Camp David formula does not have adequate linkage with other aspects of the overall Middle East problem, they feel that al-Sadat's initiative will ultimately succeed because it forces Israel to deal with the real issues of peace. What the other Arabs do not understand, in their view, is that the Egyptian tactic involves a certain finesse which will in the long run lead to a satisfactory resolution of such problems as the return of the occupied territories and the right of the Palestinians to self-determination. They also believe that the Arab-Egyptian rupture is only temporary and that a return to normal relations will follow the evacuation of eastern Sinai by Israel on April 25, 1982. In the meantime, they insist that functional relations continue to exist with many Arab states on various levels, despite the diplomatic break.[7]

King Husayn, on the other hand, believes that the Egyptian initiative threatened a disintegration of the Arab system. Because of his own opposition to it, he thinks that Jordan came to be trusted by most Arab states and therefore exercises greater influence over them. He considers this appropriate because of what he sees as a special Hashimite link with the past. In general, Jordanian leaders feel that they play a stabilizing role in inter-Arab politics and that by resorting to a diversification of options in the context of their own economic vulnerability, they will eventually become the major architects of a peaceful solution to the Arab-Israeli conflict. They insist, however, that the Palestinians are the major party of a settlement with Israel, and that this role cannot be assumed by Egypt, Jordan, or any other Arab state. They also deny that there is any pact among Jordan, Iraq, and Saudi Arabia, but rather a natural strategic consensus based on common interests and military and economic interdependence.[8]

The differences in Egyptian and Jordanian perceptions are only one example of a much more extensive divergence of viewpoints within the

7. The information in this paragraph is based on interviews with Boutros Ghali and Usama al-Bazz at the Egyptian Foreign Ministry in Cairo in May 1981.

8. The information in this paragraph in based on interviews with King Husayn, Foreign Minister Marwan Qasem, and Information Minister Adnan Abu Odeh of Jordan in Amman in May and June 1981.

Arab system. Though there is agreement on major issues among aligned states, rival blocs are often far apart in orientation. This discrepancy in the way political developments are seen by various regimes perpetuates anomosities and divisiveness. But like all the sources of disunity, new circumstances can introduce extensive changes in the pattern of relationships.

The succession of Husni Mubarak as president of Egypt following the assassination of Anwar al-Sadat on October 6, 1981, may well alter the course of Egypt's Arab policies. It is still too early to predict what will evolve in this regard, but the public indifference to al-Sadat's death suggests that his policies were not as popular as they seemed to be. Mubarak has already indicated a desire to achieve a rapprochement with the political opposition within his own country, while remaining fully aware of the need to contain the radical Islamic fundamentalists and reaffirming his support for the peace process with Israel.[9] He also clearly wants to improve Egypt's relations with the other Arab states, and refused to accept the highly restrictive Israeli plan for West Bank autonomy.[10] Similarly, on his first state visit to Washington in early February 1982, he declared emphatically that "the key to peace and stability in the area is to solve the Palestinian problem."[11] His principal foreign policy advisor, Usama al-Bazz, has stated that the peace proposal of Saudi Arabia's Prince Fahd is basically sound, but lacks the details to make it viable and fails to take into consideration the objections of Israel.[12] These recent developments in Egypt point to an eventual change in Egyptian-Arab relations, a development which would profoundly affect the Arab system.

THE ROAD TO COOPERATION

The dilemma confronting the Arabs in the last quarter of the twentieth century lies in the difficulty they have in finding a way to settle their

9. Howard Simons and David Ottaway, "Mubarak Sets Focus on Domestic Matters," *Washington Post*, November 1, 1981.
10. Don Oberdorfer, "State Department Official Sees Chance of Egypt Improving Relations with Moderate Arab States," *Washington Post*, October 22, 1981; Loren Jenkins, "Talks on Palestinian Autonomy Stymied by Council Issue," *Washington Post*, November 13, 1981.
11. John M. Goshko, "Mubarak Dims Hopes on Mideast," *Washington Post*, February 4, 1982.
12. Loren Jenkins, "Egypt Discounts Saudi Mideast Peace Plan," *Washington Post*, November, 11, 1981.

differences and construct a viable system of cooperation. Though they recognize that they are interdependent and would gain a lot from working together, genuine solidarity has so far proved an elusive goal. Nevertheless, since the 1967 war, they have made considerable progress in the art of diplomacy and in forming practical alliances geared to limited and therefore realizable aims. The question now is how far they can progress from this beginning.

A more promising future depends first of all on the ability of the Arabs to develop a balance between the ideal and the pragmatic. The extravagant ideologies of the 1950s and 1960s were ultimately counterproductive and left the Arab system in a shambles. Then the shock of the 1967 war gave rise to a new pragmatism which produced more affirmative results. The major shortcoming of this approach was that it gave priority to the special concerns of particular regimes, which formed pacts designed to achieve their own objectives, sometimes at the expense of broader Arab interests. Following the October war, this eventually led to divisiveness and polarization. The current Iraqi-Saudi-Jordanian axis has come closer to striking a balance than the preceding alliance and bilateral accords. But it has yet to mend the rift with Egypt and Syria, which are key countries in the system.

The primary task before Iraq, Saudi Arabia, and Jordan in the coming few years is one of formulating an Arab political doctrine. This should establish guidelines for inter-Arab cooperation which take into account the long-range interests of the Arabs as a community of nations. It should also seek to formalize a system of political legitimacy to be used as a model by all Arab states. To be effective, this must define certain restrictions on official authority and state policy, and specify the inalienable rights of citizens. The emergence of such a doctrine and its ratification by the Arab states would do much to promote the legitimacy and continuity of established regimes and to foster a mutually beneficial system of cooperation.

Finally, the Arabs should explore the possibilities of regional integration. The pan-Arab approach has done more to impede than to promote unity, whereas regional projects have never really been tried. The advancement of schemes of federation or confederation in the Fertile Crescent, the Arabian Peninsula, the Nile Valley, and the Maghreb could ultimately transform the whole character of inter-Arab politics. The rise of larger and more viable states would not only make the Arab bloc more influential in world politics; it might also lead to an even more comprehensive unification. But it seems certain that if there is ever to be an "Arab Nation," regional integration has to come first.

The Arabs are now at a turning point in their history. Though preoccupied at the moment with achieving and maintaining a delicate balance of power, the prospects of a more cooperative and viable Arab system are perhaps better than ever before. The future will depend on sound judgment, fair practice, and a determination to pursue common goals.

Appendices

APPENDIX 1

MEMBERSHIP OF THE ARAB LEAGUE

Member	Date of Admission
Egypt	March 22, 1945
Saudi Arabia	March 22, 1945
Iraq	March 22, 1945
Transjordan	March 22, 1945
Syria	March 22, 1945
Lebanon	March 22, 1945
North Yemen	May 5, 1945
Sudan	January 19, 1956
Libya	March 28, 1956
Morocco	October 1, 1958
Tunisia	October 1, 1958
Kuwait	July 20, 1961
Algeria	August 16, 1962
South Yemen	December 12, 1967
Bahrain	September 11, 1971
Qatar	September 11, 1971
Oman	September 29, 1971
United Arab Emirates	December 6, 1971
Mauritania	November 26, 1973
Somalia	February 14, 1974
PLO	September 9, 1976
Djibouti	September 4, 1977

APPENDIX 2

ARAB SUMMIT CONFERENCES

Date	Location	Major Topic
1. January 13–17, 1964	Cairo	Diversion of Jordan River
2. September 5–11, 1964	Alexandria	Opposition to Jordan River Conversion Plan
3. September 13–18, 1965	Casablanca	Solidarity and Peaceful Coexistence among Arab States
4. August 29– September 2, 1967	Khartum	The June 1967 War
5. December 21–23, 1969	Rabat	The Arab Situation
6. November 26–28, 1973	Algeirs	Consequences of the 1973 War
7. October 26–29, 1974	Rabat	Recognition of PLO as Sole Legitimate Representative of the Palestinian People
8. October 25–26, 1976	Cairo	The War in Lebanon
9. November 2–5, 1878	Baghdad	Rejection of Camp David Accords: Reiteration of Support for PLO
10. November 20–22, 1979	Tunis	Confirmation of Baghdad II Resolution
11. November 25–28, 1980	Amman	Economic Development
12. November 25, 1981	Fez	Prematurely Adjourned

APPENDIX 3

ARAB ALIGNMENTS, 1945–1955

Hashimite Bloc	Neutral States	Anti-Hashimite Bloc
Iraq	Syria ⟶	Egypt
Transjordan (Jordan)	Lebanon	Saudi Arabia
	Yemen (N. Yemen)	

Arrow indicates directional drift in affiliation after 1949.

APPENDIX 4

ARAB ALIGNMENTS, 1965

Revolutionary States	*Moderate States*	*Conservative States*
Egypt	Lebanon	Saudi Arabia
Sudan	Tunisia	Kuwait
Syria ⟵	Yemen (N. Yemen)	Jordan
Iraq		Libya
Algeria		Morocco

Arrow indicates directional drift in affiliation after 1962.

APPENDIX 5

ARAB ALIGNMENTS, 1971–1975

Rejection Front (October 1974)	*Neutral States*	*Trilateral Alliance*
Iraq	PLO	Egypt
Radical PLO	Lebanon	Syria
Libya	Tunisia	Saudi Arabia
S. Yemen	Algeria	*Affiliates*
	Morocco	Sudan
	Mauritania	Jordan
	Somalia	Kuwait
		UAE
		Bahrain
		Qatar
		Oman
		N. Yemen

APPENDIX 6

ARAB ALIGNMENTS, DECEMBER 1977–MARCH 1979

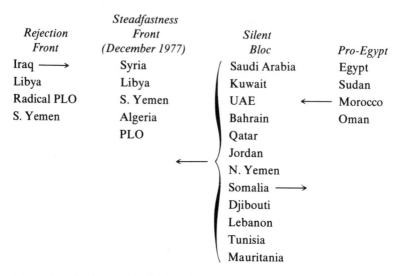

Rejection Front	Steadfastness Front (December 1977)	Silent Bloc	Pro-Egypt
Iraq ⟶	Syria	Saudi Arabia	Egypt
Libya	Libya	Kuwait	Sudan
Radical PLO	S. Yemen	UAE ⟵	Morocco
S. Yemen	Algeria	Bahrain	Oman
	PLO	Qatar	
		Jordan	
	⟵	N. Yemen	
		Somalia ⟶	
		Djibouti	
		Lebanon	
		Tunisia	
		Mauritania	

Arrows indicate directional drift in affiliation after September 1978.

APPENDIX 7
ARAB ALIGNMENTS SINCE MARCH 1979

Syrian-Libyan Counter-Axis	Egyptian Bloc	Iraqi-Saudi-Jordanian Axis
Syria	Egypt	Iraq
Libya	Sudan	Saudi Arabia
	Oman	Jordan
Affiliates	Morocco	
PLO	Somalia	*Affiliates*
Algeria		Kuwait
S. Yemen	*Neutral States*	UAE
Lebanon	Tunisia	Bahrain
	Mauritania	Qatar
	Djibouti	N. Yemen

APPENDIX 8

TREATY OF JOINT DEFENCE AND ECONOMIC COOPERATION
AMONG THE STATES OF THE ARAB LEAGUE. APRIL 13, 1950

The Treaty was approved by the Council of the League on April 13, 1950, during its Twelfth Ordinary Session. It was signed on June 17, 1950, by Syria, Saudi Arabia, Lebanon, Yaman, and Egypt. It was also signed by Iraq on February 2, 1951, and by Jordan on February 16, 1952.

The instruments of ratification were deposited at the Secretariat-General by:

1.	Syria	on October 13, 1951
2.	Egypt	on November 22, 1951
3.	Jordan	on March 13, 1952
4.	Iraq	on August 7, 1952
5.	Saudi Arabia	on August 19, 1952
6.	Lebanon	on December 24, 1952
7.	Yaman	on October 11, 1953.

Being desirous of consolidating the ties, and of strengthening cooperation among the States of the Arab League, in order to maintain their independence and to preserve their common heritage,

And in response to the desire of their peoples to join forces for realizing the common defence of their existence and for maintaining security and peace in conformity with the principles and purposes of both the Arab League Pact and the United Nations Charter, and in order to reinforce stability and reassurance, and to provide means of welfare and prosperity in their countries,

Have agreed to conclude a treaty to this end, and have delegated the following plenipotentiaries, who, having exchanged credentials which invest them with full authority, and which were found to be duly correct and in good form, have agreed upon the following:

Article 1. Being anxious to maintain and stabilize security and peace, the Contracting States hereby confirm their determination to settle all their international disputes by peaceful means, whether in their mutual relations or in their relations with other States.

Article 2. The Contracting States shall consider that an armed aggression committed against any one or more of them, or against their forces, to be an aggression against them all. For this reason, and in accordance with the right of legitimate self-defence, both individual and collective, they undertake to hasten to the aid of the State or States against whom an aggression is committed, and to take immediately, individually and collectively, all measures and to utilize all means available, including the use of armed force, to repulse the aggression and to restore security and peace.

And, in application of Article 6 of the Arab League Pact and Article 51 of the United Nations Charter, the Council of the Arab League and the (U.N.) Security Council shall be immediately notified of the act of aggression and of the measures and procedures adopted concerning same.

Article 3. The Contracting States shall consult together at the request of any one of them, whenever the territoral integrity, independence or security of any of them is threatened.

In the event of the danger of an impending war, or of the emergence of an international contingency the danger of which is apprehended, the Contracting States shall immediately proceed to unify their plans and efforts for adopting such preventive and defensive measures as the situation requires.

Article 4. In a desire to discharge fully the above-mentioned obligations, the Contracting States shall co-operate with each other for consolidating and strengthening their military power. They shall participate, according to their resources and needs, in preparing the individual and collective means of defence to resist any armed aggression.

Article 5. A Permanent Military Commission shall be formed of representatives of the General Staffs of the Contracting States in order to organise the plans of joint defence and to prepare their means and methods.

The powers of this Permanent Military Commission, including the drawing up of the necessary reports embodying the elements of co-operation and participation mentioned in Article 4 shall be defined in an Annex to this Treaty. This Permanent Commission shall submit its reports concerning matters falling within its jurisdiction to the Joint Defence Council provided for the next Article.

Article 6. A Joint Defence Council shall be constituted under the control of the Council of the Arab League, and shall have authority over all matters relating to the implementation of the provisions of the Articles 2, 3, 4, and 5 of this Treaty. In this, it shall be assisted by the Permanent Military Commission referred to in the preceding Article.

The Joint Defence Council shall consist of the Foreign Ministers and the National Defence Ministers of the Contracting States, or their representatives.

Decisions adopted by a majority of two-thirds of the (Contracting) States shall be binding on all the Contracting States.

Article 7. In order to realize the objectives of this Treaty and its aims of promoting reassurance, of ensuring prosperity in the Arab countries and of raising the standard of living therein, the Contracting States shall co-operate for the advancement of the economies of their countries, the exploitation of their natural resources, the facilitation of the exchange of their national agricultural and industrial products, and generally for the organisation and co-ordination of their economic activities and for the conclusion of such special agreements as may be necessary for realizing these objectives.

Article 8. An Economic Council shall be created and shall consist of the Ministers of the Contracting States concerned with economic affairs, or their representatives in case of necessity, in order to make proposals to the Governments of these States concerning whatever it considers guarantees to the realization of the aims indicated in the preceding Article.

The Council may, in the course of its work, seek the assistance of the Committee for Economic and Financial Affairs refered to in Article 4 of the Pact of the League of Arab States.

Article 9. The Annex to this Treaty shall be considered as an integral part of it.

Article 10. Each of the Contracting States undertakes not to conclude any international agreement which may be inconsistent with this Treaty, and not to adopt in its international relations any course which may be contrary to the aims of the Treaty.

Article 11. None of the provisions of this Treaty shall in any way affect, or be intended to affect, the rights or obligations incurred, or which may be incurred, by the Contracting Parties by virtue of the United Nations Charter of the responsibilities incumbent upon the (U.N.) Security Council for the maintenance of international peace and security.

Article 12. Any one of the Contracting States may, after the lapse of ten years from the entry into force of this Treaty, withdraw from it at the end of one year from the date of notification of its withdrawal to the Secretariat-General of the League of Arab States. The Secretariat-General shall inform the other Contracting States of such notification.

Article 13. This Treaty shall be ratified by each Contracting State in accordance with the constitutional processes in force therein.

The instruments of ratification shall be deposited at the Secretariat-General of the League of Arab States.

The Treaty shall come into force, in regard to every country which has ratified it, fifteen days after the receipt by the Secretariat-General of the instruments of ratification of at least four States.

This Treaty was drawn up in Arabic in Cairo on *Jumad al-Akhira*, 1369 A.H. (corresponding to April 13, 1950), in one original copy to be kept at the Secretariat-General of the League of Arab States. An authentic copy of the original shall be delivered to each of the Contracting States.

Source: Muhammad Khalil, *The Arab States and the Arab League: A Documentary Record,* Vol. II: *International Affairs* (Beirut: Khayats, 1962), pp. 101–104.

APPENDIX 9

PROCLAMATION OF THE UNITED ARAB REPUBLIC. FEBRUARY 1, 1958

On February 1, 1958, in an historic session held at al-Qubba Palace in Cairo, His Excellency President Shukry al-Quwwatly of Syria, and President Jamal 'Abd an-Nasir (Nasser) of Egypt, met the representatives of the Republics of Syria and Egypt: as Sayyid Sabry al-Asaly, as-Sayyid 'Abd al-Latif al-Baghdady, as-Sayyid

Khalid al-'Azm, as-Sayyid Zakariyya Muhieddin, as-Sayyid Hamid Ma'mun al-Kuzbary, as-Sayyid Husayn ash-Shifi'y, as-Sayyid As'ad Harun, General 'Abd al-Hakim'Amir, as-Sayyid Salah ad-Din al-Bitar, as-Sayyid Kamal ad-Din Husayn, as-Sayyid Khalil al-Kallas, as-Sayyid Nur ad-Din Tarraf, as-Sayyid Salih 'Aqil, as-Sayyid Fathy Radwan, General 'Afif al-Bizry, as-Sayyid Mahmud Fawzy, as-Sayyid Kamal Ramzy Stinu, as-Sayyid 'Ali Sabry, as-Sayyid 'Abd ar-Rahman al-'Azm, and as-Sayyid Mahmud Riyad.

The purpose of this meeting was to discuss the final measures (to be taken) for the realization of the Arab people's will and the carrying out of the provisions of the Constitutions of both Republics, namely that the people of each of these (Republics) form a part of the Arab Nation.

They, therefore, discussed the decisions unanimously reached by the Egyptian National Assembly and the Syrian Chamber of Deputies, to the effect that unity should be established between the two countries as a first step towards the realization of complete Arab unity. They also discussed the decisive proofs borne out (by the experience) of the past few years, showing that Arab nationalism, throughout a long history of domination (by others) of the Arabs in their various countries, has acted as an inspiration for both a common cheerful present and for a future that is the hope of every single Arab.

They came to the conclusion that this unity, which is the fruit of Arab nationalism, is the Arab's path to freedom and sovereignty, and that it is one of humanity's gateways to co-operation and peace. For this (reason), it is their duty with perseverance and determination to take this unity from its state of (mere) aspiration to where it can develop into reality. From all this, the participants concluded that the elements conducive to the success of the union of the two Republics were fully present; particulary recently, after their joint struggle had brought them even closer together, had made the meaning of freedom still clearer, and demonstrated that it was a movement for liberation and positive achievement and one for co-operation and peace.

In all this, the participants declared their total agreement as well as their complete faith and deep conviction in the necessity of uniting Egypt and Syria into one State to be called "The United Arab Republic."

They likewise declare their unanimous agreement on the adoption of a presidential democratic system of government for the United Arab Republic, according to which executive authority shall be vested in the head of the State, who will be assisted by ministers appointed by him and responsible to him. Legislative authority shall be vested in one legislative assembly.

The new Republic shall have one flag which shall bring under it one people and one army, within the framework of a union in which all will have equal rights and duties, in which all will be called upon to protect their country with heart and soul, and (in which) all will compete in the consolidation of its dignity and the safeguarding of its invulnerability.

His Excellency President Shukry al-Quwwatly and President Jamal 'Abd an-Nasir will each deliver a statement to the people, to be made (respectively) in the Syrian Chamber of Deputies and in the Egyptian National Assembly, on

Wednesday, Rajab 16, 1377 (A.H.), corresponding to February 5, 1958. In it they will announce the decisions reached at this meeting and explain the bases of the unity of (this) young State of the Arabs.

The peoples of Egypt and Syria will also be called upon within thirty days to participate in a general plebiscite on the principles of unity and on (the choice of) the person of the head of the State.

In announcing these decisions, the participants feel exceedingly happy and proud for having taken part in this positive step for the sake of Arab unity and solidarity—a unity which has been for many an epoch and many a generation the Arabs' long-cherished hope and greatly coveted objective. In deciding on the unity of both countries, the participants declare that their unity purports to unify all the Arabs, and (affirm) that the door is open for participation by each and every Arab State desirous of joining them in a union or federation for the purpose of protecting the Arab peoples from harm and evil, reinforcing Arab sovereignty and safeguarding its existence.

May God bestow His protection on this step which we have taken as well as on those which will follow, and so ordain that Arabdom shall live in unity, in pride and in peace.

[Signatures follow]

Source: Muhammad Khalil, *The Arab States and the Arab League: A Documentary Record,* Vol. I: *Constitutional Developments* (Beirut: Khayats, 1962), pp. 601–602.

APPENDIX 10

RESOLUTIONS AND RECOMMENDATIONS ADOPTED BY THE 4TH
ARAB SUMMIT CONFERENCE. KHARTUM, SEPTEMBER 1, 1967

1. The Conference affirmed the unity of the Arab ranks and the unity of collective Arab action which has been cleared of all differences. The Arab Heads of State, either personally or through their representatives, affirmed their countries' adherence to the Arab Solidarity Pact which was issued at the third Arab Summit Conference held in Casablanca, and undertook to implement it.

2. The Conference resolved that it was essential that all Arab efforts should be unified to eliminate the consequences of the aggression, in view of the fact that the occupied territories are Arab territories, so that the responsibility for their recovery must be borne by all the Arab countries.

3. The Arab Heads of State agreed to unify their efforts in political action at the international diplomatic level to eliminate the consequences of aggression and to ensure the withdrawal of Israeli forces from the Arab territories occupied during the June War, provided that it be consistent with the principles to which all

Arab nations adhere: that there shall be no peace with Israel, no recognition of Israel, no negotations with Israel, and that the Arab nations shall take action to safeguard the right of the people of Palestine to their homeland.

4. The Conference of Arab Ministers of Finance, Economy and Oil had recommended that an embargo on the flow of oil be used as a weapon in the war; the Summit Conference, after a careful study of the issue, decided that the oil flow could be used as a positive weapon, in view of the fact that oil is one of the resources of the Arab World, which could serve to support the economies of Arab nations which have been directly affected by the aggression and enable these nations to stand firm in the battle.

The Conference therefore resolved that oil pumping should be resumed, in view of the fact that oil is a positive Arab resource that can be exploited in the service of Arab objectives and play its part in enabling the Arab countries which were the victims of aggression, and had thereby lost part of their revenues, to stand fast in the battle for the elimination of the consequences of the aggression.

Moreover, the oil-producing countries have in fact played their part in enabling the nations which were the victims of the aggression to withstand economic pressures.

5. The delegates to the Conference endorsed the proposal submitted by Kuwait for the establishment of an Arab economic and social development fund as recommended by the Conference of Arab Ministers of Finance, Economy and Oil.

6. The delegates to the Conference resolved that it was essential that all requisite steps should be taken to ensure the provision of military supplies to meet all eventualities.

7. The Conference resolved to bring about the early liquidation of foreign bases in Arab countries.

The Conference also issued the follosing separate resolutions:

Each of the Kingdom of Saudi Arabia, the State of Kuwait and the Kingdom of Libya undertake to pay the following annual sums, in quarterly installments in advance, as from the middle of October , until such time as all consequences of the aggression shall be eliminated:

The Kingdom of Saudi Arabia	—L50 million
The State of Kuwait	—L55 million
The Kingdom of Libya	—L30 million

On the basis of which the Arab nation is certain of being able to continue the battle until the elimination of the consequences of the aggression is completed.

Source: Fuad Jaber, ed., *International Documents on Palestine, 1967* (Beirut: Institute for Palestine Studies, 1970), pp. 655–657.

APPENDIX 11

1. This Charter shall be known as "the Palestine National Charter."
Articles of the Charter:

Article 1. Palestine, the homeland of the Palestinian Arab people, is an inseparable part of the greater Arab homeland, and the Palestinian people are a part of the Arab Nation.

Article 2. Palestine, within the frontiers that existed under the British Mandate, is an indivisible territorial unit.

Article 3. The Palestinian Arab people alone have legitimate rights to their homeland, and shall exercise the right of self-determination after the liberation of their homeland, in keeping with their wishes and entirely of their own accord.

Article 4. The Palestinian identity is an authentic, intrinsic and indissoluble quality that is transmitted from father to son. Neither the Zionist occupation nor the dispersal of the Palestinian Arab people as a result of the afflictions they have suffered can efface this Palestinian identity.

Article 5. Palestinians are Arab citizens who were normally resident in Palestine until 1947. This includes both those who were forced to leave or who stayed in Palestine. Anyone born to a Palestinian father after that date, whether inside or outside Palestine, is a Palestinian.

Article 6. Jews who were normally resident in Palestine up to the beginning of the Zionist invasion are Palestinians.

Article 7. Palestinian identity, and material, spiritual and historical links with Palestine are immutable realities. It is a national obligation to provide every Palestinian with a revolutionary Arab upbringing, and to instil in him a profound spiritual and material familiarity with his homeland and a readiness both for armed struggle and for the sacrifice of his material possessions and his life, for the recovery of his homeland. All available educational means of guidance must be enlisted to that end, until liberation is achieved.

Article 8. The Palestinian people is at the stage of national struggle for the liberation of its homeland. For that reason, differences between Palestinian national forces must give way to the fundamental difference that exists between Zionism and imperialism on the one hand and the Palestinian Arab people on the other. On that basis, the Palestinian masses, both as organisations and as individuals, whether in the homeland or in such places as they now live as refugees, constitute a single national force working for the recovery and liberation of Palestine through armed struggle.

Article 9. Armed struggle is the only way of liberating Palestine, and is thus strategic, not tactical. The Palestinian Arab people hereby affirm their unwavering determination to carry on the armed struggle and to press on towards popular revolution for the liberation of and return to their homeland. They also affirm their right to a normal life in their homeland, to the exercise of their right of self-determination therein and to sovereignty over it.

Article 10.   Commando action constitutes the nucleus of the Palestinian popular war of liberation. This requires that commando action should be escalated, expanded and protected and that all resources of the Palestinian masses and all scientific potentials available to them should be mobilised and organised to play their part in the armed Palestinian revolution. It also requires solidarity in national struggle among the different groups within the Palestinian people and between that people and the Arab masses, to ensure the continuity of the escalation and victory of the revolution.

Article 11. Palestinians shall have three slogans: national unity, national mobilisation and liberation.

Article 12. The Palestinian Arab people believe in Arab unity. To fulfill their role in the achievement of that objective, they must, at the present stage in their national struggle, retain their Palestinian identity and all that it involves, work for increased awareness of it and oppose all measures liable to weaken or dissolve it.

Article 13.   Arab unity and the liberation of Palestine are complementary objectives; each leads to the achievement of the other. Arab unity will lead to the liberation of Palestine, and the liberation of Palestine will lead to Arab unity. To work for one is to work for both.

Article 14.   The destiny of the Arab nation, indeed the continued existence of the Arabs, depends on the fate of the Palestinian cause. This interrelationship is the point of departure of the Arab endeavour to liberate Palestine. The Palestinian people are the vanguard of the movement to achieve this sacred national objective.

Article 15.   The liberation of Palestine is a national obligation for the Arabs. It is their duty to repel the Zionist and imperialist invasion of the greater Arab homeland and to liquidate the Zionist presence in Palestine. The full responsibility for this belongs to the peoples and governments of the Arab nation and to the Palestinian people first and foremost.

For this reason, the task of the Arab nation is to enlist all the military, human, moral and material resources at its command to play an effective part, along with the Palestinian people, in the liberation of Palestine. Moreover, it is the task of the Arab nation, particularly at the present stage of the Palestinian armed revolution, to offer the Palestinian people all possible aid, material and manpower support, and to place at their disposal all the means and opportunities that will enable them to continue to perform their role as the vanguard of their armed revolution until the liberation of their homeland is achieved.

Article 16.   On the spiritual plane, the liberation of Palestine will establish in the Holy Land an atmosphere of peace and tranquility in which all religious institutions will be safeguarded and freedom of worship and the right of visit guaranteed to all without discrimination or distinction of race, colour, language or creed. For this reason, the people of Palestine look to all spiritual forces in the world for support.

Article 17. On the human plane, the liberation of Palestine will restore to the Palestinians their dignity, integrity and freedom. For this reason, the Palestinian Arab people look to all those who believe in the dignity and freedom of man for support.

Article 18. On the international plane, the liberation of Palestine is a defensive measure dictated by the requirements of self-defence. This is why the Palestinian people, who seek to win the friendship of all peoples, look for the support of all freedom, justice and peace-loving countries in restoring the legitimate state of affairs in Palestine, establishing security and peace in it and enabling its people to exercise national sovereignty and freedom.

Article 19. The partition of Palestine, which took place in 1947, and the establishment of Israel, are fundamentally invalid, however long they last, for they contravene the will of the people of Palestine and their natural right to their homeland and contradict the principles of the United Nations Charter, foremost among which is the right of self-determination.

Article 20. The Balfour Declaration, the Mandate Instrument, and all their consequences, are hereby declared null and void. The claim of historical or spiritual links between the Jews and Palestine is neither in conformity with historical fact nor does it satisfy the requirements for statehood. Judaism is a revealed religion; it is not a separate nationality, nor are the Jews a single people with a separate identity; they are citizens of their respective countries.

Article 21. The Palestinian Arab people, expressing themselves through the Palestinian armed revolution, reject all alternatives to the total liberation of Palestine. They also reject all proposals for the liquidation or internationalisation of the Palestine problem.

Article 22. Zionism is a political movement that is organically linked with world imperialism and is opposed to all liberation movements or movements for progress in the world. The Zionist movement is essentially fanatical and racialist; its objectives involve aggression, expansion and the establishment of colonial settlements, and its methods are those of the Fascists and the Nazis. Israel acts as cat's paw for the Zionist movement, a geographic and manpower base for world imperialism and a springboard for its thrust into the Arab homeland to frustrate the aspirations of the Arab nation to liberation, unity and progress. Israel is a constant threat to peace in the Middle East and the whole world. Inasmuch as the liberation of Palestine will eliminate the Zionist and imperialist presence in that country and bring peace to the Middle East, the Palestinian people look for support to all liberals and to all forces of good, peace and progress in the world, and call on them, whatever their political convictions, for all possible aid and support in their just and legitimate struggle to liberate their homeland.

Article 23. The demands of peace and security and the exigencies of right and justice require that all nations should regard Zionism as an illegal movement and outlaw it and its activities, out of consideration for the ties of friendship between peoples and for the loyalty of citizens to their homelands.

Article 24. The Palestinian Arab people believe in justice, freedom, sovereignty, self-determination, human dignity and the right of peoples to enjoy them.

Article 25.   In pursuance of the objectives set out in this charter, the Palestine Liberation Organisation shall perform its proper role in the liberation of Palestine in the full.

Article 26.   The Palestine Liberation Organisation, as the representative of the forces of the Palestinian revolution, is responsible for the struggle of the Palestinian Arab people to regain, liberate and return to their homeland and to exercise the right of self-determination in that homeland, in the military, political and financial fields, and for all else that the Palestinian cause may demand, both at Arab and international levels.

Article 27.   The Palestine Liberation Organisation shall cooperate with all Arab countries, each according to its means, maintaining a neutral attitude vis-à-vis these countries in accordance with the requirements of the battle of liberation, and on the basis of that factor. The Organisation shall not interfere in the internal affairs of any Arab country.

Article 28.   The Palestinian Arab people hereby affirm the authenticity and independence of their national revolution and reject interference, tutelage or dependency.

Article 29.   The Palestinian Arab people have the legitimate and prior right to liberate and recover their homeland, and shall define their attitude to all countries and forces in accordance with the attitude adopted by such countries and forces to the cause of the Palestinian people and with the extent of their support for that people in their revolution to achieve their objectives.

Article 30.   Those who fight or bear arms in the battle of liberation form the nucleus of the popular army which will shield the achievements of the Palestinian Arab people.

Article 31.   The Organisation shall have a flag, an oath of allegiance and an anthem, to be decided in accordance with appropriate regulations.

Article 32.   Regulations, to be known as Basic Regulations for the Palestine Liberation Organisation, shall be appended to this Charter. These regulations shall define the structure of the Organisation, its bodies and institutions, and the powers, duties and obligations of each of them, in accordance with this Charter.

Article 33.   This Charter may only be amended with a majority of two thirds of the total number of the members of the National Assembly of the Palestine Liberation Organisation at a special meeting called for that purpose.

Source: Zuhair Diab, ed., *International Documents on Palestine, 1968* (Beirut: Institute for Palestine Studies and University of Kuwait, 1971), pp. 393–395.

APPENDIX 12

On Monday, November 3, 1969, a meeting took place in Cairo between the Lebanese delegation, headed by General Emile Bustani, and the delegation from the Palestine Liberation Organisation, headed by Mr. Yasser Arafat, head of the Organisation. The United Arab Republic was represented at the meeting by Mr. Mahmud Riyad, Minister for Foreign Affairs, and Lieutenant General Muhammad Fawzi, Minster for War.

In keeping with the principles of brotherhood and common destiny, Lebanon's relations with the Palestinian Revolution should always be characterised by trust, frankness and positive cooperation; this is in the interest of both Lebanon and the Palestine Revolution, while also respecting the sovereignty and security of Lebanon. Both delegations agree to the following measures and principles:

THE PALESTINE PRESENCE

It is agreed that the Palestine presence in Lebanon shall be reorganized along the following lines:

1. Palestinians at present residing in Lebanon shall have the right to work, reside and move about in Lebanon.

2. Local Palestinian Committees are to be set up in refugee camps to look after the interests of Palestinian residents of the camps, in cooperation with the local authorities and in keeping with the principle of Lebanese sovereignty.

3. There shall be Palestine Armed Struggle Posts in the camps which will cooperate with the local Committees so as to ensure good relations with the authorities. These Posts shall be responsible for controlling and limiting the presence of arms in the camps, in keeping with the requirements of Lebanese security and the interests of the Palestinian Revolution.

4. Palestinians residing in Lebanon are to be allowed to take part in the Palestinian Revolution through the Armed Struggle while acting in conformity with the Lebanese sovereignty and security.

COMMANDO ACTION

It is agreed that commando action is to be accorded the following facilities:

1. Passage for the commandos is to be facilitated. They are to be assigned crossing points and observation posts along the frontiers.

2. The commandos shall have the right of passage to the Arqub district.

3. The Armed Struggle Command is to control the activities of all those belonging to its member organisations and is responsible for ensuring that they do not interfere in Lebanese affairs.

4. A joint disciplinary board is to be set up comprising members from the Armed Struggle and the Lebanese Army.

5. Both sides are to stop their propaganda campaigns.

6. A census is to be carried out of the number of elements in the Armed Struggle in Lebanon, through the Armed Struggle Command.

7. Representatives of the Armed Struggle are to be attached to the Lebanese General Staff to help resolve sudden difficulties as they arise.

8. The distribution of commando bases along the frontiers is to be re-examined and determined after agreement with the Lebanese General Staff.

9. The entry, exit and movements of all elements belonging to the Armed Struggle are to be regulated.

10. The Jirun base is to be evacuated.

11. The Lebanese army shall facilitate the activities of medical evacuation and supply centres belonging to the commando movement.

12. All detainees and confiscated arms are to be released.

13. It is understood that all Lebanese civil and military authorities shall continue to exercise their authority and discharge their responsibilities in full throughout Lebanese territory under all circumstances.

14. Both sides affirm that Palestinian Armed Struggle is in the interest of Lebanon, the Palestinians and all Arabs.

15. This agreement shall remain top secret. It shall only be accessible to the commands.

Signed:

Head of the Lebanese Delegation
    Emile Bustani

Head of the Palestinian Delegation
    Yasser Arafat
November 3, 1969.

Source: Walid Khalidi, ed., *International Documents on Palestine, 1969* (Beirut: Institute for Palestine Studies and University of Kuwait, 1972), pp. 804–805.

APPENDIX 13

SPEECH BY THE UNITED ARAB REPUBLIC PRESIDENT NASSER AT THE CLOSED SESSION OF THE 5TH ARAB SUMMIT CONFERENCE (EXCERPT). RABAT, DECEMBER 21, 1969

We are not begging for mobilisation for the battle, we are demanding it.

We might beg from others who are not menaced by the danger, but we do not beg from Arab countries, we make demands of them.

Tell me, does the danger threaten Egypt alone, or is the entire Arab nation threatened?

Is it Sinai alone that we seek to liberate... or more than that?

If our aim was to liberate Sinai alone, then we should want absolutely nothing from you. . . we are capable of liberating Sinai by ourselves, whatever the means employed, whatever the sacrifice involved.

If it were a matter of liberating Sinai, then what you gave us at Khartum would be enough; we would be content with it and thank you.

However, the Egyptian people do not consider the objective to be the liberation of Sinai. They consider it to be the liberation of all occupied territory. That is why they set no limits to what they offer for the battle.

The Egyptian people have half a million soldiers on the battle front and supporting it. They are in the process of increasing that number to one million.

The Egyptian people are spending 500 million Egyptian pounds on the arms budget.

The Egyptian people have lost 250 million Egyptian pounds as a result of the closing down of the Suez Canal and the factories in the Canal Zone.

In other words, the Egyptian people have given 750 million Egyptian pounds to support the battle. They do not regard this as an act of generosity, they consider it to be their duty, for they are aware of the extent of the danger.

We want to know whether you are in this battle only to help us out. . . or because the danger threatens the entire Arab nation?

Those who help others might place a limit on the help they give.

Those who are helping themselves know no limits.

What we must agree on here, in the first place, is: what is the extent of the danger?

If we agree on that, our way is clear. If we fail to agree, we have lost the way.

SPEECH BY THE UNITED ARAB REPUBLIC PRESIDENT NASSER AT THE 5TH ARAB SUMMIT CONFERENCE (EXCERPT). RABAT, DECEMBER 22, 1969

It seems to me that, in fact, the Conference has not accomplished anything at all. It is my honest opinion that we should tell the people in our final joint communiqué that the Conference has failed so as not to deceive them by giving them false hopes.

I should like to know whether you want to fight the battle nor not? I have no intention of complaining, but I want to know and I am prepared for either alternative. Do you want to be faithful to your obligations and enter the battle alongside the United Arab Republic? Or do you want to declare that you are not bound by these obligations? If so I will draw up my plans on the understanding that I shall be fighting the battle alone. We do not ask for money; the United Arab Republic has not made such a request. But it believes that the responsibility is the responsibility of all and this requires total mobilisation by all the Arab States with each state performing its duty. It is not only Egypt's problem; it it had been we should have solved it long ago. But the battle involves all of you. And this is why I appeal to you to be frank with me. First, do you want to fight?

Source: Walid Khaldid, ed., *International Documents on Palestine, 1969* (Beirut: Institute for Palestine Studies and University of Kuwait, 1972), pp. 830–831.

APPENDIX 14

RESOLUTION ON PALESTINE ADOPTED BY THE 7TH ARAB SUMMIT
CONFERENCE. RABAT, OCTOBER 28, 1974

The Seventh Arab Summit Conference after exhaustive and detailed discussions
conducted by their Majesties, Excellencies, and Highnesses, the Kings, Presidents
and Amirs on the Arab situation in general and the Palestine problem in particular, within their national and international frameworks; and after hearing the
statements submitted by His Majesty King Hussein, King of the Hashemite
Kingdom of Jordan and His Excellency Brother Yasser Arafat, Chairman of the
Palestine Liberation Organisation, and after the statements of their Majesties and
Excellencies the Kings and Presidents, in an atmosphere of candour and sincerity
and full responsibility; and in view of the Arab leaders' appreciation of the joint
national responsibility required of them at present for confronting aggression and
performing duties of liberation, enjoined by the unity of the Arab cause and the
unity of its struggle; and in view of the fact that all are aware of Zionist schemes
still being made to eliminate the Palestinian existence and to obliterate the Palestinian national entity; and in view of the Arab leaders' belief in the necessity to
frustrate these attempts and schemes and to counteract them by supporting and
strengthening this Palestinian national entity, by providing all requirements to
develop and increase its ability to ensure that the Palestinian people recover their
rights in full; and by meeting responsibilities of close cooperation with its brothers
within the framework of collective Arab commitment;

    And in light of the victories achieved by Palestinian struggle in the con-
frontation with the Zionist enemy, at the Arab and international levels, at the
United Nations, and of the obligation imposed thereby to continue joint Arab
action to develop and increase the scope of these victories; and having received the
views of all on all the above, and having succeeded in cooling the differences
between brethren within the framework of consolidating Arab solidarity, the
Seventh Arab Summit Conference resolves the following:

    1. To affirm the right of the Palestinian people to self-determination and to
return to their homeland;

    2. To affirm the right of the Palestinian people to establish an independent
national authority under the command of the Palestine Liberation Organization,
the sole legitimate representative of the Palestinian people in any Palestinian
territory that is liberated. This authority, once it is established, shall enjoy the
support of the Arab states in all fields and at all levels;

    3. To support the Palestine Liberation Organization in the exercise of its
responsibility at the national and international levels within the framework of
Arab commitment;

    4. To call on the Hashemite Kingdom of Jordan, the Syrian Arab Republic,
the Arab Republic of Egypt and the Palestine Liberation Organization to devise a
formula for the regulation of relations between them in the light of these decisions
so as to ensure their implementation;

5. That all the Arab states undertake to defend Palestinian national unity and not to interfere in the internal affairs of Palestinian action.

Source: Jorgen Nielson, ed., *International Documents on Palestine, 1974* (Beirut: Institute for Palestine Studies and University of Kuwait, 1977), p. 525.

APPENDIX 15

RESOLUTION OF THE SIX-NATION ARAB SUMMIT CONFERENCE HELD TO CONSIDER THE WAR IN LEBANON. RIYADH, OCTOBER 18, 1976

The limited Arab summit conference held in Riyadh, Shawwal 25-28, 1396 AH (October 16-18, 1976 AD), on the initiative of His Majesty King Khalid ibn Abd al-Aziz al-Saud of Saudi Arabia and His Highness Shaykh Sabah al-Salim Sabah, Emir of the State of Kuwait, having reviewed the resolutions adopted by the Council of the Arab League at its extraordinary sessions held June 8-10, 1976, and on June 23, 1976, and July 1, 1976, and at the session of September 4, 1976, and in light of the national commitment to maintain the unity, security and sovereignty of Lebanon, and also to protect the Palestine resistance, as represented by the PLO, the sole legitimate representative of the Palestinian people, in conformity with the Rabat resolutions, and to enhance its capacity to hold out in the face of all attacks on the entity of the Palestinian people and their right to self-determination and to recover their national soil; from a belief in the common goals and destiny of the Lebanese and Palestinian peoples and the impossibility of any conflict of interests arising between them; and from the conviction that the past and its negative heritage must be forgotten so that the future may be faced in a spirit of concilia-tion, dialogue and cooperation; and from appreciation of the need for rapid action to ensure the re-establishment of normal life in Lebanon and to strengthen its political, economic and other institutions, and to enable the PLO to achieve its national goals; and in light of the positive and constructive spirit evinced by the leaders attending this conference, which disclosed that they were all moved by a sincere desire to end the crisis in Lebanon once and for all and to contain any dispute that might arise in the future, resolves the following:

1. That all parties shall stop fighting and observe a final ceasefire throughout Lebanese territory as from 6 a.m. on October 21, 1976, and that the parties shall adhere to this decision.

2. That the present Arab security forces be reinforced so as to constitute a deterrent force to operate in Lebanon under the personal orders of the president of the Lebanese Republic. The force shall number not more than thirty thousand men and its principal tasks shall be the following:

    a) To impose adherence to the ceasefire, to separate conflicting parties and to prevent any violations.

   b) To enforce the Cairo agreement and its annexes.

   c) To maintain internal security.

   d) To supervise the withdrawal of armed elements to the positions they occupied before April 13, 1975, and to eliminate armed manifestations in accordance with the timetable in the attached annex.

   e) To supervise the collection of all heavy armaments, including artillery, mortars, rocket-launchers, armoured vehicles, etc., under the control of the parties concerned.

   f) To assist the Lebanese authorities, when necessary, to take over public utilities and institutions in preparation for resuming control of them, and to protect military and civil installations.

   3. That normal life in Lebanon, as it was before the incidents started, that is before April 13, 1975, shall be restored as a first step in conformity with the time-table in the attached annex.

   4. That the Cairo agreement and its annexes shall be implemented and adhered to in letter and in spirit, under guarantees provided by the Arab countries here assembled, and a committee consisting of representatives of Saudi Arabia, Egypt, Syria and Kuwait shall be formed to coordinate with the president of the Lebanese Republic on matters related to the implementation of the Cairo agreement and its annexes, this committee to remain in existence for ninety days as from the announcement of the ceasefire.

   5. The Palestine Liberation Organization affirms its respect for the sovereignty and integrity of Lebanon and that it has no intention of interfering in its internal affairs, in the light of its total commitment to the national goals of the Palestine cause, and the legitimate Lebanese authorities similarly guarantee the presence and operation of the Palestine Liberation Organization in Lebanese territory within the framework of the Cairo agreement and its annexes.

   6. The Arab states here assembled undertake to respect Lebanon's sovereignty and integrity and the unity of its people and territory.

   7. The Arab states here assembled affirm their commitment to the resolutions of the Algiers and Rabat summit conferences to support and assist the Palestine resistance and to respect the right of the Palestinian people to struggle by all available means for the recovery of their national rights.

   8. Information Affairs

   a) All parties shall refrain from information campaigns and negative psychological mobilization.

   b) Information activity shall be directed towards securing a ceasefire, achieving peace and promoting a spirit of cooperation and brotherhood.

   c) Efforts shall be made to unify official information activity.

   9. The attached time-table for the implementation of these resolutions shall be regarded as an integral part of them.

   Time-table for the implementation of the resolutions of the Riyadh conference:

   1. A ceasefire shall be declared and fighting by all parties shall stop once and for all in all Lebanese territory as from 6 a.m. on October 21, 1976.

2. Once buffer zones have been established, observation posts shall be set up in locations of tension to enforce the ceasefire and stop the fighting.

3. Armed elements and all heavy arms shall be withdrawn and armed manifestations shall be eliminated in accordance with the following time-table:

    a) Mount Lebanon: within five days.

    b) The South: within five days.

    c) Beirut and its environs: within seven days.

    d) The North: within ten days.

4. The reopening of main roads

    a) The following main roads shall be reopened within five days: Beirut-Masnaa, Beirut-Tripoli, the frontier, Beirut-Tyre, Beirut-Sidon-Marjayun-Masnaa.

    b) Observation patrol points manned by members of the Deterrent Forces shall be set up on insecure roads by agreement with the parties concerned and the commander of the said forces.

5. The legitimate Lebanese authorities shall take over public utilities, installations and institutions, both military and civil, the following measures being taken:

    a) They shall be cleared of armed elements and all who do not regularly work in them, and the Arab Deterrent Force shall be called in to guard them to facilitate their operation by their regular employees, when they have taken them over, which shall take place within ten days.

    b) They shall be handed over to an official Lebanese central committee which in turn shall entrust sub-committees, one for each utility or installation, with the task of taking inventories of their contents before handing them over.

6. The forces required to reinforce the Arab Deterrent Forces shall be formed by agreement with the president of the Lebanese Republic, and these forces shall arrive within two weeks.

7. The Cairo agreement and its annexes shall be implemented as a second stage. This applies particularly to arms and ammunition in the camps and the departure of Palestinian forces which entered after the start of the incidents. This shall be implemented within 45 days of the formation of the Arab Deterrent Force.

Source: Jorgen Nielson, ed., *International Documents on Palestine, 1976* (Beirut: Institute for Palestine Studies and University of Kuwait, 1978), pp. 491–493.

APPENDIX 16

COMMUNIQUÉ ISSUED BY THE 8TH ARAB SUMMIT CONFERENCE CONVENED TO DISCUSS THE ENDING OF THE WAR IN LEBANON. CAIRO, OCTOBER 26, 1976

The kings and presidents of the Arab League states meeting in Cairo at the Arab League headquarters on Dhu al-Qaada 2–3, 1396 AH, corresponding to October

25–26, 1976, AD; having examined the current situation in Lebanon and the resolutions adopted by the six-party Arab summit held in Riyad in October 1976; having in mind the importance of Arab solidarity, resolve the following:

I. The current situation in Lebanon

1. To ratify the communiqué, resolutions and appendices issued by the six-party Arab summit conference held in Riyad on October 18, 1976.

2. Each Arab country is to contribute, in accordance with its capability, to the reconstruction of Lebanon and to furnish the financial aid necessary to remove the traces of armed conflict and the damage sustained by the Lebanese and the Palestinian peoples. The Arab states are to offer speedy aid to the Lebanese government and the PLO.

II. Strengthening Arab solidarity

Arab kings and presidents reaffirm their commitment to the provisions of the resolutions of summit conferences and of the Arab League Council in this regard, especially to the provisions of the Arab Solidarity Pact issued at the Casablanca Summit on September 15, 1965, and to work to implement these provisions at once.

III. Financing the Arab security force

The Arab summit conference, desiring to furnish the necessary funds to be spent upon the Arab security forces in Lebanon as stipulated by the second of the Riyad summit resolutions, and having examined the report of the Military Secretariat of the Arab League in this regard, resolves the following:

1. To set up a special fund which would be responsible for meeting the requirements of the Arab security forces in Lebanon.

2. Each Arab member state of the League is to contribute to this fund at a percentage ratio to be determined by each state in accordance with its abilities.

3. The president of the Lebanese republic is to supervise this fund and to formulate, in consultation with the General Secretariat of the Arab League and with states contributing at least 10 percent, general regulations governing this fund and outlining the means of payment and of liquidating the fund when its term is ended. The present system currently followed with respect to the Arab forces shall be maintained until new regulations are formulated.

4. The fund shall operate for a period of six months which may be renewed by decision of the League Council which would meet at the request of the president of the Lebanese republic.

RESOLUTIONS OF THE 8TH ARAB SUMMIT CONFERENCE CONVENED TO DISCUSS THE ENDING OF THE WAR IN LEBANON. CAIRO, OCTOBER 26, 1976

The kings and presidents of the Arab League states meeting in Cairo to discuss the crisis in Lebanon and the means for resolving it; in order to maintain Lebanon's security, sovereignty and unity and to protect the Palestine resistance as represented by the PLO; in furtherance of Arab solidarity and motivated by a sense of national and historic responsibility regarding the necessity for a collective Arab role in order to ensure a decisive settlement in Lebanon and to prevent a future explosion; in furtherance of guarantees necessary for the return of normal life and stability; in order to protect Lebanon's political, economic and other institutions and to preserve Lebanon's sovereignty as well as the Palestine resistance; convinced that the liberation of Arab lands occupied by Israel and the recovery of Palestinian national rights, foremost among which is their right to return and establish their independent state upon their national soil, that all these require the strengthening of Arab solidarity and the direction of all Arab efforts and potentialities towards the service of the cause of destiny; motivated by their feelings regarding the necessity of helping Lebanon to overcome its ordeal and to rebuild its economy, institutions and public utilities to the end that normal life may be restored and Lebanon may once more play its effective role in the Arab sphere;

The conference examined the current situation in Lebanon with a view to preserving its sovereignty and independence as well as the solidarity of the Lebanese and Palestinian peoples. The conference welcomed the resolutions of the six-party Arab Summit Conference in Riyad and expressed its appreciation for what it had accomplished regarding a settlement of the crisis in Lebanon, protection for the Palestine resistance and actions adopted to bolster Arab solidarity.

The conference decided to ratify the resolutions adopted by the six-party summit conference on October 18, 1976. The Arab kings and presidents reaffirmed their resolve to work in order to furnish the guarantees required for consolidating the ceasefire declared to have come into effect at 6:00 a.m. on October 21, 1976, and bringing all the fighting, whatever its form, to an end, in preparation for the return to normal life. They further affirmed the need to strengthen the Arab peace keeping force in order that it may become a deterrent force operating in Lebanon under personal command of the Lebanese president. They unanimously agreed to reject any partition of Lebanon in any guise or any legal or actual form, explicit or implicit. They affirmed their commitment to protect Lebanon's national unity and territorial integrity and to refrain from harming its territorial integrity and to refrain from harming its territorial unity and from interfering in its internal affairs in any way. They examined with great care the situation in South Lebanon, expressing their concern regarding the escalation of Israeli attacks on Lebanese territory, especially in the South, as well as Israel's insistence upon following a policy of aggression and expansion against Arab lands. They emphasized the necessity of implementing the Cairo agreement and its annexes to which the chairman of the PLO has expressed his full commitment. They agreed to form a committee to include representatives from the Kingdom of Saudi Arabia, the Arab Republic of Egypt, the Syrian Arab Republic and the State of Kuwait entrusted with coordinating action with the president of Lebanon regarding the implementation of the Cairo agreement. Its term of office shall be for a period of 90 days following announcement of the ceasefire.

The Arab kings and presidents reaffirmed their commitment to the resolutions of the seventh Arab summit held in Rabat which declared the PLO to be the sole and legitimate representative of the Palestinian people and where all Arab member states of the League undertook to support the PLO and not to interfere in its affairs. The PLO in turn affirmed its policy of noninterference in the internal affairs of any Arab country. The Arab kings and presidents agreed that the Arab states should contribute to the reconstruction of Lebanon and to removing the traces of armed conflict and the damage sustained by the Lebanese and Palestinian peoples and to furnish them with aid quickly.

The Arab kings and presidents paid special attention to the question of strengthening Arab solidarity as an essential condition for the success of common Arab efforts and for the realization of the objectives of the Arab nation for liberation and development.

They further reasserted their total commitment to abide by the provisions of the resolutions of the Arab summit conferences and of the Arab League Council in this regard, especially the Arab Solidarity Pact issued by the Casablanca summit on September 15, 1965, and their determination to implement them.

They expressed the gravest concern in their discussions of the explosive situation inside the occupied Arab territories, which has resulted from continued Israeli occupation, and the escalation of acts of suppression, terrorism, and expropriation and acts of sacrilege against religious sanctuaries, especially the sanctuary of Abraham. These acts are being committed by the occupying authorities and constitute a glaring violation of international law and of the UN Charter. They salute the Arab people who are standing fast in the occupied territories and salute their legitimate national struggle. They affirm the solidarity of the Arab states with them. They call upon the states and peoples of the world to condemn this Israeli aggression and to foil it. They call upon them to cease any dealings with Israel that might contribute to the entrenchment of Israeli occupation of Arab lands or of Israeli repressive measures against their inhabitants.

Source: Jorgen Nielson, ed., *International Documents on Palestine, 1976* (Beirut: Institute for Palestine Studies and University of Kuwait, 1978), pp. 500–502.

APPENDIX 17

PALESTINE NATIONAL COUNCIL DECLARATION. CAIRO, MARCH 20, 1977

1. The PNC affirms that the Palestine issue is the essence and root of the Arab-Zionist conflict. Security Council Resolution 242 ignores the Palestinian people and their firm rights and therefore the PNC confirms its rejection of this resolution and rejects dealings on the Arab and international levels on the basis of this resolution.

2. The PNC affirms the PLO's stand in its determination to continue the armed struggle and its concomitant forms of political and mass struggle to achieve inalienable national rights.

3. The PNC affirms that the struggle in the occupied territory in all its military, political and popular forms constitutes the central link of its program of struggle. On this basis, the PLO will strive to escalate the armed struggle in the occupied land, to escalate all forms of concomitant struggle, and to give all kinds of moral support to the masses of our people in the occupied land so as to escalate this struggle and strengthen their steadfastness to defeat and liquidate the occupation.

4. The PNC affirms the PLO's stand which rejects all kinds of American capitulationist settlements and all liquidationist projects. The council affirms the PLO's determination to abort any settlement achieved at the expense of our people's firm national rights. The PNC calls upon the Arab nation to shoulder its pan-Arab responsibilities and to pool all its energies to confront these imperialist and Zionist plans.

5. The PNC stresses the importance and necessity of national unity, political and military, among all contingents of the Palestine revolution within the framework of the PLO, because this is one of the basic conditions for victory. That is why it is necessary to coordinate national unity of all levels and in all spheres on the basis of commitment to all these resolutions and to draw up programs that will insure the implementation of this.

6. The PNC affirms the right of the Palestinian revolution to be present on the soil of fraternal Lebanon within the framework of the Cairo Agreement and its appendices concluded between the PLO and the Lebanese authorities. The council also affirms adherence to implementation of the Cairo Agreement in letter and spirit, including the preservation of the revolution's position and the security of the camps. The PNC rejects any unilateral interpretation of this agreement. Meanwhile, it affirms its concern over Lebanon's sovereignty and security.

7. The PNC greets the heroic fraternal Lebanese people and affirms the PLO's concern over Lebanon's territorial integrity, the unity of its people, and its security, independence, sovereignty and Arabism. The PNC affirms its pride in the support rendered by this heroic fraternal people to the PLO, which is struggling for our people's regaining their national rights to their homeland as well as their right to return to this homeland. The PNC strongly affirms the need for deepening and consolidating cohesion between all Lebanese nationalist forces and the Palestinian revolution.

8. The council affirms the need to strengthen the Arab front participating in the Palestinian revolution and to deepen cohesion with all forces participating in it in all Arab countries, as well as to escalate the joint Arab struggle and to further strengthen the Palestinian revolution in order to cope with the imperialist and Zionist designs.

9. The PNC has decided to consolidate Arab struggle and solidarity on the basis of struggle against imperialism and Zionism, to work for the liberation of all the occupied Arab areas, and to continue to support the Palestinian revolution in order to regain the eternal national rights of the Palestinian Arab people without any conciliation (sulh) or recognition (of Israel).

10. The PNC affirms the PLO's right to exercise its struggle responsibilities on the pan-Arab level and through any Arab land for the sake of liberating the occupied areas.

11. The PNC has decided to continue the struggle to regain the national rights of our people, particularly their rights of return, self-determination and establishing their independent national state on their national soil.

12. The PNC affirms the significance of cooperation and solidarity with socialist, nonaligned, Islamic and African countries, and with all the national liberation movements in the world.

13. The PNC hails the stands and struggle of all democratic countries and forces against Zionism, in its capacity as one form of racism, as well as against its aggressive practices.

14. The PNC affirms the significance of establishing relations and coordinating with the progressive and democratic Jewish forces inside and outside the occupied homeland, since these forces are struggling against Zionism as a doctrine and practice. The PNC calls upon all states and forces who love freedom, justice and peace in the world to cut off all forms of assistance to and cooperation with the racist Zionist regime and to stop contacting it and its tools.

15. Taking into consideration the important accomplishments achieved in the Arab and international arenas since the conclusion of the PNC's 12th session, the PNC, which has reviewed the political report submitted by the PLO, has decided the following:

A. The council confirms its care for the PLO's rights to participate in an independent manner and on an equal footing in all conferences and international forums concerned with the Palestine issue and the Arab-Zionist conflict, with a view to achieving our inalienable national rights as approved by the UN General Assembly in 1974, specifically, in Resolution 3236.

B. The council declares that any settlement of agreement affecting the rights of our Palestinian people in the absence of this people will be completely null and void. Long live the Palestine revolution, long live Palestinian unity among the revolution's contingents, glory and immortality for our innocent martyrs! This revolution will continue until victory!

PNC official spokesman Mahmud al-Labadi said that the Arab Front for the Liberation of Palestine, headed by 'Abd al-Wahhab al-Kayyali, and the PFLP-GC, headed by Ahmad Jubril—two organizations which are well known for their position within the rejectionist front—voted for the Political Declaration approved by the council. However, 13 members who attended on behalf of the Popular Front (presumably the PFLP) voted against the Political Declaration and the PNC resolutions.

Source: U.S. Dept. of Commerce, *Foreign Broadcast Information Service: Middle East and North Africa*, March 21, 1977, Vol. V, No. 54, pp. A8–A9.

APPENDIX 18

FINAL STATEMENT ISSUED BY THE 9TH ARAB SUMMIT CONFERENCE.
BAGHDAD, NOVEMBER 5, 1978

The Arab summit conference issued a final statement at the conclusion of its meetings,which lasted for 4 days. The following is the text of the final statement:

By the initiative of the Government of the Republic of Iraq and at the invitation of President Ahmad Hasan al-Bakr, the ninth Arab summit conference convened in Baghdad 2–5 November 1978.

In a high spirit of pan-Arab responsibility and joint concern about the unity of the Arab stand, the conference studied confrontation of the dangers and challenges threatening the Arab nation, particularly after the results of the Camp David agreements signed by the Egyptian Government and the effects of these agreements on the Arab struggle to face the Zionist aggression against the Arab nation.

Proceeding from the principles in which the Arab nation believes, acting on the unity of Arab destiny and complying with the traditions of joint Arab action, the Arab summit conference has emphasized the following basic principles:

First: The Palestinian question is a fateful Arab issue and is the essence of the conflict with the Zionist enemy. The sons of the Arab nation and all the Arab countries are concerned with it and are obliged to struggle for its sake and to offer all material and moral sacrifices for this cause. The struggle to regain Arab rights in Palestine and in the occupied Arab territory is a general Arab responsibility. All Arabs must share this responsibility, each in accord with his military, economic, political and other abilities. The conflict with the Zionist enemy exceeds the framework of the conflict of the countries whose territory was occupied in 1967, and it includes the whole Arab nation because of the military, political, economic and cultural danger the Zionist enemy constitutes against the entire Arab nation and its substantial and pan-Arab interests, civilization and destiny. This places on all the countries of the Arab nation the responsibility to share in this conflict with all the resources it possesses.

Second: All the Arab countries must offer all forms of support, backing and facilities to all forms of the struggle of the Palestinian resistance, supporting the PLO in its capacity as the sole legitimate representative of the Palestinian people inside and outside the occupied land, struggling for liberation and restoration of the national rights of its people, including their right to return to their homeland, to determine their future and to establish their independent state on their national soil. The Arab states pledge to preserve Palestinian national unity and not to interfere in the internal affairs of the Palestinian action.

Third: Commitment is reaffirmed to the resolutions of the Arab summit conferences, particularly the sixth and seventh summit conferences of Algiers and Rabat.

Fourth: In light of the above principles it is impermissible for any side to act unilaterally in solving the Palestinian question in particular and the Arab-Zionist conflict in general.

Fifth: No solution shall be accepted unless it is associated with a resolution by an Arab summit conference convened for this purpose.

The conference discussed the two agreements signed by the Egyptian Government at Camp David and considered that they harm the Palestinian people's rights and the rights of the Arab nation in Palestine and the occupied Arab territory. The conference considered that these agreements took place outside the framework of collective Arab responsibility and are opposed to the resolutions of the Arab summit conferences, particularly the resolutions of the Algiers and Rabat summit conferences, the Arab League Charter and the UN resolutions of the Palestinian question. The conference considers that these agreements do not lead to the just peace that the Arab nation desires. Therefore, the conference has decided not to approve of these two agreements and not to deal with their results. The conference has also rejected all the political, economic, legal and other effects resulting from them.

The conference decided to call on the Egyptian Government to go back on these agreements and not to sign any reconciliation treaty with the enemy. The conference hopes that Egypt will return to the fold of joint Arab action and not to act unilaterally in the affairs of the Arab-Zionist conflict. In this respect the conference adopted a number of resolutions to face the new stage and to safeguard the aims and interests of the Arab nation out of faith that with its material and moral resources the Arab nation is capable of confronting the difficult circumstances and all challenges, just as it has always been throughout history, because it is defending right, justice and its national existence.

The conference stressed the need to unify all the Arab efforts in order to remedy the strategic imbalance that has resulted from Egypt's withdrawal from the confrontation arena. The conference decided that the countries that possess readiness and capability will coordinate participation with effective efforts. The conference also stressed the need to adhere to the regulations of Arab boycott and to tighten application of its provisions.

The conference studied means to develop Arab information media beamed abroad for the benefit of the just Arab issues. The conference decided to hold annual meetings for the Arab summit conference and decided that the month of November each year will be the date for holding the summit.

After studying the Arab international situation, the conference asserts the Arab nation's commitment to a just peace based on the comprehensive Israeli withdrawal from the Arab territories occupied in 1967, including Arab Jerusalem, the guaranteeing of the inalienable national rights of the Palestinian Arab people, including the right to establish their independent state on their national soil.

The conference decided to embark on large-scale international activity to explain the just rights of the Palestinian people and the Arab nation. The conference expressed its deep appreciation and gratitude for all the states that stood on the side of the Arab rights.

The conference expressed its appreciation to the Syrian Arab Republic and its heroic army, and to the Hashemite Kingdom of Jordan and its heroic army, and expressed its pride in the struggle of the Palestinian people and its steadfastness inside and outside the occupied territories, under the leadership of the PLO, the sole legitimate representative of the Palestinian people.

The conference praised the "charter for joint national action" signed by fraternal Syria and Iraq, and the conference regarded the charter as a great achievement on the way to Arab solidarity. The conference also expressed its great appreciation for the initiative of the Iraq Government under President Ahmad Hasan al-Bakr in calling for the convening of an Arab summit conference in Baghdad so as to unify Arab ranks and to organize Arab efforts to face the threats to which the Arab nation is currently exposed. The conference expressed its thanks for President Al-Bakr's efforts to make the conference a success.

The conference took a number of resolutions and measures to face the next stage and to protect the aims and interests of the Arab nation. These resolutions stem from the conviction of the conferees that the Arab nation is able, through its material and moral capabilities and through its solidarity, to face all the difficult circumstances and all the challenges, as it always faced them throughout history, because it is defending justice and right and protecting its national existence.

Source: U.S. Dept. of Commerce, *Foreign Broadcast Information Service: Middle East and North Africa*, November 6, 1978, Vol. V, No. 215, pp. A13–A15.

APPENDIX 19

RESOLUTIONS OF THE ARAB LEAGUE COUNCIL FOLLOWING MEETINGS OF THE ARAB FOREIGN AND ECONOMY MINISTERS. BAGHDAD, MARCH 31, 1979

As the Government of the Arab Republic of Egypt has ignored the Arab summit conferences' resolutions, especially those of the sixth and seventh conferences held in Algiers and Rabat; as it has at the same time ignored the ninth Arab summit conference resolutions—especially the call made by the Arab kings, presidents and princes to avoid signing the peace treaty with the Zionist enemy—and signed the peace treaty on 26 March 1979; It has thus deviated from the Arab ranks and has chosen, in collusion with the United States, to stand by the side of the Zionist enemy in one trench; has behaved unilaterally in the Arab-Zionist struggle affairs; has violated the Arab nation's rights; has exposed the nation's destiny, its struggle and aims to dangers and challenges; has relinquished its pan-Arab duty of liberating the occupied Arab territories, particularly Jerusalem, and restoring the Palestinian Arab people's inalienable national rights, including their right to repatriation, self-determination and establishment of the independent Palestinian state on their national soil.

In order to safeguard Arab solidarity and the unity of ranks in defense of the Arabs' fateful issue; in appreciation of the Egyptian people's struggle and sacrifices for Arab issues and the Palestinian issues in particular; in implementation of the resolutions adopted by the ninth Arab summit conference that convened in Baghdad 2–5 November 1978, and at the invitation of the Government of the Republic of Iraq, the Arab League Council convened in Baghdad from 27 March 1979 to 31 March 1979 on the level of Arab foreign and economy ministers.

In light of the ninth Arab summit conference resolutions, the council studied the latest developments pertaining to the Arab-Zionist conflict, especially after the signing by the Government of the Arab Republic of Egypt of the peace (as-sulh) agreement with the Zionist enemy on 26 March 1979.

The Arab League Council, on the level of Arab foreign ministers, has decided the following:

1. A. To withdraw the ambassadors of the Arab states from Egypt immediately. B. To recommend the severance of political and diplomatic relations with the Egyptian Government. The Arab governments will adopt the necessary measures to apply this recommendation within a maximum period of 1 month from the date of issuance of this decision, in accordance with the constitutional measures in force in each country.

2. To consider the suspension of the Egyptian Government's membership in the Arab League as operative from the date of the Egyptian Government's signing of the peace treaty with the Zionist enemy. This means depriving it of all rights resulting from this membership.

3. A. To make the city of Tunis, capital of the Tunisian Republic, the temporary headquarters of the Arab League, its General Secretariat, the competent ministerial councils and the permanent technical committees, as of the date of the signing of the treaty between the Egyptian Government and the Zionist enemy. This shall be communicated to all international and regional organizations and bodies. They will also be informed that dealings with the Arab League will be conducted with its secretariat in its new temporary headquarters.

B. To appeal to the Tunisian Government to offer all possible aid in facilitating the settlement of the temporary Arab League headquarters and its officials.

C. To form a committee comprising representatives of Iraq, Syria, Tunisia, Kuwait, Saudi Arabia and Algeria, in addition to a representative for the General Secretariat. The aim of this committee will be to implement this resolution's provisions and to seek the aid it requires from the member states. The committee will have all the authorization and responsibilities from the Arab League Council necessary to implement this resolution, including the protection of the Arab League's properties, deposits, documents and records. It is also entitled to take necessary measures against any action that may be taken by the Egyptian Government to hinder the transfer of the Arab League headquarters or to harm the Arab League's rights and possessions.

The committee will have to accomplish its task of transfer to the temporary headquarters within 2 months from the date of this resolution. This period of time may be extended another month if the committee so decides. The committee shall submit a report on its accomplishments to the first forthcoming meeting of the Arab League Council.

D. A sum of $5 million shall be placed at the committee's disposal to cover the transfer expenses. This sum shall be drawn from the credit accounts of various funds. The committee has the right to spend more than that amount if required. Expenditures for this purpose shall come under the supervision of the committee or of those it authorizes. The expenses shall be paid by the member states, each according to the percentage of its annual contribution to the Arab League budget.

E. To transfer the Arab League General Secretariat officials who are employed at the time of the issuance of this resolution from the permanent headquarters to the temporary one during the period defined in paragraph 3C of this resolution. The committee referred to in the above-mentioned paragraph 3 will have the responsibility of paying them financial compensation compatible with the standard of living in the new headquarters and for settling their affairs until a permanent system is drafted for this purpose.

4. The competent and specialized Arab organizations, bodies, establishments and federations named in the attached list No. 1 will take the necessary measures to suspend Egypt's membership. They will transfer their headquarters from Egypt to other Arab states on a temporary basis, similar to the action that shall be taken regarding the Council General Secretariat. The executive councils and boards of these bodies, organizations, establishments and federations shall meet immediately following the implementation of this decision within a period not to exceed the period specified in Paragraph 3C above.

5. To seek to suspend Egypt's membership in the nonaligned movement, the Islamic conference organization and the OAU for violating the resolutions of these organizations pertaining to the Arab-Zionist conflict.

6. To continue to cooperate with the fraternal Egyptian people and with Egyptian individuals, with the exception of those who cooperate with the Zionist enemy directly or indirectly.

7. The member states shall inform all foreign countries of their stand on the Egyptian-Israeli treaty and will ask these countries not to support this treaty as it constitutes an aggression against the rights of the Palestinian people and the Arab nation as well as a threat to world peace and security.

8. To condemn the policy that the United States is practicing regarding its role in concluding the Camp David agreements and the Egyptian-Israeli treaty.

9. To consider the measures in this decision to be temporary and subject to cancellation by an Arab League Council decision as soon as the circumstances that justified their adoption are eliminated.

10. The Arab countries will pass legislation, decisions and measures necessary for the implementation of this resolution.

The Arab League Council, on the level of Arab foreign and economy ministers, has also decided the following:

1. To halt all bank loans, deposits, guarantees or facilities, as well as all

financial or technical contributions and aid by Arab governments or their establishments to the Egyptian Government and its establishments as of the treaty signing date.

2. To ban the extension of economic aid by the Arab funds, banks and financial establishments within the framework of the Arab League and the joint Arab cooperation to the Egyptian Government and its establishments.

3. The Arab governments and institutions shall refrain from purchasing the bonds, shares, postals orders and public credit loans that are issued by the Egyptian Government and its financial foundations.

4. Following the suspension of the Egyptian Government's membership in the Arab League, its membership will also be suspended from the institutions, funds and organizations deriving from the Arab League. The Egyptian Government and its institutions will cease to benefit from these organizations. The headquarters of those Arab League departments residing in Egypt will be transfered to other Arab states temporarily.

5. In view of the fact that the ill-omened Egyptian-Israeli treaty and its appendices have demonstrated Egypt's commitment to sell oil to Israel, the Arab states shall refrain from providing Egypt with oil and its derivatives.

6. Trade exchange with the Egyptian state and private establishments that deal with the Zionist enemy shall be prohibited.

7. The Economic Boycott

A. The Arab boycott laws, principles and provisions shall be applied to those companies, foundations and individuals of the Arab Republic of Egypt that deal directly or indirectly with the Zionist enemy. The boycott office shall be entrusted with following up the implementation of these tasks.

B. The provisions of paragraph A shall include the intellectual, cultural and artistic activities that involve dealing with the Zionist enemy or have connections with the enemy's institutions.

C. The Arab states stress the importance of continued dealings with those private national Egyptian institutions that are confirmed not to be dealing with the Zionist enemy. Such institutions will be encouraged to work and maintain activities in the Arab countries within the framework of their fields of competence.

D. The Arab countries stress the importance of caring for the feelings of the Egyptian people's sons who are working or living in the Arab countries as well as looking after their interests and consolidating their pan-Arab affiliation with Arabism.

E. To consolidate the role of the Arab boycott and to enhance its grip at this stage, in affirmation of Arab unanimity, the assistant secretary general for economic affairs will be temporarily entrusted with the task of directly supervising the major boycott office in Damascus. He will be granted the necessary powers to reorganize and back the said department and to submit proposals on developing the boycott in method, content and scope. He shall submit a report in this regard to the first meeting of the Arab League Council.

8. The United Nations will be asked to transfer its regional offices, which serve the Arab region, from the Arab Republic of Egypt to any other Arab capital. The Arab states will work collectively toward this end.

9. The Arab League General Secretariat will be assigned the task of studying the joint Arab projects so as to take the necessary measures for protecting the Arab nation's interests in accordance with the aims of these resolutions. The General Secretariat shall submit its proposals to the Arab League Council in its first forthcoming meeting.

10. The Zionist plot must be faced by drafting an Arab strategy for economic confrontation. This will lead to utilizing the Arabs' own strength and will emphasize the need for realizing Arab economic integration in all aspects. The strategy will strengthen joint Arab development and regional development within the pan-Arab outlook and will expand the establishment of joint Arab projects—projects that serve the aims of emancipating, developing and integrating the Arab economy—and will promote the projects already in operation. The strategy will also develop the methods, systems and substances of the Arab boycott of Israel and will diversify and promote international relations with the developing countries. The Arab League General Secretariat shall rapidly submit studies relevant to the strategy of joint Arab economic action to the forthcoming session of the Arab Economic Council. This will be a prelude to the convention of a general Arab economic conference.

11. The above-mentioned committee shall be assigned the task of supervising the implementation of these decisions and of submitting a followup report to the Arab League Council in its first forthcoming meeting.

12. The Arab states will issue the decisions and legislations pertaining to these decisions and will take the necessary measures to implement them.

13. These measures taken by the Arab and economy ministers are considered minimal requirements to face the threats of the treaty. Individual governments can take whatever measures they deem necessary in addition to these measures.

14. The Arab foreign and economy ministers call on the Arab nation in all Arab countries to support the economic measures taken against the Zionist enemy and the Egyptian regime.

Source: U.S. Dept. of Commerce, *Foreign Broadcast Information Service: Middle East and North Africa*, April 2, 1979, Vol. V, No. 064, pp. A1–A5.

APPENDIX 20

NATIONAL COVENANT PROPOSED BY IRAQ. BAGHDAD, FEBRUARY 8, 1980

In light of the current international situation and the possibilities of its future development and in light of the dangerous possibilities that might ensue from this development, threatening pan-Arab sovereignty and security on the one hand, and world peace and security on the other; in response to the dictates of pan-Arab responsibility toward the Arab nation and its people, land, culture, civilization and heritage; and in accordance with the principles of the nonalined movement, Iraq finds itself called upon to initiate the issuance of this declaration so that it can serve first as a charter to regulate relations among the Arab countries and second, as a pledge by the nation to neighboring countries which proclaim their respect for and commitment to this charter.

The declaration is based on the following principles:

1. The rejection of the presence or the facilitation of the presence of any foreign armies, bases or armed forces in the Arab homeland in any form, under any pretext and guise or for any reason; the isolation of any Arab regime which does not adhere to this principle, boycotting such an Arab regime politically and economically and resisting its policies by all available means.

2. Banning any Arab state from resorting to armed force against any other Arab state and resolving any dispute that might arise among the Arab countries by peaceful means and within the context of the principles of joint pan-Arab action and the supreme Arab interests.

3. The application of the principle cited in clause two above to the relations between the Arab nation and its countries and nations and states neighboring the Arab homeland.

Of course, you know that the Zionist entity is not included because it is not considered a state. It is a freak entity occupying Arab land and is not included in these principles.

It is not permissible to resort to the armed forces in disputes with these states, except in the case of self–defense and the defense of sovereignty against the threats which undermine the security and basic interests of the Arab countries.

4. The solidarity of all the Arab countries against any aggression, violation or state of actual war which any foreign side might undertake against the territorial integrity of any Arab country. These countries will jointly repulse this aggression or violation and will thwart it by using all ways and means, including military action, collective political and economic boycott and any other methods dictated by necessity and pan-Arab interests.

5. The affirmation of the Arab countries' commitment to international laws and norms pertaining to the use of waters, airspace and zones by any state which is not in a state of war with any Arab country.

6. Keeping the Arab countries away from the circle of international conflicts or wars, and commitment to total neutrality and nonalinement toward any party to the conflict or war as long as these parties to the conflict or war have not violated Arab tertitorial integrity and the inalienable rights of the Arab countries, which are guaranteed by international laws and norms. The Arab countries will not allow their military forces to participate in part or whole in military conflicts and wars inside and outside the area on behalf of any foreign state or quarter.

7. The commitment of the Arab countries to establish developing and constructive economic relations among themselves in order to provide and strengthen a joint groundwork for a developed Arab economic edifice and Arab unity. The Arab countries will shun any behavior which might harm these relations or impede their continuity and development, irrespective of the diversity of

Arab regimes and the peripheral political differences among them, as long as the parties concerned are commited to the principles of this declaration. The Arab countries will adhere to the principles of pan-Arab economic integration. The Arab countries which are economically capable will pledge to offer all kinds of economic assistance to other Arab countries so as to prevent their possible dependence upon foreign forces, which might undermine their independence and pan-Arab will.

8. While drawing up the principles of this declaration, Iraq affirms its readiness to be committed to this declaration before every Arab country and before any party which is committed to it. Iraq is ready to discuss this declaration with the Arab brothers and to listen to their remarks in order to enhance this declaration's effectiveness and to deepen its context.

Iraq also affirms that this declaration does not constitute a substitute to the Arab League Charter, the joint defense treaty and the economic cooperation among the members of the Arab League. Iraq considers this declaration as a strengthening of the charter and treaty commensurate with the current international circumstances, the dangers which threaten the Arab nation and the pan-Arab responsibilities which result from the current and future circumstances.

Source: U.S. Dept. of Commerce, *Foreign Broadcast Information Service: Middle East and North Africa,* February 11, 1980, Vol. V, No. 029, pp. E2–E4.

APPENDIX 21

JOINT SYRIAN-LIBYAN DECLARATION FORMING A UNITARY STATE. DAMASCUS, AND TRIPOLI, LIBYA, SEPTEMBER 10, 1980

Proceeding from the basic objectives of the Arab masses throughout the Arab homeland—represented in achieving Arab unity, building socialism and liberating the occupied parts of the Arab homeland; out of the belief that Arab unity is the fate of this nation, in which its future and salvation from its sufferings lie; and in accordance with the resolutions of the national and regional commands of the Arab Socialist Ba'th Party and the decisions made by the people's congresses in the Socialist People's Libyan Arab Jamahiriyah at their extraordinary session in 1980, the two revolutionary leaderships in Libya and Syria declare the formation of one single state (dawlat wahidah) consisting of the two countries and on the following bases:

1. One single state will enjoy full sovereignty over the two states and enjoy a single identity (shakhisiyyah wahidah) on the international level, which would achieve the complete political, economic, military and cultural unity between the two countries. This also applies to all fields.

2. This state shall have democratic popular institutions that will enable the masses to practice their full role in building their society and future. This state shall shoulder its responsibilities to the effect that the authority belongs to the

people. The unitary state shall struggle to set up a socialist, popular and unified society. The authority in this society belongs to the people through their democratic institutions, congresses and popular committees in order to achieve the final freeing from all aspects of hegemony, exploitation and subservience.

3. The all-out Arab revolution is an existing and constant necessity to achieve the Arab nation's objectives in building an Arab socialist, popular and unified society. The revolution in our Arab state is part of the all-out Arab revolution and its policies in all domains that emanate from its general strategy.

4. All accomplishments achieved and that will be achieved by any Arab state given the present division shall continue to be incapable of being fully developed and to be exposed to mutilation and setback unless these accomplishments are supported and protected by Arab unity. Any danger menacing any Arab part menaces, at the same time, the entire Arab nation.

5. Building socialism, in addition to the fact that it is a necessity stemming from the Arab society's needs, is also a basic means to bring forth the energies of the masses and to deploy them in their battle for unity and against Zionism, imperialism and all factors of backwardness and reaction. Therefore, the struggle for building socialism is a basic issue in the unitary state.

6. This state forms a base for the Arab revolutionary movement.

7. This state is a base and a tool for confronting the Zionist presence in the Arab homeland and for liberating Palestine.

8. The Arab masses are the fence and shield of this state. The revolutionary forces are also its tools to achieve its strategy and objectives.

9. The unitary state, in its capacity as a base hostile to Zionism, imperialism and reaction, is a base for the Arab Palestinian struggle and for the Palestinian revolution, for the Palestinian revolution is a principal group of the Arab revolution's groups.

10. This state shall work to consolidate the pan-Arab Front for Steadfastness and Confrontation in its capacity as a major Arab link in the confrontation of the tripartite Camp David scheme, represented by U.S. imperialism, the Zionist enemy and As-Sadat's agent regime.

11. This state shall work to deploy the Arab's capabilities and their human, economic and military energies in the arena of the Arab-Zionist struggle. This work stems from the pan-Arab dimensions of this struggle.

12. This state is a nucleus for all-out Arab unity. Consequently, it is open for every Arab state wishing to join its unity and struggling march and to adhere to its principles.

13. This unitary state is a part of the national liberation movement in the world and an ally of forces of socialism and liberation struggling against Zionism, racism, imperialism, colonialism, reaction, injustice and all kinds of exploitation and subservience.

The two revolutionary leaderships in the two Arab Countries—Syria and Lybia—out of their faith that unity is the road of honor and dignity of the nation, announce these historic bases to the Arab nation, asserting that this state will be the state for all the Arabs struggling for the sake of their issues, fighting for their objectives and building for their future. The two leaderships announce that they will hold a joint meeting to draw up formulae and to adopt measures to implement these bases and principles and to build the unitary state and its popular institutions.

Source: U.S. Dept. of Commerce, *Foreign Broadcast Information Service: Middle East and North Africa,* September 10, 1980, Vol. V, No. 177, pp. 16–17.

Index

Abbasid Caliphate, 2–4, 6, 10
Abd al-Nasir, Gamal:
  views of, 30–31
  comes to power (1954), 30
  policies of, 30–32
  relations with Syrian Baath, 33–36, 42
  and UAR, 34, 37, 42
  and Yemen war, 39–40, 44
  and Cairo negotiations, 40–41
  and Iraq, 40–41
  and Jordan, 43–44
  and Saudi Arabia, 39, 51
  and Soviet Union, 49
  convenes first Arab summit, 42
  at Khartum Summit, 43–44
  and Qaddhafi, 59
  Egyptianism of, 41
  pan-Arabism of, 10, 31–32, 34, 37–38,
    42, 110
  as advocate of "unity of purpose," 60
  old bourgeoisie under, 54
  revolutionary image of, 42
  pragmatism of, 35–36, 43
  death of, 49
Abduh, Muhammad, 7–9
Abd ul-Ilah, 15, 25, 27
Abdullah, Emir, 21, 24–25
Achaemenid Empire, 6
Aden, 14, 17, 39, 45, 101
al-Afghani, Jamal al-Din, 7
Afghanistan, 79, 83–84, 86, 105, 114
Aflaq, Nichel, 18

Ahali Group (Iraq), 17–18
al-Ahd, 13
Ahmad, Imam, 38
Algeria, 14, 16, 46–47, 70, 73–74, 90, 93,
    97–100
Alexandria Protocol, 22–23
Amal (Hope), 95
Amin, Qasim, 8–9
Amir, Abd al-Hakim, 36
al-Amri, Hasan, 40
Anglo-Abyssinian Treaty (1897), 106
Anglo-Egyptian Treaty (1936), 10, 14, 30
Arab Awakening, 12
Arab Deterrent Force (Lebanon), 69, 95
Arab League:
  Nuri al-Said's conception of, 22
  foundation of, 22–23
  principles of, 24, 28
  initial alignments in, 25
  and Lebanese crisis, 69–70
  removal from Cairo, 74, 80
  mediation role in North and South
    Yemen, 101–103
  increased membership of, 46
  Council of creates Arab Solidarity
    Committee, 75
  Secretariat of, 75
  al-Sadat and members of, 73, 76, 80
  Red Sea members of, 105
Arab Liberation Front (ALF), 47, 55
Arab Liberation Movement (al-Shish-
    akli), 27–28

Arab Nationalist Movement (AMN), 41
Arab Solidarity Committee (see Arab
   League), 75
Arafat, Yasir:
   elected chairman PLO executive
      committee, 47
   leader of Fatah, 47, 61
   and King Husayn, 70, 76
   and Lebanese crisis, 68
   and Qaddhafi, 59
   diplomatic maneuvering of, 95
   mediator role of, 60, 71
   pragmatism of, 60–61, 95
Arif, Abd al-Rahman, 45
Arif, Abd al-Salam, 38, 41, 45
al-Asad, Hafiz:
   comes to power (1970), 45, 50
   and Abd al-Nasir, 47
   and King Husayn, 65–66, 76, 86,
      93–94
   and Saddam Husayn, 77–78
   and Iraq, 72
   and Iran, 92–94
   and Israel, 51, 68, 73
   and Lebanon, 62–68, 72, 95
   and PLO 51, 59, 69, 93
   and Qaddhafi, 89, 91
   and al-Sadat, 51–52, 67–69, 73
   and Saudi Arabia, 51–52, 67
   and Soviet Union, 91
   and Federation of Arab Republics, 50
   and Greater Syrian federation, 63–66
   and Steadfastness Front, 74, 89
   and trilateral alliance, 68–69
   and United Nations, 51, 53
   internal opposition to, 89, 110
   isolation within Arab system, 67, 89
   pragmatism of, 52, 64
Assad, Kamal, 65
al-Atassi, Hashim, 27
Aziz, Tariq, 77
al-Azm, Khalid, 33

al-Badr, Imam Muhammad, 38
Badran, Mudar, 94
Baghdad Pact, 31–32
Bahrain, 46, 82, 92, 114
al-Bakr, Ahmad Hasan, 38, 45, 71, 78
Baktiar, Shahpur, 81
Balfour Declaration, 15
Bani Sadr, Abul Hasan, 92
Baqdash, Khalid, 33
Bazargan, Mehdi, 92

Barre, Muhammad Siad, 106
Baath Party (Syria):
   foundation of, 18
   emergence of, 19, 26, 28, 33
   and SSNP, 32
   role in forming UAR, 33–34
   relations with Abd al-Nasir, 34, 36, 42
   comes to power (1963), 41
   and Cairo negotiations, 40–41
   military wing under al-Asad, 45
   and Iraqi Baath, 41, 71, 77–78, 86, 111
   ideological discontinuity of, 110
Baath Party (Iraq):
   overthrows Qasim (1963), 38
   and Cairo negotiations, 40–41
   and Communists, 83
   relinquishes power to Abd al-Salam
      Arif (1963), 41–42
   comes to power under al-Bakr (1968),
      45
   and Syrian Baath, 41, 71, 77–78, 86,
      111
   self-image of, 71
   Shiite members purged, 81
   prominent members visit Saudi
      Arabia, 85
   ideological discontinuity of, 110
al-Bazz, Usama, 118
Begin, Menachem, 72, 75
Benjedid, Chadli, 99
al-Bitar, Salah al-Din, 38
Boumedienne, Houari, 97, 99
Bourguiba, Habib, 89

Cairo Agreement (1969), 56, 62
Cairo negotiations (1963), 40–41
Camp David, 75–77, 79, 85, 88, 104,
   111–112, 117
Carter, Jimmy, 72, 75
Chad, 90–91
Chamun, Camille, 65
Committee of Union and Progress
   (CUP), 12
Communists, 17, 28–29, 32–34, 37–38,
   45–46, 79, 83, 101, 104
Conferences:
   Arab-African (1977), 70
   Arab Foreign and Economy Minis-
      ters (Baghdad, 1979), 79–83, 94
   Arab Summits:
      1. Cairo (1964), 40, 42, 47
      2. Alexandria (1964), 42
      3. Casablanca (1965), 42

4. Khartum (1967), 40
5. Rabat (1969), 44
7. Rabat (1974), 56, 59, 70
8. Cairo (1976), 69
9. Baghdad (1978), 76–77, 79–84, 94, 99
11. Amman (1980), 93–95
12. Fez (1981), 112
Erkwith Conference (1964), 39
Harad Conference (1965), 39
Inter-Parliamentary Congress of the Arab and Islamic Countries for the Defense of Palestine (Cairo, 1938), 20
Islamic Congress (Jerusalem, 1931), 20
Pan-Arab Congress (Bludan, Syria, 1937), 20
Quadripartite Summit (Taiz, 1977), 106
Six-Nation Arab Summit (Riyadh, 1976), 67–72
Syrian Congress (Damascus, 1919), 13, 24
Crusaders, 6
Cuba, 91, 106

al-Dajani, Ahmad Sidqi, 58
Damascus Protocol, 13
al-Dawah al-Islamiyya (The Islamic Call), 81
Destour Party, 16
Djibouti, 75, 80
Dulles, John Foster, 31–32

Eden, Anthony, 21–22
Egypt, 3–5, 7–11, 14, 16–17, 22, 24–34, 38, 40–47, 49–55, 59, 62, 64–81, 85–86, 90–91, 93–94, 99–100, 106, 109, 111–112, 115–119.
Egyptian-Israeli treaty, 79–81
Eisenhower, Dwight, 31
Equatorial Guinea, 90
Ethiopia, 83–84, 86, 105–106, 114

Fahd, Crown Prince:
political role in Saudi Arabia, 80
and al-Sadat, 76–77
reaction to Israeli annexation of Jerusalem, 84
peace plan of, 112, 118

Faisal, King (Saudi Arabia):
innovative policies of, 17
and al-Asad, 52
and al-Sadat, 52
and Islamic conference, 39
and Yemen war, 39–40, 44
Faisal I, King (son of Sherif Husayn), 13, 15
Faisal II (son of Faisal I), 35
al-Faisal, Saud, 84
Farah, Tawfiq, 109
Faruq, King, 27, 30
al-Fasi, Allal, 16
Fatah (Movement of Palestinian Liberation), 47, 54, 59, 61
al-Fatat (Young Arab Society), 13
Fatamid dynasty, 3, 10
Federation of Arab Republics (1971), 45, 50–52
France, 30, 32, 46, 62–63
Free Officers (Egypt), 30
Front for the Liberation of South Yemen (FLOSY), 46
Front of Steadfastness and Confrontation, 74–76, 79, 89, 91, 93, 99
Front of Support, 73–74

Gambia, 90
Ghana, 90
al-Ghashmi, Husayn, 102–103
Great Britain, 13–15, 19, 21–22, 29–30, 32, 45–46, 62, 106
Greater Syria, 10–12, 21–22, 62, 66, 109
Gulf Cooperation Council, 114, 116

Habash, George, 47
Habré, Hissène, 90–91
Haddad, Major Saad, 95–96
al-Hafiz, Amin, 41, 45
Haile Mariam, Mengistu, 106
Haile Selassie, Emperor, 106
Haitham, Muhammad Ali, 46
al-Hakim, Tawfiq, 10
al-Hamdi, Ibrahim, 101–102
Hammami, Said, 59
Hammurabic Code, 5
Hannibal, 6
al-Hariri, Ziyad, 41
Hasan, King (Morocco), 97–100
Hawatmeh, Nayif, 47
al-Hinnawi, Sami, 27

al-Hourani, Akram, 18, 27
Husayn, King:
  and Abd al-Nasir, 42–44
  and Arafat, 70, 76
  and Kamal Asaad, 65
  and al-Asad, 65, 76, 86, 93–94
  and Camille Chamun, 65
  and Faisal II, 35
  and Saddam Husayn, 86, 88, 112
  and Lebanon, 65
  and PLO, 42, 58–59, 65, 70, 72
  and Qaddhafi, 76
  and al-Sadat, 70, 74–76, 85, 87
  and Saudi Arabia, 42, 86, 112
  and Khartum Summit, 43–44
  assumes role as Arab spokesman, 88, 112
  opposition to Camp David, 76, 85, 88, 112
  self-image of, 117
Husayn, Saddam:
  and al-Asad, 77–78
  and Gulf states, 85
  and King Husayn, 86, 88
  and Iran, 79, 85
  and Iraq-Iran war, 92–94, 114
  and radical Palestinian organizations, 88
  and al-Sadat, 82, 86
  and Saudi Arabia, 79
  and Soviet Union, 82–83
  and Western Sahara controversy, 100
  and North and South Yemen, 85–87,
  assumes Arab leadership role, 78–79, 81–82, 86
  and Iraqi Communists, 79, 83
  and Iraqi Shiites, 82
  and Iraqi-Saudi-Jordanian axis, 81
  National Covenant of, 87
  pragmatism of, 78–79, 86, 110
Husayn, Sherif, 13
al-Husri, Sati, 18

Ibn Tulun, 10
Idris, King (Libya), 45
Interim Sinai agreement (Sinai II), 52, 55, 66–68
Iran, 31, 77, 81–85, 88, 92–95, 113–115
Iraq, 5, 13–16, 18–19, 22, 24–28, 31–32, 34–35, 38, 40–42, 44–45, 47, 55, 58–59, 62, 64–65, 70–71, 73–74, 77–89, 92–95, 103, 105, 110–112, 114–117, 119

Iraq-Iran war, 92–94, 96
Iryani, Abd al-Rahman, 40
Iskander, Ahmad, 94
Ismail, Abd al-Fattah, 105
Israel, 27, 30–32, 36, 40, 42–44, 47, 50–55, 57, 62–63, 65–68, 72–77, 79–80, 82, 84, 86–87, 95–96, 117–118
Istiqlal Party (Morocco), 16
Italy, 106

Jadid, Salah, 45
Jarring, Gunnar, 49–50
Jidda Agreement (1965), 39
Joint Political Command (Egypt, Syria, Sudan), 69, 71
Joint Supreme Leadership Council (Jordan, Syria), 70
Jordan, 5, 35–36, 42–44, 47, 49, 56, 58, 62, 65–66, 70, 72, 74–75, 79, 81, 85–88, 92–94, 99–100, 112, 116–117, 119
Jumblat, Kamal, 62–63

Kamil, Mustafa, 9–10
al-Kawakibi, Abd al-Rahman, 8, 11
Kazziha, Walid, 57–58
Khalid, King (Saudi Arabia), 68–69, 106
Khomeni, Ayatollah, 77, 81
Kissinger, Henry, 54–55
Kurds, 38
Kuwait, 18, 44, 46, 66, 75, 80, 85, 87, 92, 114

Lebanon, 11, 13–14, 16, 18, 21–22, 25–26, 28, 34, 56, 59, 61–72, 75, 77, 93, 95–96, 100, 116
Libya, 14, 44–47, 50–51, 55, 58–59, 62, 64–65, 70–74, 84, 88–94, 98–100, 107, 116
Lutfi al-Sayyid, Ahmad, 8–9

MacDonald, Ramsey, 20
Maher, Ali, 30
al-Malki, Adnan, 33
al-Manar, 8
Maronites, 62–63
Mauritania, 46–47, 75, 90, 97–100
mawali, 1
Middle East Defense Command, 29
millets, 4
Morocco, 14, 16, 46–47, 73, 90, 92, 97–100

Mubarak, Husni, 94, 118
Muhammad Ali, 4
Muslim Brotherhood, 29, 86, 89

Nagib, Muhammad, 30
al-Nahas, Mustafa, 22, 29-30
Nasir Muhammad, Ali, 105
National Bloc (Syria), 16, 26, 32
National Covenant (Iraq), 87
National Guidance Committee (West
    Bank), 61
National Liberation Front (South Ye-
    men), 46
National Pact (Lebanon), 25
National Party (Egypt), 8-9
National Progressive Front (Lebanon),
    62
National Revolutionary Command
    Council (Syria), 38
National Union (UAR), 34, 37
Niger, 90
Nigeria, 90
Numan, Ahmad Muhammad, 40
Numeiri, Muhammad Jafar, 45, 70-71,
    85, 91, 106

Oman, 46, 73, 80, 85, 87, 115
OPEC, 81
Organization of African Unity (OAU),
    50
Ottoman Empire, 4, 6, 11, 108
Ottoman Party of Administrative De-
    centralization, 12
Ouddei, Goukouni, 90
Ould Daddah, Mukhtar, 97
Ould Haidallah, Khuna, 100
Ould Salek, Mustafa, 98-99

Pact of the Arab League, 23
Palestine (Palestinians), 13-15, 19-21, 26,
    29-30, 36, 52-53, 57, 59, 79, 83, 95-96
Palestine Liberation Organization
    (PLO):
    creation of, 42
    and Arab regimes, 47, 57-58, 60
    and Arab system, 46, 73, 96
    and Egypt, 64, 69
    and King Husayn, 42, 57-59, 65, 72
    and Iraq, 59, 88
    and Israel, 57, 67
    and Lebanon, 56, 59, 62-67, 95-96,
        116

and Libya, 59-60
and Saudi Arabia, 88
and Syria, 59, 62-67, 69, 93, 95
fragmentation of, 47
radical factions of, 47, 55, 73, 88
and Camp David, 76
and National Guidance Committee,
    61
and Steadfastness Front, 74
and Western Sahara controversy, 100
admitted to Arab League, 57
recognized as Palestinian representa-
    tive, 59, 70
concept of a secular democratic Pal-
    estine, 57, 63
democratic character of, 58
increased influence of, 46, 56
pragmatism of, 61
reduced political leverage of, 95-96
boycotts Amman Summit, 93
endorses mini-state idea, 54-55, 59
opposes Fahad's peace plan, 112
Pakistan, 31
Palestine National Charter, 56
Palestine National Council, 47, 56, 59
Pan-African Legion, 90
Pan-Arabism, 10, 18-19, 28, 33-35,
    37-38, 42, 52, 65-66, 72, 110-111, 119
Passfield White Paper, 20
People's Party (Syria), 26, 32
Pharoanism, 15
People's Democratic Republic of Yemen
    (South Yemen), 17, 46-47, 55, 73-74,
    79, 83-84, 86, 88, 93, 100-107, 114
People's Republic of China, 46
Philosophy of the Revolution (Abd al-
    Nasir), 30-31
Polisario Front, 90, 98-100
Popular Democratic Front for the Liber-
    ation of Palestine (PDFLP), 47, 54,
    59, 88
Popular Front for the Liberation of
    Palestine (PFLP), 47, 55, 88
Popular Front for the Liberation of
    Palestine—General Command
    (PFLPGC), 55
Popular Struggle Front (PSF), 55
Punic Wars, 6

Qabus bin Saidd Sultan, 87
Qaddhafi, Muammar:
    comes to power, 45
    and Abd al-Nasir, 59
    and Algeria, 90, 98-100

and al-Asad, 89
and Chad, 90
and Iran, 92–93
and Iraq, 92–93
and Jordan, 76
and Lebanon, 65
and Mauritania, 90, 98–100
and Morocco, 90, 98–100
and PLO 59–60
and Polisario Front, 90, 98–100
and al-Sadat, 51, 70–71
and Saudi Arabia, 93
and Soviet Union, 91–92
and Sudan, 71, 91
and Tunisia, 89–90, 99
and Federation of Arab Republics, 50
isolation within Arab system, 90–91
al-Qahtaniyya, 13
Qasim, Abd al-Karim, 34–35, 38
Qatar, 46, 80, 92, 114
al-Quwatli, Shukri, 26, 33

Randal, Jonathan, 60, 116
Reagan, Ronald, 88
Rejection Front, 55, 59, 70–71, 73–75, 79
Revolutionary Command Council
   (Egypt), 30
Rida, Muhammad Rashid, 8, 11
Rogers plan, 44
Rouhani, Ayatollah, 82, 85
Rubayyi Ali, Salim, 46, 101–102

Saadeh, Antun, 18
Saadist Party (Egypt), 29
al-Sadat, Anwar:
   Egyptianism of, 10, 54, 75, 116
   comes to power, 49
   early policies of, 49
   and al-Asad, 51–52, 67–69, 73
   and Begin, 75
   and Israel, 50, 52–53, 72–73, 77, 80, 82
   and Kissinger, 54–55
   and King Husayn, 70, 74, 87
   and Saddam Husayn, 82
   and Lebanon, 64, 68
   and Mubarak, 94, 118
   and Numeiri, 70–71
   and Qaddhafi, 51, 70–71
   and Saudi Arabia, 51–52, 76–77, 80,
      83–84
   and Soviet Union, 49
   and United States, 50, 53–54, 83
   and Arab system, 72–75, 78, 81–82
   and Camp David, 75–76, 85, 117
   and Federation of Arab Republics, 50
   and interim Sinai agreement, 52, 55,
      64
   and October war, 53
   and Riyadh mini-summit, 68–69
   and trilateral alliance, 68–69, 73
   and Western Sahara controversy, 99
   Egyptian official support of, 117
   initiates Security Council debate
      (1973), 53
   Jerusalem visit of, 74–75, 94
   new Egyptian bourgeoisie under, 54
   paternalism of, 58
   policies after October war, 81, 116
   pragmatism of, 49, 52
   unilateralism of, 72–73, 78, 80–81
   death of, 118
Saharan Arab Democratic Republic
   (SADR), 98
Saharan Islamic empire, 90
al-Said, Nuri, 22, 24, 27
Saiqa, 47, 54, 59
salafiyya movement, 7–11, 16–17, 109
Salih, Ali Abdullah, 104
al-Sallal, Abdullah, 38, 40
Sarraj, Abd al-Hamid, 33, 36
Saudi Arabia, 14, 16–17, 22, 25–28,
   35–40, 42, 45–47, 49, 51–54, 62,
   66–68, 71–72, 74–77, 79–88, 93–94,
   99–107, 112, 114, 116–119
Senegal, 90
al-Shabi, Qahtan, 46
Shah of Iran, 77, 81, 113
Sharaf, Abd al-Hamid, 86
sharia (Islamic law), 9
Shaw Commission, 19
al-Shisakli, Adib, 27–28, 32–33, 109
shura, 58
shuubiyya movement, 1
Sidqi, Bekr, 19
"silent" states, 75–76
Simpson, Sir John Hope, 19
Somalia, 75, 83, 105–107
Spain, 97–98
Sudan, 14–15, 29, 39, 45–47, 70–73, 75,
   80, 85, 90, 100, 106
Suleiman, Hikmat, 19
Sultan ben Abd al-Aziz, 80
Sykes-Picot agreement, 13
Syria, 5, 11, 13–14, 16, 18–21, 26–28,
   32–34, 36–38, 41–44, 47, 50–54,
   58–59, 62–75, 77–80, 86–89, 91–95,
   98, 100, 103, 110–112, 116, 119
Syrian-Libyan declaration, 91

Syrian Protestant College (American
    University of Beirut), 11
Syrian Social Nationalist Party (SSNP),
    18 19, 25, 28, 32–33

Toynbee, Arnold, 9
Transjordan, 14–15, 21–22, 24–25, 58
Treaty of Brotherhood and Alliance
    (Iraq, Transjordan), 25
Treaties of Friendship and Cooperation:
    USSR, Egypt, 49
    USSR, Iraq, 83
    USSR, South Yemen, 104
    USSR, Syria, 91
Treaty of Joint Defense and Economic
    Cooperation (Arab Collective Secu-
    rity Pact), 28
Tunisia, 14, 16, 46–47, 74–75, 90, 92,
    99–100
Turkey, 30–31

Umayyad Caliphate, 1, 3
umma (Islamic community), 9
Union of Soviet Socialist Republics,
    30–31, 33, 46, 49, 51, 72, 77, 81–85,
    87–88, 91–93, 103–107, 114–115
United Arab Emirates (UAE), 46, 75, 80,
    87, 92, 115

United Arab Republic (UAR), 34–36,
    41–42, 110
United Nations, 51, 53
United States of America, 30–32, 44,
    50–51, 53–55, 69, 75–76, 79–80, 83,
    87–88, 104, 107
al-Urabi, Ahmad, 8

Vance, Cyrus, 69
Voice of the Arabs (Radio Cairo), 31

Wafd Party, 10, 14, 29
Waldheim, Kurt, 50
Weizmann, Chaim, 20
Western Sahara, 90, 97–101, 105
White Paper, 1939, 21

Yemen (North Yemen, Yemen Arab
    Republic), 14, 17, 25–26, 35, 38–40,
    42, 44, 47, 75, 79, 85, 87, 92, 101–105
Young Egypt, 29
Young Turks, 8, 12

Zaghlul, Saad, 10, 14
Zaim, Husni, 26–27
al-Zubeiri, Mahmud, 40

THE ARAB BALANCE OF POWER

was composed in 10-point Fototronic Times Roman and leaded two points
by Dharma Press,
with display type in photocomposition
by J. M. Bundscho, Inc.;
printed on 55-pound acid-free Glatfelter Antique Cream,
Smythe-sewn and bound over boards with Columbia Bayside Linen,
also adhesive-bound with Corvon 220-13 covers,
by Maple-Vail Book Manufacturing Group, Inc.;
and published by

SYRACUSE UNIVERSITY PRESS
SYRACUSE, NEW YORK 13210